QUIET COURAGE

Kansas Congressman
Clifford R. Hope

QUIET COURAGE

Kansas Congressman
Clifford R. Hope

by
Cliff Hope, Jr.

Sunflower University Press®
1531 Yuma • P. O. Box 1009 • Manhattan, Kansas 66505-1009 USA

ISBN 0-89745-209-7

Edited by Ruth Ann Warren

Layout by Lori L. Daniel

To my wife and helpmate of forty-eight years,

Dolores Sulzman Hope

and

to Virgil W. Dean, Ph.D., editor of *Kansas History*,

Historian at the Kansas State Historical Society,

and my friend and history mentor.

Contents

Acknowledgments

I AM INDEBTED TO MANY PEOPLE for both their help and counsel in writing this memoir-biography of my father, Clifford R. Hope. My wife, Dolores, a professional journalist, as she has with my several writing projects over the years, provided initial typing from my long-hand, yellow page drafts, with editing and helpful suggestions. Dr. Virgil W. Dean, editor of **Kansas History** *and historian with the Kansas State Historical Society, volunteered many hours of research and editorial assistance on his own time. He became my history mentor in 1992 and has continued in that capacity to this date. My daughter, Dr. Holly T. Hope, provided constructive criticism of the original manuscript. Edward Cade, a research specialist in congressional files, provided much of the research necessary in the Clifford R. Hope collection of letters, speeches, and documents at the Kansas State Historical Society.*

My thanks also to the many staff members of the Society for their help and many kindnesses in connection with my personal research in the Society collections, including Dr. Ramon Powers, Executive Director, and Dr. Patricia A. Michaelis, Director of the Library and Archives Division. The staff of the Finney County Historical Museum, especially WenDee LaPlant and Olga Montgomery, were most helpful in locating photographs and miscellaneous information. Earlene Nicholson and others on the staff of the Finney County Public Library provided valuable assistance in obtaining hard-to-locate books through the interlibrary loan system. Marx Koehnke, through his self-published book, *Kernals and Chaff — A History of Wheat Marketing Development*, provided needed information on Great Plains Wheat, Inc., and other wheat promotion organizations. The late Dr. Donald R. McCoy, Distinguished Professor of history at the University of Kansas, gave helpful criticism of the revised manuscript.

My thanks to Pat Toneges for initial typing of notes and to Pam Lenow for typing the revised manuscript. My thanks also to Dr. Robin Higham, Carol A. Williams, and Ruth Ann Warren of Sunflower University Press. My association with them has been most pleasant.

Finally, but by no means least, I am indebted to my sister, Martha Hope West, and to my son, Quentin C. Hope, for financial assistance for research, travel, and other costs, and to my former law partners, Jim D. Mills, William B. Bolin, Michael E. Collins, and Michael K. Ramsey, for providing me with research and writing space without compensation.

Needless to mention, I alone am responsible for any and all errors or deficiencies in the text.

Foreword

*I*N THE YEARS BETWEEN 1927 and 1957, when Clifford R. Hope represented the then southwest Congressional District in Kansas, there were momentous events taking place in our nation's history. Congressman Hope's span of dedicated public service covered the Depression years and the Dust Bowl days, World War II and the Korean War, the McCarthy era and the beginning of the "Cold War," the Brown v. Topeka Board of Education school desegregation case, and the fundamental change in the relationship between the federal government and the American people.

*I am in awe of the thoughtful, dedicated representation that Clifford Hope gave, not just to his district but to his country. He spent time thinking about the responsibilities he undertook. It was a different era in the political arena. Television was not a factor. One communicated by means of letters or radio or newspapers; as a result, I believe, issues were cast in a broader perspective. Today politics seems more like **Entertainment To-***

night, and audiences want ever-changing faces and events. As the pace escalates, our attention span and interest become ever narrower.

Everyone involved in public service should read the story of Congressman Hope's life and reflect on his dignified, principled representation in Congress. His decisions and the legislation with which he worked over the years did make a difference -- not because of a press secretary's "spin" in a press release, but because he devoted his time in making sure he exercised his best judgment as he believed it to be.

Clifford Hope's impressive career is a walk through the formative years of the 20th century by a man who had the courage of his convictions. As we look back on this period it seems a more secure time, at least in the certainties of the issues before the nation. It wasn't. However, if we are to better understand our own times and prepare for the future, it is of benefit to reflect on the tensions and decisions of the past.

John Dos Passos said, "In times of change and danger when there is a quicksand of fear under men's reasoning, a sense of continuity with generations gone before can stretch like a lifeline across the scary present."

We are reassured in reading about the career of Clifford R. Hope: reassured that men and women of good will and dedicated concern for their fellow man do come forth and serve. Clifford Hope's legacy is the lifeline he laid for future generations to follow.

Nancy Kassebaum Baker
U.S. Senator, Kansas (Ret.)

A Note to the Reader

*C*LIFFORD RAGSDALE HOPE, *of Garden City, Kansas, was one of those extraordinary politicians whose temperament suited the process of lawmaking in the best tradition. His son, Clifford Hope, Jr., has written a biography of his father based on the senior Hope's papers, newspaper accounts, and personal recollections. This work of scholarship and appreciation brings to life a figure in Kansas history whose service to the people of this state greatly enhanced the fortunes of his constituents and the general public. This biography concentrates on Hope's congressional career representing the people of southwest Kansas. Using the extensive correspondence that Congressman Hope carried on with his constituents, we observe the process by which a skilled politician carried on a dialogue with those he served. One wonders whether elected officials today maintain constituents' correspondence with similar rigor.*

The important contributions of Congressman Hope in crafting legislation to support agriculture from 1927 to 1956, particularly in the areas of soil and water conservation, agricultural research and marketing, and the Food for Peace program are told here with admiration and respect. However, the side of Congressman Hope that is most enduring will be the qualities of his character that provide a model for politicians and those they serve. As his son Cliff Hope, Jr., asserts, his father's work ethic, his honesty, his guilelessness, his sense of responsibility, and his courage are revealed in a political life that warrants our attention and gratitude.

There are few references in our public canon to the "Quiet Courage" of this important figure in Kansas and U.S. history. This biography serves as a tribute to Clifford Ragsdale Hope's contributions and sheds additional light on this most interesting period in "America's century."

Ramon Powers
Executive Director
Kansas State Historical Society

Prologue

Now will I praise those godly men,
  our ancestors, each in his own time . . .

All these were glorious in their time,
  each illustrious in his day.
Some of them have left behind a name
  and men recount their praiseworthy deeds;
But of others there is no memory,
  for when they ceased, they ceased.
And they are as though they had not lived,
  they and their children after them.
Yet these also were godly men
  whose virtues have not been forgotten.

  The Book of Sirach, Chapter 44:1,7-10[1]

Clifford R. Hope, my father, was a member of Congress from the southwest Kansas district for 30 years (1927-1957), and thereafter spent most of his time, until his death in 1970, in national, state, and community service. He was a well-known, important member of the House of Representatives during the latter part of this period. My friend, James F. Forsythe, professor of history and presently Dean of the Graduate School at Fort Hays State University, has been researching and writing a "practical Congressman and agrarian idealist" biography of my father for more than 20 years, but his administrative duties and other activities have precluded completion of the work. Other scholars have covered various events in my father's career such as his reaction to President Franklin D. Roosevelt's proposed court-packing plan in 1937, and his and other Kansas congressmen's views and votes on such issues as the 1940 Selective Service Act, the 1941 Lend-Lease Act, and the Brannan Plan, 1949-1950.

I am certain that Dr. Forsythe's comprehensive biography and, perhaps, other biographies will be completed in due course. In the meantime, the years are hastening on. As a son who was close to his father for many years and who has memories as well as substantive documentation, I feel compelled at the risk of filiopietism to write a biography while I am still able to do so.

Except for a brief period in 1945, my father did not keep a diary or journal. The written record of his life is found primarily in his voluminous correspondence, most of which has been donated to the library and archives division of the Kansas State Historical Society. Other sources are his newspaper columns, interviews given by him and interviews with some of his contemporaries, numerous books and monographs, and my memories of events and of our many discussions, both profound and trivial, over the years. In addition, during the past several years, I have retraced the route our family usually took in driving from Garden City to Washington and have revisited the sites of our various residences in Washington.

Professor James T. Patterson, noted American historian at Indiana University, attested to the value of Hope's papers at the historical society in a 1965 letter:

> . . . Your papers contain a good deal more relevant and revealing material than do the vast majority of collections which I have examined (and I have examined some 30 others). I am grateful — and I am sure other researchers have also been

Clifford R. Hope, Sr.　　　　　　　　　　　*Rudy Valenzuela Photo, Garden City, KS*

— that you didn't go through . . . and remove all the valuable stuff. Many others have done just this, you know.

Let me also express my admiration for the devotion which you obviously felt for your constituents. Your letters make it quite clear that you considered your constituents mature, intelligent people; thus you answered them in a forthright and detailed manner. I have not seen such careful letters in any other collection.

I realize, of course, that many citizens consider the subjects of agriculture, federal farm programs, and related matters to be of little interest, if not downright boring. David McCullough, in his splendid biography of Harry S. Truman, makes no mention whatsoever of Secretary of Agriculture Charles F. Brannan or of the Brannan Plan (proposed controversial agricultural legislation), although Brannan played a major role in Truman's election of 1948 and the Brannan Plan was a major issue before Congress during 1949-1950. This general lack of interest in agricultural matters makes it more difficult to write an interesting biography of a man who spent a great deal of his time on agricultural problems and legislation.

However, Clifford Hope, Sr., was not a one-issue representative. He carefully studied all major issues before Congress, particularly during World War II and the postwar years, and wrote lengthy letters to constituents explaining his views. He perceived it his duty to tell the reasons for his views in detail whether the letter writer wanted to know them or not. One of his frequent correspondents wrote, "I'm writing to tell you what *I* think. I don't care what *you* think." (On occasion, especially to those letter writers who considered themselves oracles of knowledge and virtue, Hope could be quite sarcastic and feisty in his replies. This aspect of his personality was not generally known; years later, his daughter Martha was greatly surprised to read some of these Truman-like responses.)

Hope answered every letter, whether the writer expected an answer or not. A friend of mine in Liberal observed, "If you'd write ol' Cliff and say 'Hello,' he'd write back and say 'hi.'" If a letter required research, an acknowledgement would be sent, followed by a detailed letter as soon as he had time to dictate — often on Saturday. He worked six, sometimes seven, days a week and on many nights spent hours studying current issues.

My father was a man of considerable courage — not flamboyant courage, but quiet courage. In 1925, at the age of 31, he ran for speaker of the Kansas House of Representatives. One of the main issues in the two-man race involved legislation to legalize the Ku Klux Klan in Kansas after the Kansas Supreme Court had held that the Klan was a foreign corporation not authorized to do business in the state. His opponent supported this legislation; my father was vehemently opposed, determined to rid Kansas of the bigoted, hate-mongering group. He greatly underestimated the strength of the Klan. He thought he would win the Republican caucus vote hands down, but, in fact, he won by only two votes. "Politics as usual" would have dictated that he back off, especially when he was seriously considering running for Congress the next year. Instead, he met the issue head-on. After complicated legislative maneuvering, the legalizing bill was defeated, sounding the death knell for the Klan in Kansas.

Much later, in the spring of 1951, President Truman's sudden firing of General Douglas MacArthur created an emotional upsurge of support for the General in Kansas as well as in the nation. Clifford Hope alone among the Kansas congressional delegation defended Truman's action on the grounds of upholding the supremacy of civilian authority over the military. Thousands in Hope's district, especially in Sumner County, south of Wichita, were angry. Some vowed to defeat him in the next election. But he did not give in. By 1952 the emotional fervor had subsided, and the controversy was not an issue in the election.

Hope's quiet courage was evident throughout his congressional career. Despite pressure, he opposed the Republican Party line and leadership on occasion, especially during the Eisenhower administration when Secretary of Agriculture Ezra Taft Benson embarked on his "moral crusade" to lower and eventually abolish farm crop price supports.

The advent of World War II had changed my father's views from moderate isolationist to internationalist. He supported assistance to struggling democracies, especially the Marshall Plan. In this, he was ahead of most of his constituents, and he spent much time explaining to them his position.

In a ceremony honoring my father at the end of his 30 years in the House of Representatives, his longtime friend Senator Frank Carlson of Concordia called him, in what may seem a quaint description today, a "perfect gentleman." Carlson cited nine virtues as marks of a gentleman, emphasizing the virtue of guilelessness. I can vouch for that one. Never have I known anyone who personified that virtue more. My father believed in rewarding friends, but he did not believe in punishing enemies or those who had done him wrong. He never tried to "get even," however tempting that might have been on occasion. He believed in the biblical admonition, "Recompense no man evil for evil." This was part of his fundamental honesty and integrity.

My father grew up in poverty, laying out of high school for two years or more to help support his parents and younger siblings. This was not unusual for those times, but he went out of his way to do more than his part for his family when they were in need. Although he did not preach or even express it in words, as a public servant he believed in dedication and duty to community and country. His belief in duty to country was similar to that of a good soldier, such as George Marshall or Dwight Eisenhower. As long as he was in Congress, his duty to his constituents and to all the people came before his duty to his wife and children, but he did not neglect his family. Although I have not discovered that he ever used the expression "A man should not live for his generation alone but for countless generations to follow," I am certain this was his belief.

And though he held some conservative views, Hope never viewed himself as a conservative with a capital "C," in contrast with many Republicans, including his successors in Congress from western Kansas. From boyhood, he was an admirer of Teddy Roosevelt and his progressive views. In later life, when he read more about Abraham Lincoln, Hope came to venerate him more than the great Teddy. He especially admired Lincoln's principled pragmatism, as Lincoln's political tenets and skills have been described by recent historians. Hope saw himself as one who "took a middle-ground view" and the practical approach in solving problems. Concerning any proposed legislation, he first asked, "Will it work?"

My father was modest, unassuming, and self-effacing. During the gasoline rationing period of World War II when, as a congressman, he could have received unlimited rations, he spent an hour each way riding the bus to and from the Capitol every day. He always maintained a judicious temperament (except in some of those rare sarcastic letters), avoiding snap judgments. While he was seeking a solution to a particular problem, one of his favorite expressions was "Let's sleep on it."

Clifford R. Hope was not without faults, but his mistakes, as he said of Teddy Roosevelt, were honest ones.

Chapter 1

Birmingham, Ripley, Garden City (1893-1913)

*O*N MARCH 1893 President Grover Cleveland was inaugu-
*rated for his second term. Democrats controlled both
houses of Congress and the Presidency for the first time
since 1859. And soon a 4½-year, nationwide depression
would begin, sparked by a drop in the gold reserve, precipitating
the Panic of 1893. Farmers, already suffering from glutted markets and drought, were especially hard hit.*

*The year 1893 was also distinguished by the official opening
of the World's Columbian Exposition in Chicago and the Cherokee Strip in Oklahoma Territory. Although land in the Great
Plains would still be available for homesteading for some years,
the Western frontier, for all practical purposes, was gone, and
naturalists estimated there probably were not more than 1,000
buffalo left on the Plains. Jeremiah "Sockless Jerry" Simpson, a
colorful, brilliant Populist leader and friend of the farmer, was
serving the second of his three terms in Congress, representing
the new, large 7th District of southwest Kansas.*

On June 9, 1893, Clifford Ragsdale Hope was born to Armitta Ragsdale and Harry M. Hope in the village of Birmingham in southeastern Iowa. Birmingham, in Van Buren County, had been settled in 1839, seven years before Iowa became a state. It was about 15 miles north of Keosauqua, the county seat on the Des Moines River, near the Missouri line. John Harrison, owner of the town site, named the town after Birmingham, England. In its early years, Birmingham had been a center for small industries: a saw and grist mill, a woolen mill, a plow and wagon factory, a tannery later converted to a pork-packing plant, and a cheese factory. Its population reached 700 in the 1870s when Van Buren County's population was at its zenith. By 1900, however, most of the industries had moved or closed down, and Birmingham had become a small, quiet village. The 1895 census listed 159 families, among them a goodly number of Hopes.

The Hope and Ragsdale families had been early-day settlers in the Birmingham area. John Stewart Hope, Harry's father, was 17 when he came to a farm near Birmingham in 1852 from Westmoreland County, Pennsylvania, with his parents, James Hope and Margaret Paden Dinsmore. Margaret was an Irish immigrant. John did not serve in the Civil War. He married Margaret Jane McDonald of Scotch-Irish ancestry in 1862. Harry, their first child, born in 1863, was followed by four siblings: Bird Norris, James Walter, Daisy Jennesse, and Rose Marie. Bird became a dentist and the family's genealogist in Oklahoma; Walter, a cattleman in Kansas; Jennesse, a nurse in Iowa; and Rose, an Iowa housewife.

John Stewart Hope was reared to be a farmer. In 1866 he moved his family to a farm near Ottawa in northeast Kansas, but their crops were destroyed by grasshoppers, and within a year they returned to Birmingham. Later he and his son Harry operated a grocery store, which was sold in 1901. John, a lifelong, active Presbyterian, spent his last years as an insurance agent. Upon his death in 1924, an obituary noted:

> We have known Mr. Hope for many years as one of Van Buren County's most highly esteemed and most useful citizens. He was pure gold, and it is with deep regret that we hear of his taking off.

John's wife, Margaret Jane, had died years before, in 1897, of heart disease at the age of 55.

The family of Armitta Ragsdale Hope traced its ancestry back to the owners of Raglan Castle in Wales, according to a flowery genealogy. Godfrey Ragsdale came to America in 1606, a year before the founding of the first permanent English settlement at Jamestown. The various Lords Raglan were his descendants. One of the several Lords Raglan was the British Commander in the Crimean War. His great-grandson, FitzRoy Richard Somerset, Fourth Baron Raglan, attended Eton and Sandhurst, served in the Grenadier Guards, fought slave traders in the Sudan, and was stationed in India, Afghanistan, and Hong Kong. He was also a scholar of note, and upon his death received a two-column obituary in *The New York Times*. Whether the Iowa Ragsdales were related to the Lords Raglan is not known for certain, but some family members — especially Armitta's sister Cora Lee — liked to think so.

John S. Ragsdale, Armitta's father, born in Owen County, Indiana, in 1840, came to Iowa with his parents, Daniel and Elizabeth Lindsay Ragsdale, in the early 1850s. John married his first wife, Rachel A. Cupp, in 1860. She died in 1884. A year later he married Isora M. Norris. After her death, he married Hattie M. Brooks (1907). By 1863 John had enlisted as first lieutenant in Company I, 19th Regiment of Iowa Infantry Volunteers. He was captured in Louisiana in September, confined in military prisons at Shreveport and Tyler, Texas, and escaped in March 1864, 40 miles above Natchez, Mississippi. According to an early, informal family history,

> He and three others made their way over 400 miles through the enemy's country, traveling at night, swimming streams, living on nuts and such supplies as they could get from fields and from Negroes, always loyal; the escapees succeeded after 30 days of extreme hardship in reaching their command at or near Vicksburg.

As if that ordeal were not enough for one war, John re-enlisted in May in his same outfit and served until his discharge at Mobile, Alabama, in July 1865. There is no record of John Ragsdale's feelings concerning the Confederacy and its leaders, but his strong-willed daughter Cora spent her long life proclaiming that Robert E. Lee should have been hanged.

Ragsdale spent the remainder of his life in Birmingham, serving as a druggist, postmaster, mayor, and editor until his death in 1916. In addition to Armitta and Cora, John and Rachel Ragsdale had four other children: George Wilson, who served in the U.S. foreign service in St. Petersburg (Russia), Tientsin (China), and Nova Scotia; Elmer Ellsworth, named after the heroic Colonel Ephraim Elmer Ellsworth, the first Union soldier killed in the Civil War; Ella, who married James Walter Hope, Harry's brother; and Wilmot Proviso, named for the amendment introduced in the U.S. House of Representatives in 1846 by David Wilmot, prohibiting slavery in any territory that might be acquired as a result of the Mexican War. Although the amendment did not become law, it did become a rallying principle for the Free Soil forces. Thus two of John Ragsdale's sons bore the imprint of the Civil War.

Wilmot Proviso Ragsdale, known in the family as "Uncle Pro," became a druggist and led a sedate life in Tacoma, Washington. Not so his son and only child, Wilmot (he was not inflicted with "Proviso"). A college drop-out in the 1930s, he was a seaman on a tramp steamer, a gardener and handyman, and, eventually, head of a ragamuffin (small-time) radio news service in Washington, D.C. Then he became a Washington correspondent for *The Wall Street Journal* and a war correspondent for *Time* magazine, covering D-Day in Normandy. In 1960 he accepted a position as professor of journalism at the University of Wisconsin, where he remained for 20 years, inspiring two generations of students. When he left the university in 1981, a headline read: "Legendary Ragsdale leaves UW. Eminent Reporter Became Unforgettable Teacher." Without question, Wilmot was the most talented and famous Ragsdale in the family — in this country, at any rate.

Armitta, always called "Mitta," was born in 1866 at Hermitage, Missouri, but was raised in Birmingham. Unfortunately no record of her early life there has been found. Harry Hope attended grade school in Birmingham (the town had no high school at that time) and Parsons College in nearby Fairfield. He then operated a grocery store with his father until 1901. Mitta and Harry were married in June 1891. Clifford was their first child (1893), followed by Mary (1895), Mildred (1896), John Cecil (1898), Hollis Raymond (1901), and Ralph Maurice (1904).

Harry, a devout Presbyterian, had a prickly moustache from the time he was a young man and most of the time thereafter until he died. He was a man of very, very few words. He mumbled table blessings. When he thought there was too much talk at the dinner table, he directed an older child sitting next to the one doing the talking to "thump him" with a thumb

Clifford, Mary, Mildred, and Cecil Hope, *ca*. 1905, Birmingham, Iowa.

on the side of his head. It must have seemed as if the spirit of John Calvin hovered over the meal — a brooding omnipresence.

Mitta was a devout Methodist at the time of her marriage, at which time she became an equally devout Presbyterian. Although she did not express hatred of the South as did her sister Cora, she had strong negative feelings toward the Democratic Party and the Roman Catholic Church. Slight of build, she was full of nervous energy. Her dominant physical characteristic was her long reddish-brown hair, which never turned gray or white.

Mitta and Harry instilled in their children the virtues of hard work, thrift, duty, struggle, and self-improvement. Sunday was a day of worship; and liquor, tobacco, card playing, and dancing were shunned. Later, movie attendance on Sunday was added to the proscribed list. The children characterized their parents simply as "poor but honest."

Harry and Mitta's political values and politics were determined in the aftermath of the Civil War. It would be difficult to overemphasize the lingering influence of the war on the state of Iowa and the town of Birming-

ham. About half the state's male population of military age took some part
in the war. Few states paid a higher cost per capita in lives lost; there were
13,000 military deaths. Fifteen thousand Iowa soldiers marched with Sherman's Army in the great victory parade down Pennsylvania Avenue on
May 4, 1865, and John Ragsdale may have been among them. They
looked "like the lords of the world," said one observer.[1] Concerning the
war, Iowa historian Joseph Frazier Wall wrote:

> It was the great determinant of our political structure and
> in many important ways of our social attitudes for the next
> one hundred years. In these respects, the Civil War was as
> important to Iowa as it was to Alabama or Mississippi. It cre-
> ated a one-party state with all the implications that that histori-
> cal fact has politically, socially, and economically. It was the
> great temporal landmark by which thousands of Iowans would
> fix their family calendars, and our museum and courthouse
> squares are filled with the artifacts and memorials of that con-
> flict.[2]

Although there were Democrats in state and local offices in Iowa in the
1890s, to the majority of citizens — including the Ragsdales and the
Hopes — the Union and the Grand Old Party still were one and the same.
Young Clifford, at the age of seven or eight, took a more pragmatic
approach to partisan politics. His only written memory of Birmingham
days was expressed in one of his newspaper columns in 1965. He reminisced:

> My first political argument, or at least the first I remember,
> took place in the little southeast Iowa town of Birmingham,
> where I was born. It must have been about 1900 or 1901. It
> couldn't have been any later, because we left Iowa in August of
> the latter year.
> This discussion was with a dear old lady who lived next door.
> Her husband's name was D. P. Wilson. He was a Civil War vet-
> eran. We children in the neighborhood called her "Mrs. D. P."
> and she was a popular figure, no doubt in part because she usu-
> ally had a well-filled cookie jar. Someone had told her that the
> Hills, who lived down the street, were Democrats. She just

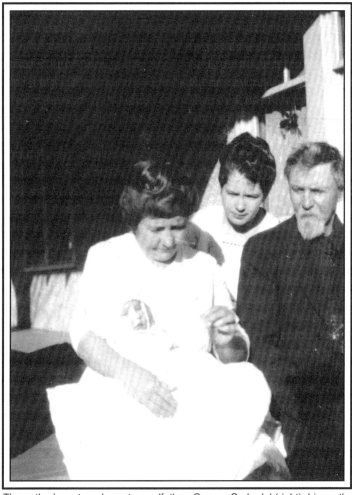

The author's maternal great-grandfather, George Corkadel (right), his mother (center), and his great-grandmother Laura Sanders holding him.

couldn't believe it. She had always thought they were such nice people. I don't remember just what started the argument, but in my innocence, I must have made some favorable references to Democrats. Whatever I said, I soon got my comeuppance. "In the first place," said Mrs. D. P., "It is a well-known fact that all Democrats were rebels and in the second place, more Democrats drink than Republicans."

Birmingham was a hard place to challenge the rebel argument which had long been accepted, since Union veterans and their descendants comprised most of the population of the community. There seemed to be some basis for the drinking argument also, since one of the four or five people in town who admitted Democratic leanings was the town drunkard.

In spite of her arguments, I wasn't entirely convinced of the perfidy of all Democrats and this apparently added to Mrs. D. P.'s worries. A day or so later, I overheard her discussing the Hill case with a neighbor and in the course of explaining how shocked she was, she added, ". . . and from the way Clifford talks, I'm not sure about Harry" (my father).

She needn't have worried about Harry. He lived to be 86 and I'm sure he never voted for a Democrat in all that time.

However, my career as a Democrat didn't last long. I'm afraid in the first place it was based mainly on my sympathy for the underdog. In the fall of 1901, we moved to Oklahoma. The little town of Ripley where we lived was something of a duplicate of Birmingham, except that there, the Republicans were the underdogs. This in itself might have swung me back to the Republicanism of my father.[3]

Harry Hope had been comfortable with Birmingham's political environment, but the business climate was another matter. His grocery business simply was not providing adequate income for a family of seven. Possibly influenced by his brother Bird, then a dentist practicing in Pawnee, Oklahoma Territory, in 1901 Harry participated unsuccessfully in an Oklahoma land lottery. By August conditions were such that a move from Birmingham had to be made. Harry had an opportunity to take over a general merchandise store in Ripley, a small town on the Cimarron River in Payne County.

Ripley had been established in April 1900, just after the Santa Fe Railway constructed a bridge across the Cimarron. The town was named after the president of the Santa Fe. The population quickly grew to a thousand inhabitants. Many new businesses were established, including ten grocery stores and four saloons.

Stillwater, founded at the time the Indian Territory was opened to white settlement in 1889, was the county seat. It became the home of Oklahoma

Agricultural and Mechanical College, later Oklahoma State University. The town of Cushing, in eastern Payne County, became Ripley's arch rival. Guthrie, in Logan County to the west, was the territorial capital.

Harry operated the store under the name of Hope and Byers. There is no record of whether Byers was a resident partner or not. The Hope family lived over the store; Ralph Hope, the last child, was born there in 1904.

Clifford finished the eighth grade in Ripley. Because there was no high school then, he repeated his last year of grade school, hoping to learn more. In his spare time he worked in the nearby cotton fields, earning ten cents a day to help with the family finances.

Ripley's boom soon declined, and Harry's business went from bad to worse. One reason for its failure, my father once told me, was Harry's kindness in extending credit to customers. The family moved in 1906, but Harry did not forget his creditors. His daughter Mary recalled years later that he took 10 to 15 years to pay his Oklahoma debts down to the last penny. It never occurred to him to try to default on his creditors when he left the state. Harry was still poor and still honest.

Harry's brother, James Walter, known as Walt, had in the meantime left Birmingham and settled in Finney County in southwest Kansas. He told Harry about an opportunity to manage a ranch near Holcomb, in the western part of the county, and Harry jumped at the chance. The ranch (later part of the L. L. Jones ranch) was owned by an absentee landlord named Carcher. The children performed daily farm chores. Among Clifford's tasks was hauling hay southeast of Garden City to the cattalo herd of the legendary Charles J. "Buffalo" Jones (not a relative of L. L. Jones). Cattalos were a crossbreed of cattle and bison, which Jones experimented with unsuccessfully for several years.

During this time Clifford rode horseback to high school in Garden City, the county seat. The high school was located on the second floor of the stately Garfield School building, named after the martyred President. The other children walked to the two-room grade school in Holcomb. The ranch was sold in 1909, and the Hope family moved to Garden City.

Finney County's first permanent settlers arrived soon after the Atchison, Topeka, and Santa Fe Railway tracks were laid across Kansas in 1872. Pierceville and Sherlock (later Holcomb) were the first towns along the railroad, which followed the Arkansas River across the county. In gen-

eral the railroad followed the route of the Santa Fe Trail. Sequoyah
County, named after the great Cherokee chief, was designated by the Kansas Legislature in 1873 and ten years later was renamed for Lieutenant
Governor David W. Finney. The next year the county was formally organized with a population of 1,569.

The first permanent settlers arrived at the site of Garden City in 1878.
William D. and James R. Fulton, John A. Stevens, and Buffalo Jones filed
homestead claims on the land. Frederick Finnup arrived from Indiana the
next year. Luticia Fulton, wife of William D., is credited with naming the
settlement Garden City, either at the suggestion of a tramp who admired
her garden or upon her own initiative. For the next few years, the county's
population grew rapidly, reaching more than 14,000 in 1886. Associations
of farmers developed irrigation ditch systems served by the Arkansas
River. Predictions of a prairie metropolis were made.

The great blizzard of 1886, which devastated the Great Plains, was followed by droughts and crop failures and almost made a ghost town of Garden City. In 1890 its population was only 400, with the county population
reduced to 3,350. By the time the Hope family arrived, the city and county
were gradually recovering, but the county would not reach its 1886 peak
again until after World War II.

In 1906 the United States Sugar and Land Company (later The Garden
City Company), owned by the Penrose family of Pennsylvania and Colorado Springs, opened a sugar beet refining factory. According to a promotion booklet put out by the Industrial Club of Garden City in 1907,
200,000 acres of fine beet land "were in the vicinity of Garden City." The
booklet claimed a population of 4,000 for Garden City, "the metropolis of
the west half of the state." Alfalfa, wheat, dairy farming, bees and honey,
and cantaloupes were promoted.

Economic conditions in 1909 were better for the city and county in
general, but not for the Hopes. Harry worked at Keep's Grocery for $45
a month, and Clifford dropped out of school for two years to work at
Mack's Grocery Store in the Windsor Hotel building, where he continued
working full time or part time for the next seven years. The grocery experience gave Clifford insight into the lives of the area people, their daily
problems, and their needs — knowledge that became invaluable when he
later took public office.

In two newspaper columns written in the 1960s, Clifford fondly recalled Mack's Grocery:

My first job was that of delivery boy. However, that was only part of my duties. When not out on the route, I worked at all of the many chores around a grocery store. As delivery boy, part of my job was feeding and caring for the two rather wild, nondescript ponies which constituted our horse power.

This was long before the forty-hour week. What we had in 1909 was closer to eighty hours. The store opened at six A.M. and closed at seven P.M., except on Saturday, when the closing hour was eleven. Employees put in full time, except an hour off for lunch. . . .

I opened the store at six, swept it, including the sidewalks, dusted off the showcases, put out fresh fly paper in strategic spots and slicked up things generally. . . .

Being a delivery boy was not a bad job. It enabled one to get away from the monotony of the store and see something of what was going on around town. In the forenoon, there was always a chance of arriving in someone's kitchen about the time a batch of cookies or other goodies were being taken out of the oven. I probably looked hungry and frequently was invited to help myself.

While some housewives came to the store to shop personally, most of them telephoned their orders in during the early part of the day. However, there were a good many customers who came to the store. These included husbands whose wives asked them to pick up something on the way home, children to buy candy or chewing gum, and men to buy a plug of chewing tobacco or a cigar.

Saturday was always a busy day as none of the stores remained open on Sunday. Also it was the day when most farmers and their families came to town. Many of them brought butter and eggs or other produce to exchange for groceries.

One of the most interesting, as well as mysterious, parts of the store was the back room. Stored there were cases of canned goods, flour in 24 and 48 pound sacks, potatoes, onions and other vegetables. Also kerosene, better known as coal oil, gasoline, lard, bacon, hams and other bulk commodities. The combination of smells was fascinating.

It was an adventuresome place also because one could never

tell when he might run into a large, fat rat. There were plenty of mice also and two or three cats lived well and sumptiously, apparently without greatly diminishing the rodent population.

This was before the day of modern insecticides and insect life was abundant. Flies were everywhere in spite of fly paper and poison. Bugs and weevils had a way of getting into flour and even in the packaged breakfast food. All of this was generally accepted as unavoidable, both by the proprietors and customers.

The only refrigeration was a large icebox which had little more capacity than some present day home refrigerators and freezers. . . .

Food preservation was based largely upon the use of salt (either dry or in the form of brine), smoke, dehydration, and, of course, canning. . . .

Pork was a big item, either as salt fat sides known as sowbelly or smoked in the form of hams and bacon. This was in a day when women were paying more attention to the figures on the grocery bill than to their own silhouettes. Dried apples, peaches, prunes, and raisins were big items. There were large barrels of pickles, fish, and sauerkraut packed in brine. One of the most profitable items in the store must have been sauerkraut. A large hogshead was purchased in the fall, lightly packed in brine. One of my jobs every Saturday night was to put some fresh brine in the barrel. This new brine was absorbed by the kraut and by the end of the winter we had probably sold considerably more brine than sauerkraut. . . .

Aside from canned goods, most groceries were sold in bulk. Packaging was only beginning to come in. The National Biscuit Company had come out with Uneeda Biscuit. Post and Kellogg were packaging breakfast food. Quaker Oats came in packages although rolled oats were to be had in bulk. However, most customers continued to prefer purchasing in bulk, partly because the packaged goods were higher and offered no opportunities for inspection. The sanitary advantages of packaging were stressed by the manufacturers, but up to that time their arguments had made little impression on customers.

Tobacco, chewing and smoking, was an important item. Star

and Horseshoe were the most popular brands of chewing tobacco, with exotic brands like Piper Heidsick favored by some
of the luxury-loving and sporting element. Popular brands of
smoking tobacco were Bull Durham, Duke's Mixture, and a relatively new brand, Prince Albert. The sale of cigarettes and
cigarette papers was prohibited. There was a small demand for
snuff.

Fresh fruits outside of oranges and bananas were available
only in season. The same was true of vegetables. . . .

One of the breaks in the monotony was the visits of drum-
mers [traveling salesmen] from wholesale grocery and produce
houses. . . . They were voices from the great outside world,
although probably not as wise and sophisticated as they
appeared to be. Most of them had at least some new stories to
tell.[4]

Through waiting on customers and making deliveries Clifford became known as a friendly, hard-working young man. The friends he made
then would serve him well when he began his political career a decade
later.

Hope family members, parents and children alike, spent much of their
non-working hours in Presbyterian church activities. The church met in a
white frame building at the corner of Spruce Street and Garden City
Avenue. Clifford was president of the Christian Endeavor Youth Group for
two years. Harry and Mitta served as church and Sunday school officers
for many years.

Harry and the family had a red-letter year in 1910, when he was
appointed assistant postmaster of Garden City, a position he held until his
retirement, 23 years later. His $75-per-month starting salary brought the
family into the middle class. Clifford was able to return to high school, and
Harry and Mitta became homeowners for the first time. After moving to
Garden City, they had lived in a succession of small, crowded rental
houses, the last of which was the somewhat roomier Buffalo Jones homestead on north Ninth Street. The house they bought at 604 St. John Street
provided them with indoor plumbing, telephone service, and electricity for
the first time.

After Clifford left home, Harry and Mitta filed a homestead claim in the
sandhills south of Holcomb. The law required them to live on the home-

stead part of the year, so they constructed a small house. Once a tornado upended the house and carried it 60 feet from its foundation with Harry and Mitta inside, but they suffered only minor injuries. As soon as they proved up on their claim by keeping it the required time and improving the land, they sold the property to Orange J. Brown for $3,000. (Orange was Mr. Brown's real name; he had a brother named Lemon.) For the first time, Harry and Mitta not only had their debts paid, but they also had savings. In 1923 they bought a home at 619 Garden City Avenue, where they lived for the rest of their long lives.

I do not remember my father telling my sister and me much about his high school days. Fortunately he shared many of his recollections in an interview in 1953 with Marilyn Alexander, then editor of the high school newspaper, *The Sugar Beet*. Alexander's article was reprinted in *The Garden City Telegram*. My father recalled that the March 1912 issue of *The Sugar Beet* had included this ditty:

> Cliff H. take notice:
> You can have your new title Live Wire.
> For you've certainly earned that and more.
> But there's one thing the boys won't stand.
> That's to see such a stiff pompadour.

The "live wire" designation probably was prompted by Clifford's service as business manager of *The Sugar Beet* and participation in debate and the senior play. However, his achievements in these extracurricular activities were apparently not too impressive. Clifford's classmate, Ruby Sheaks Olomon, observed in the same news story:

> I admire him because he has had to work for everything he's got. In high school he was a rather poor speaker and not an exceptional leader. He's overcome all of that and is really successful now.

Hope recalled, "I had only one ambition in high school — to become a lawyer and a politician, though I didn't think too much about politics."

Clifford's social activities were mainly confined to Sundays.

> We went to church, and in the afternoons we had dates. Since

we didn't have many cars then, some of the "kids" rode up and down Main on Sundays, but not very much.

Jeannette Wheeler was his high school sweetheart, but they drifted apart when he left for college in the fall of 1913. Years later Eleanor Counsell Riley recalled Clifford as a "very popular, almost prim person" with whom she had had several dates. On one, ginger-haired, spirited Eleanor, on a dare from other students, stole a watermelon from a patch in town, losing a shoe in the process. The owner of the patch was irate, and Clifford was upset with Eleanor.

During his high school days, Clifford became noticeably round-shoul-dered, possibly a result of the heavy, constant lifting at Mack's Grocery. At that time in Garden City there was a lawyer and abstractor, W. C. Pearce, who was a hunchback. Passing Clifford on the street one day, he exclaimed, "Straighten up, boy. Do you want to look like me?" That admonition cured Clifford on the spot. He recalled it frequently in later years.

Despite his rather dignified demeanor, Clifford had a lighter side. In his youth, he had learned several poems and songs that he frequently recited or sang throughout his life. One of his favorite versifiers was Eugene Fitch "Ironquill" Ware, a lawyer from Fort Scott, Kansas, who was then known as the poet laureate of Kansas. Ware was not a great poet, but his work was a good commentary on current events. One of his more famous poems was composed in the Creamerie Restaurant in the 700 block of Kansas Avenue in Topeka after Admiral George Dewey's May 1, 1898, victory in Manila Bay. Clifford recited this poem every May Day:

> Oh dewy was the morning upon the first of May,
> And Dewey was the Admiral down in Manila Bay,
> And Dewey were the Regent's eyes,
> Them orbs of royal blue,
> And do we feel discouraged?
> I do not think we do.

(The Regent referred to was the Regent of Spain, mother of King Alfon-so, who was then a minor.)

I remember well another of Clifford's favorite poems, "The Teacher and the Toad":

> As I went down the new cut road,
> I met the teacher and the toad,
> And every time the toad would jump,
> The teacher'd hide behind the stump.

From boyhood on he loved to sing or hum "Annie Laurie," and his daughter Martha remembered him singing "Moonlight and Roses" and "Smoke Gets in Your Eyes" during his morning shower.

In his spare time as a youth, Clifford read his favorite magazines, *The Youth's Companion* and *The Saturday Evening Post*. And like other members of his family, he was an avid newspaper reader. (Later on, Harry's and Mitta's daughters-in-law were amazed and sometimes chagrined to observe the entire family with noses buried in newspapers for long periods of time.)

Unlike Harry Truman, my father never claimed to have read all the history books in the public library, but he had a deep, abiding love and knowledge of history. As the years went by, his knowledge of the past served him well in analyzing events of his time. When I was growing up he related to me in detail historical events such as the War of the Roses, between the Houses of Lancaster and York in 15th-century England; the career of the Kansas poet, Eugene Fitch Ware; the story of Alfred Dreyfus and anti-Semitism in France in the 1890s and thereafter; the heavyweight boxing championship fights between John L. Sullivan and Gentleman Jim Corbett and their successors; the story of how John J. Pershing, a captain in the Army, married the daughter of Francis E. Warren, sheep farmer and senator from Wyoming (he was described as "the greatest shepherd since Abraham") — and thereafter Pershing was promoted to the rank of Brigadier General in one fell swoop; the stories in Francis Parkman's *Oregon Trail* and the Western writings of Theodore Roosevelt (he especially enjoyed Western authors); and the sequence of events following the assassination of the Austrian Archduke Franz Ferdinand in June 1914, leading to World War I.

During 1958, Roosevelt's centennial year, and in the 1960s, Clifford wrote newspaper columns extolling Roosevelt's accomplishments and virtues. In one column he recalled:

> Theodore Roosevelt was the first President I ever saw, and
> that was long after he was out of the Presidential office. If my

memory is correct, it was 1914 or 1915, at one of the railroad stations in Topeka. His train stopped for about five minutes and he made a short talk in characteristic fashion. That was certainly one of the high spots of my life, at least up to that time.

All of us, I guess, are hero worshippers to some extent, and I must admit that Theodore Roosevelt was the greatest hero of my boyhood days and remained such throughout the years. I was eight years old when he became President, and from that time on I followed all of his activities. I read everything about him that I could lay my hands on.

As a premium for securing subscriptions to the *The Youth's Companion*, I received a copy of one of Theodore Roosevelt's earliest books, *Hunting Trips of a Ranchman*. I literally wore it out with reading. Afterward, I read others of his books, particularly those about the west and the accounts of his trips and explorations.

Upon retiring from the Presidency, he made his famous hunting trip to Africa, followed by visits to several western European countries on his way home. He had not been home long before he again began to take an active part in politics. He felt the Taft Administration had gone back on many of the principles that he favored. Although he had strongly supported Taft in 1908 — in fact had made him President — he did not hesitate to break with him over governmental policies. This took him into the campaign of 1912 where, denied a nomination by the Republicans, he accepted the Progressive nomination after his friends in the Republican Convention had withdrawn and organized the Progressive Party.

How well I remember that campaign of 1912. I wasn't old enough to vote and I never wanted to vote so badly in my life. I was for Roosevelt all the way and can well remember the disappointment and chagrin I felt when my father and grandfather — both standpat Republicans — voted for Taft. . . .[5]

To those who knew my father, it may be difficult to explain his great admiration for Roosevelt, when — on the surface at least — they had such different personalities. Roosevelt was flamboyant, egotistical, and domineering. My father was reserved, self-effacing, and quietly persuasive. He never told me why he admired Roosevelt so much, and I regret I never asked him. I can only hazard a guess: my father admired Roosevelt's courage — political and physical, his telling the truth as he saw it, his sincere belief in family values, and his talent for putting first things first. I also believe my father, perhaps, was envious of Roosevelt's leadership style and ability to persuade by fiery speeches. Such attributes did not come naturally to my father, and he never attempted to be something he was not for the sake of popularity and momentary glory.

Without a doubt, the reading he did in his early years had much to do with the formation of his philosophy of what constituted the great and the good and the stuff of heroes and role models.

At last, in May 1913, when almost 20, Clifford graduated from high school. The class of 27 included his sister Mary and his cousin, Joe Harold Hope. Mary was the salutatorian. Years later in a graduation address at Garden City High School, Clifford remembered those days:

> In these times, I would be called a drop-out. I was out a year after graduating from grade school and two more between my sophomore and junior years. I was fortunate in being able to return. Many of my contemporaries could not do so.
>
> But they were good days to us. I was reminded of them a few years ago when President Eisenhower, speaking at Abilene about his boyhood, said, in substance: I realize now that we were desperately poor, but the nice thing about it was that we didn't know it. That's much like my recollection of those times.

In the fall Clifford left for college. Harry, at long last, had financial security under Civil Service as assistant postmaster, and Mitta remained a housewife and a good mother. They could take pride in their children in the years ahead. Mary became a bookkeeper, teller, and eventually an assistant vice president of a Garden City bank. Mildred taught Spanish and French in Kansas high schools. And, after a period of illness, she worked for the Red Cross as a volunteer, office secretary, and as executive secretary, serving for 37 years before her retirement at 75. Cecil, a dispatcher with the Santa Fe Railway in La Junta, Colorado, and Las Vegas, New Mexico, was a loyal defender of his employer. Active in the Presbyterian church and Rotary Club, he was the only one of the Hope children to become a Democrat. He explained to his daughter that he liked being contrary. Hollis was a high school coach and teacher in Wisconsin. Although he was overage for military service in World War II, he volunteered for the National Park Service and, with his family, endured frigid winters in Yellowstone National Park. Ralph was a skilled, accomplished lawyer in Atchison and Wichita, Kansas. After retiring he wrote an interesting memoir about growing up in Garden City. As for Clifford, he became a lawyer, state legislator, and U.S. Representative. In the eyes of his parents, he could do no wrong.

Chapter 2

Lincoln, Topeka, and Fountainbleau (1913-1919)

LIFFORD'S QUANDARY OF where to attend college was settled by an offer from his uncle, Elmer Ellsworth Ragsdale, who lived in Lincoln, Nebraska. Uncle Elmer, the brother of Clifford's mother, lived with his two daughters, Wilma and Georgia. (I believe his wife, Alice Suit, had died by this time.) His offer of free lodging was too good to refuse.

Clifford's original intention was to attend the University of Nebraska, a land-grant college that required all males to take military training in afternoon classes. Because he had to work afternoons, Clifford could not arrange a suitable schedule at the university. And thus he opted to attend Nebraska Wesleyan College, enrolling in advanced U.S. history, European history, freshman rhetoric, the novel, the essay, debate, and two German courses. He maintained grades in the A and B range, with his highest mark, 95, earned in debate.

Little is known of the year at Lincoln except for a story Clifford loved to tell about his afternoon employment — at a grocery store, of course. When he was not waiting on a customer, his employer would order, "Move these packing cases (from the curb into the store) while you're resting."

At first Clifford planned to obtain an A.B. degree in three or four years and then enter law school. However, by the end of the year in Lincoln, he had decided that if he followed that program he would be "too old" by the time he finished. After years of being poor, he was eager to start making a good living as a lawyer as soon as possible. His Aunt Cora Lee, known as "Coe," and her physician husband, Charles B. Van Horn, offered him room and board at their home in Topeka in return for household chores. Again this was an offer that suited his needs, one that enabled him to attend Washburn Law School in Topeka at minimum expense.

Aunt Coe was a remarkable, formidable woman, the exact opposite of her diminutive, quiet older sister Mitta. She described herself as a "large woman." Indeed, she was that in every sense of the word, and she was proud of it. She had attended Highland Park College in Des Moines, majoring in physical education and speech. Her first and last job outside the home was teaching at the Quaker Academy in Washington, Kansas, where she met and married one of the teachers, Charles Van Horn. In a few years she and Charlie decided he should become a physician, thus he entered the Kansas Medical College in Topeka. Together they worked his way through medical school. Coe rented rooms, took in washing, and started a family. By 1914 they had built a comfortable home at 1215 Mulvane. This was Clifford's home during the three years he attended Washburn Law School.

To earn his keep Clifford helped Aunt Coe clean house and wash dishes, work he detested. More pleasant was his job of delivering *The Topeka State Journal* in the afternoons and sitting with the neighbors' children. One child he baby-sat was Bernard Fink, who later married Ruth Garvey, daughter of Raymond and Olive Garvey, the noted Kansas entrepreneurs. Another was Arthur Carruth, Jr., whose father was editor of the *The Topeka State Journal*. The Carruth family connection proved to be valuable for Clifford a decade later when he ran for Congress.

Washburn Law School had been established in 1903 under the leadership of the president of Washburn College, Norman Plass, and Robert Stone, a prominent Topeka attorney. In 1914 the school was housed in a downtown business building at 211 West Sixth. It was known as "one of the finest law buildings in the West." Far from the college campus in southwest Topeka, it was close to the courts.

Clifford became an outstanding debater and captain of one of the two debate teams. He was president of his class in his senior year and the only Law School honor graduate. Kansas Supreme Court Justice Henry F. Mason of Garden City, an adjunct law professor at Washburn, reportedly said Clifford was the best law student he had ever taught. When the United States entered World War I in April 1917, Washburn's graduating seniors — including Clifford — who were entering officer training camps in May were automatically granted degrees. Even more accommodating was the action of the Kansas Board of Law Examiners. Clifford passed the bar examination, ordinarily a frightening ordeal, by answering one oral question. That, too, was a story he enjoyed telling many times in later years.

Clifford's college years were not all work and study. An item in the 1916 *Kaw*, Washburn's yearbook, alluded to another interest:

> He made the highest grade in "domestic relations." Why he
> did, we don't know. But we are told that someone has Hope.

The young lady alluded to is not known, but it was not Pauline Elizabeth Sanders, a senior at Topeka High School, for it wasn't until the next year, when she was a freshman at Washburn, that she and Clifford became serious friends. And so the year 1917 was significant for Clifford, beyond the coming of war and the passing of the bar.

Pauline was born in Topeka on March 2, 1899, the daughter of Martin Jesse Sanders and Laura Bridwell Corkadel. Little is known of Martin's family and early life except that he was born of Simeon Sanders and Elizabeth Storer in 1867 in Perry County, Ohio. A carpenter by trade, he came to Kansas as a young man and married Laura in 1895.

Laura's parents were George F. Corkadel and Tinetta Hogan. George was born in Oxford, Pennsylvania, and at 17, in 1862, enlisted in Company C of the 124th Regiment, Pennsylvania Volunteers. He fought in the battles of Antietam and Chancellorsville and came to Valley Falls, Kansas, with his cousin, Wall Dickey, in 1866. He and Tinetta were married in 1868.

Little is known of Tinetta and the Hogan family, but she had a famous uncle on her mother's side of the family — Charles Reynolds, better

Aunt Coe — Cora Lee Van Horn, the sister of Armitta Hope.

known as Lonesome Charley Reynolds. Lonesome Charley, George Custer's favorite white scout, was admired by Custer's wife, Elizabeth, for his gentlemanly ways. During his time off, Charley preferred to hunt and fish and think by himself rather than drink and chase women in the frontier towns. Before June 25, 1876, he and others warned Custer of the vast Indian forces near the Little Bighorn River, all to no avail. Assigned to Major Marcus Reno's detachment, Charley was killed in the valley fight on June 25, earlier in the day of Custer's famous "Last Stand."

Two months to the day later, Laura was born to Charley's niece and George Corkadel. As she was growing up, and later as her daughter Pauline was growing up, family members expressed little interest in Uncle Charley or his fate in General Custer's command. They just surmised he had been at the Little Bighorn and was never heard from again. In 1938 a marker with a fence around it was placed at the spot where Charley had fallen.

Like Clifford's parents, Pauline's were endowed with the Protestant work ethic and a puritanical moral code. They were members of the Disciples of Christ church — known to some at the time as the Campbellites — and diligent students of the Bible.

Pauline was an only child. In her later years she intimated that her parents, Martin and Laura, became estranged but reconciled shortly before his untimely death at 59. Pauline felt much closer to her father than to her mother, and she was the apple of his eye. She delighted in telling of his buying her an orange — in simpler times, a rare treat — once when she had an earache.

Martin Sanders wanted to get rich quick. About 1909 he filed a claim for a homestead on the shores of Goose Lake, near Lakeview, Oregon. He hoped to discover oil or something else of value on or under the land. The family moved to Oregon for five years or so, Martin to the homestead and Laura and Pauline to Portland, where Laura taught Chinese children. Martin worked as a carpenter in Lakeview to help make ends meet.

In the fall of 1912, Pauline returned alone from Portland to Topeka to begin high school while her parents remained in Oregon to meet the five-year residence requirement on the homestead. On the long train ride east to Topeka, Pauline was befriended by a young woman, Nellie M. Thone. Although they never met again, they became lifelong pen pals.

In 1916 Pauline graduated from Topeka High School, majoring in math and music. She had a role in the senior play and was president of the girls' glee club. She was an active member of the Central Park Christian Church, singing in the choir and serving as soloist at a number of weddings.

In the meantime, her parents had moved back from Oregon. No oil or minerals had been found on the homesteaded land. It was sheep pasture then and is to this day. In Topeka Martin became a building contractor and later purchased and operated the College Hill Hardware Store near the Washburn campus. Laura resumed her housewifely duties, canning fruits and vegetables, quilting, and working hard. Pauline once commented that the ambitious Laura would have been happier if she had been a single businesswoman, something virtually impossible for women at that time.

In the fall of 1916 Pauline entered Washburn College, graduating in 1920 with a major in mathematics. In 1990 John Troxall, a classmate, remembered her affectionately. She was known then as Polly, he recalled. She and John read the plays of J. M. Barrie and the poetry of Edna St. Vincent Millay and Carl Sandburg. "She had sparkling wit and an enchanting laugh," John remembered. The young Polly was a student council representative and was active in the YMCA on campus and the Alpha Phi social sorority. She and John talked of becoming foreign missionaries. The highlight of their college years was attending the Eighth International Student Volunteer Convention in Des Moines at the beginning of 1920. About 7,000 students from 40 nations representing 1,000 colleges heard speeches from the ablest men and women in the world. It was a global, mind-expanding experience.

Pauline, much like her mother, had career ambitions. For a time, she worked for a Topeka physician, giving thought to becoming a doctor. Though her dreams, much as her mother's had been, were given up for marriage, throughout her life she retained an interest in "doctoring," always willing, almost eager, to attend to cuts and abrasions. Her family recalled that even when cutting up a chicken for a meal, she spoke with interest and admiration of surgical procedures performed by physicians of the time.

Pauline's outstanding attributes from an early age were concern and compassion for individuals and their problems. As years went by, such matters received her attention over national or world problems or politics. Because she was an only child, she nurtured close kinship with many of her cousins and other relatives and maintained contact with them throughout her life. She used her talents to establish a round-robin letter through which about 35 classmates received news of one another once or twice a year for many years. And she had a keen sense of humor, which never diminished, even when she developed serious health problems in later years.

As the romance between Pauline and Clifford blossomed during the years of World War I, the four adult children of Harry and Mitta Hope volunteered for duty. (Clifford undoubtedly would have been drafted in due course.) Cecil, 19, enlisted in the Navy, where he served for 15 months, including a tour in the West Indies. Mary and Mildred worked as clerks in the War Department in Washington, D.C. Mary's office was in the newly constructed Munitions Building on Constitution Avenue, where she answered inquiries from parents and wives who had not heard from their men in service for some time. Mary stayed in Washington several years after the war before returning to her bank job in Garden City. Mildred worked in the old State, War, and Navy Building (now the Old Executive Office Building) directly west of the White House. She returned to Kansas in 1919, becoming the first graduate of Garden City Junior College the following year.

Clifford left for the first officer's training camp at Fort Riley in May 1917. He was commissioned a second lieutenant in the infantry in August. Pauline visited him at Fort Riley on weekends whenever possible, and they became quite serious about each other during those four months. He was stationed first at Camp Cody near Deming, New Mexico, and then at Camp Doniphan in Fort Sill, Oklahoma, where he was assigned to Company D, 137th Infantry Regiment of the 35th Division (Kansas-Missouri National Guard). In February Clifford was transferred to Company K, 340th Infantry of the 85th Division at Camp Custer, Michigan. In July 1918 he arrived at Camp Mills, New York, a port of embarkation. He sailed on a converted British cargo ship in a convoy to Liverpool, arriving August 11. Taking a train across what he described as the "fresh and green" English countryside, he arrived in Le Havre, France, on August 14. U.S. flags were everywhere. He wrote to Pauline, "Never did Old Glory look so beautiful."

Between that August 1918 and April 1919, when he was discharged, Clifford wrote Pauline 65 letters. She saved all of them. Unfortunately, he did not save any of her numerous letters to him, so one may only surmise what she wrote to him by reading his responses to her. These letters are the only preserved written record of Clifford's thoughts and deeds during his first 24 years. Most of the letters are long and detailed, revealing Clifford as a keen observer of French history, customs, and culture — and of Army ways. He was especially sympathetic to the war roles and responsibilities of French women. Later — after the war had ended in November — his great desire to return home and to Pauline led him to criticize the French

Clifford Hope was commissioned a second lieutenant in the Infantry in August 1917.

as being "set in their ways" and to castigate the Army for its interminable red tape and delays. Yet, overall, the letters were indicative of his interest in other people and their problems, hopes, and despairs. Primarily, of course, they were love letters.

Clifford wrote tenderly in each letter. He wished to return and "be with her always" instead of being together for "a few hours snatched between trains." And he always assured her that he was "just fine." Frequently he complained that she didn't write often enough — only once a week or so, and he lamented the delay in receiving what she did write. It was evident that he was much more interested than she in marrying as soon as possible. Pauline, only 19 in 1918, was thoroughly enjoying college life. Nevertheless, Clifford displayed the same determination in winning her that he later displayed in pursuing political office.

Clifford wrote of a touching incident at Le Havre, telling Pauline of an orphan asylum there for Belgian children who had lost their parents in the war:

> I was marching a detail down the road, and we met a group of the children out for a walk. As we passed them, they all took their hats off and held them until we had gone by. It wasn't much, but it made me awfully proud of being an American.

Between Le Havre and Paris, Clifford's battalion was stopped on its journey to the front and diverted to Recloses, a small, 1,100-year-old village near Fountainbleau, southeast of Paris. They were the first Americans in this village. The Inter-Allied tank school had just been established at Fountainbleau to teach the coordination of infantry advancing with tanks. The French were in command. But there were also British, Italian, and Algerian troops. (Hope described the Algerians as "wild, savage-looking fellows who carry knives almost as large as they are.")

In a letter written in late August 1918, Clifford expressed his admiration of the French:

> They have borne the brunt of this thing for over four years, borne every privation and all the desolation that the cruelest of wars can cause — there is scarcely a family that hasn't sacrificed one or more of its loved ones — and yet, they are just as smiling, confident, and hopeful as they ever were; and thru it all

they've had a "never say die" spirit that will win over everything. And now that we are over here, they can hardly find
words to express their gratitude for, and appreciation of, our
coming.

But by the end of October, Clifford had a different view of the French.
They were trying his patience. He wrote Pauline:

> The French are a wonderful people in many ways, but it's
> certianly [*sic*] painful to see how far behind the times they are.
> These peasants don't get a new idea in their heads once in a
> hundred years. They may become more progressive after the
> war but I doubt it. They are so set in the old way of doing things
> that they look on any change with suspicion. The worst trouble
> is that they like to spend their time talking about doing things,
> but they never take time to get them done. And if they do
> accomplish anything, then they must spend more time talking
> about what they've done, instead of doing something else. Time
> is no object to them at all. The woman who does my laundry
> generally takes about two weeks at it, whereas if she would get
> busy it would take about an hour. If I had charge of this coun-
> try, I'd have a billion "do it now" signs painted and stick them
> up on every street corner and crossroads in France. After this
> war is over, I haven't the slightest doubt but that they'll spend
> five or ten years talking about it before they begin any work of
> reconstruction.

Entertainment for the troops was provided by the YMCA. Among those
he met with the Y volunteers was Dr. James Naismith, the inventor of basketball, then with the University of Kansas. Occasionally there was time
for sightseeing. On a Sunday in September, Clifford visited the royal
palace in Fountainbleau — where Napoleon had abdicated in 1814 — and
the forest surrounding it. Clifford later related to his family an incident
from this visit. While walking in the woods, he felt the call of nature. He
was without toilet paper, but he had with him his old shipping orders for
which, he decided, he would have no further use. Within the next few
days, however, he found he did need the orders and had to go back to the
woods to retrieve them!

Clifford longed to go the front, but the French refused to release his battalion. Despite the good war news, he thought the war might well last another year. On November 11 Clifford's battalion was finally alerted to be ready to leave on an hour's notice. "What irony! To be ordered up to the front on the last day of the war," Clifford wrote home. That was one more grievance against the German Kaiser. He "might have waited a week or two longer. . . . He probably heard we were coming," Clifford said. Then he described the end of the war in the village of Recloses.

> France is wild tonight. They're firing cannons, ringing church bells, having parades and doing various other things by way of celebration. Yet it isn't the noisy gala occasion one would imagine it would be. Not at all like what is probably going on in the states. In a way there is a sort of solemn note in it, more like a thanksgiving service than anything else. The war is over but to these people who have suffered so much and lost so much, the world will never be quite the same as before the war. Peace has come at last, but it can never bring back what they have lost. The priest held a sort of service in the little church this afternoon. There was an old woman there who has lost her husband and four sons, all she had, in the war. With tears running down her cheeks, she was uttering a prayer of thankfulness that it was all over.

Prior to the November 11 Armistice, Clifford had mentioned the easy life he was leading much of the time — and after the armistice, at least for the officers, it got even better. In mid-November, he described a "tea party."

> . . . There is a fine old French gentleman who speaks excellent English, living in a town near here. He thinks a great deal of Americans, and this afternoon invited all the American officers here to his house for a tea party. He has a beautiful house, one of the loveliest I've ever been in. There were a lot of charming mademoiselles who could talk English present and after some fine music he turned us loose on what we came after: the tea. Well, it was some feed. They served tea, hot chocolate, chocolate glaze, champagne, sandwiches, wafers, and so many

different kinds of cake that I grew dizzy and lost count. I was quite overwhelmed because usually one has to pull out a pocket full of bread tickets to even get a slice of bread. I voted it a very good tea party.

Clifford had the duty of censoring the outgoing letters (30 or 40 a day) of enlisted men. He wrote Pauline that the bulk of the letters indicated "American girls will be appreciated as never before." He also commented, "I should be quite a connoissuer [*sic*] of love letters when I get back." At the same time, he confessed, he felt guilty reading other people's letters. He assured Pauline the beautiful mademoiselles had not turned his head. "I know that you trust me just as I trust you, and I'll do everything in the world to be worthy of it."

By December 12 Clifford had been transferred to Nantes, then the fourth largest city in France, at the mouth of the Loire River on the Atlantic coast. It was "the dirtiest city from a sanitary and moral standpoint" he had ever seen, he wrote, but he was billeted with a rich family in the suburbs, sleeping on a feather bed. Christmas dinner included "four kinds of wine and two kinds of champagne and cognac." The following night there was a dance with "beaucoup belle mademoiselles." He wrote, "If I don't get out of the army soon, I'll be so lazy that I'll just faint at the thought of doing a day's work." By year's end he was back in the barracks sleeping on a cot, but he still had a "soft job." He visited the Nantes Cathedral, the second oldest in France, "escorted by an old guide who was dolled up like a brigadier general in the Abyssinian Army." Clifford described Nantes as a cosmopolitan city with "French soldiers and sailors, Chinese coolies in French uniforms, Russians, Czechoslovakians, Belgians, Moroccans, Japanese sailors, and German prisoners."

In mid-January, Clifford was transferred to Tiffanges, a village 40 kilometers southeast of Nantes. Nearby was the infamous Bluebeard's Castle where Bluebeard had murdered his wives and many children, according to the villagers. Clifford served as chief of police for the MPs. Some soldiers of the tough 2nd Division, impatiently waiting to go home, rioted. He wrote to Pauline, "16 of the unit men are in the jug. I don't think there will be more trouble." In February he was transferred to several villages near Le Mans to the east, where a short-lived rumor surfaced that his outfit would be sent to Archangel and become involved in the Russian civil war. The 339th Regiment of the 85th Division had previously been sent there.

Now eager to return home, Clifford described France as a "beastly country." Scheduled return dates were continually moved forward, as is always the case when an army is demobilizing. Pauline marked his March 8 letter "Last letter from France." In it Clifford wrote sarcastically, "It won't be long until we walk up the gangplank and with tears streaming down my cheeks, I'll say 'Goodbye, France.' A touching scene." He said he was "half drunk over the idea of going home."

In late March Clifford sailed from Brest on the former luxury liner *Leviathan*, a striking contrast with the British cargo ship which had brought him to Liverpool. His April 3 letter from Camp Upton, New York, reported he was being "decooterized [deloused] for about the 20th time." Five days later he wrote he was

> tired of hanging around waiting for someone in Washington to unroll a thousand yards of red tape. I've seen enough inefficiency in the army before to make any ordinary man gray-haired, but this place approaches the limit.

His last letter, dated the 18th, reported he should reach Camp Funston, at Fort Riley, Tuesday night. He was going to see Pauline within a week, and then, he wrote, "I'm going to be the happiest man in the world."

Clifford was discharged at Camp Funston on April 25, 1919, but there is no record of what happened immediately after that. He and Pauline were not married until January 1921. Pauline wanted to graduate from Washburn and did not wish to be rushed into what she considered a hasty marriage.

Being an officer, living in France, and associating with the cream of French society was a heady experience for a boy who had grown up dirt poor. It gave Clifford self-esteem, confidence, and leadership training, which would be useful to him in his future political activities.

Chapter 3

The Kansas Legislature and the Ku Klux Klan (1919-1925)

O

N MAY 1919 the leading lawyer and most distinguished citizen of Garden City was William Easton Hutchison. His partner, Charles Elijah Vance, had been elected district judge the preceding November, and Judge Hutchison, as he was usually addressed, was looking for a young associate or two. The first he selected was Clifford Ragsdale Hope, just returned from two years of service in the Army. Thus began a fortuitous lifetime friendship for both. The Judge became a mentor and second father to Clifford during the 1920s.

Born on Bastille Day, July 14, 1860, on a farm near Oxford, Chester County, Pennsylvania, Judge Hutchison proudly recalled that his first memory was one of hearing the roar of the cannon in the Battle of Gettysburg in July 1863. He entered Lafayette College at Easton, Pennsylvania, in 1879. He suffered from a serious respiratory ailment, probably caused by the smog in the area. So, the story goes, upon his graduation and admission to the bar, his doctor told him he might live a few years longer but only if he moved to a cleaner, drier climate. Hence, in 1887 the young lawyer found his way west to Grant County, Kansas, to become county attorney in that wild-and-woolly pioneer settlement.

It is not known when his doctor died, but the Judge stayed in southwest Kansas to live to the age of 92. Judge Hutchison had a difficult time eking out a living at first. Shortly before his death, he told me the story of borrowing money from a cowboy to pay his rent. Engrossed in a card game at the time, the cowboy tossed his wallet to the Judge, telling him to take what he needed from it.

A courageous prosecutor, Judge Hutchison soon earned the respect of the community. His appearance and manner of dress commanded respect too. His red beard was neatly trimmed. A Prince Albert suit, complete with tails, high-top black shoes, and a white shirt with winged collar were his daily attire. This was the customary dress of Pennsylvania lawyers at the time, and he wore this mark of distinction for the rest of his life. In 1892 he was elected district judge, and four years later, while continuing as judge, he moved to Garden City. He was defeated in a race for Congress in 1906, after which he commenced law practice in Garden City. Charles Elijah Vance joined him in 1908.

When his brother, Dr. Joseph Hutchison, and his wife were killed in an automobile accident in 1913, the Judge and his wife Reba, who were childless, adopted the three orphaned children, who all grew up to be distinguished citizens. Ralph, the oldest, became president of Lafayette College and a close friend of Dwight D. Eisenhower.

Judge Hutchison continued to prosper professionally, serving as president of the State Bar Association in 1911. That same year he became secretary of the State Board of Law Examiners, a position he held until he was appointed to the Kansas Supreme Court in 1927. Upon his retirement in 1939, he returned to Garden City, living alone at the Warren Hotel, eating at a table reserved for him in the hotel's coffee shop, and climbing the long flight of stairs, with the assistance of a bellboy, to his old law office in the Walters Building just up the street from the hotel.

In 1925 the East Ward grade school was named Hutchison Grade School in the Judge's honor. He took a special interest in the students there. To encourage them to be thrifty, he established a savings program on which he paid interest on all student savings accounts. The teacher in each classroom kept track of all those nickels and dimes, no doubt driving some teachers "up the wall." When the Judge died, his will and three codicils set up many complicated trusts that required administration for 20 years. Unfortunately, his estate totaled only $60,000, and its administration was a burden on A. M. Fleming, his law partner. But the diligent, hardworking Fleming, trained by Hutchison, never complained.

In addition to his professional activities, Judge Hutchison was active in Masonic affairs, the Republican Party, and the Presbyterian church — all three to him showed the "mark of a gentleman." And though he was proper, he was not stuffy. On one occasion when I was a small boy, the Judge was invited to dinner at our home. I insisted that my father show him "how the donkey goes," a performance that required my father to stick his thumbs in his ears while saying "Ee-aw, Eee-aw." My father, with great embarrassment, obliged, and the Judge, aiming to please me, laughed politely.

There were also apocryphal stories about the Judge's always-immaculate appearance. When everyone else riding in the buggy or buckboard through the countryside was covered with dust, the legend went, nary a speck would show on the Judge's Prince Albert attire. The Judge was an intelligent, hardworking, and scrupulous lawyer and a shrewd politician. Above all, he was a good and kindly man.

Hutchison started young Clifford Hope as an associate in 1919 on a salary of $125 per month. Several years later the salary was increased to $200 and, although Clifford remained on a salary, I believe the Judge regarded the young lawyer as a partner.

The firm had an extensive practice in western Kansas, trying many cases. Yet no member owned a car. East-west travel was easy enough on the many passenger trains, but going north-south required hiring a livery vehicle — a taxi.

In 1921 Arthur Milo Fleming was added to the firm as an associate. Fleming had a young family, and unable to attend college or law school, he became the Judge's secretary in 1919 and read law under the tutelage of the Judge and C. E. Vance. For a time he also served as Vance's court reporter. Following the civic service example of his mentor, Judge Hutchison, Fleming became county attorney, a member and president of the school board, and a city commissioner and mayor. He was always a loyal supporter of Clifford's political career, which spanned 36 years. In Fleming's later years in practice, I was one of his law partners. Never have I known a harder-working lawyer or one who enjoyed the practice of law more.

In 1920 the Judge encouraged Clifford to run for the vacant Kansas Legislature seat from the Finney County 115th district. Clifford was elected without opposition; but in 17 subsequent general elections for the Kansas Legislature and the U.S. Congress, he always had an opponent. The Legislature at that time met only in odd-numbered years for a session usually not exceeding three months. Each of Kansas's 105 counties had a representative, with an additional 20 representatives distributed among the larger counties, no county having more than 3. The rural counties controlled the Legislature.

That same year of his election, Clifford and Pauline made preparations for marriage — but not too hastily. Pauline insisted upon graduating from Washburn first. The summer of 1920, after graduation, she lived in the Alpha Phi house. In the fall she taught the sophomore class at the high school in Nortonville, a small town in Atchison County. And thus the wedding was postponed until a few days before the Legislature convened in January. There is no record of their visits during 1919 and 1920, but the Santa Fe ran many trains daily between Garden City and Topeka. It can be assumed that Clifford was a frequent passenger.

In preparation for marriage, Clifford purchased a residence on a 1½-acre tract near Garden City's east city limits on a quiet, short street named Gillespie Place. Built around 1911, the three-bedroom house had an unfinished basement and attic. On the back acre, there was a chicken house and an orchard. The residential development had been initiated by Frank Gillespie, who had come to Garden City in 1907 as superintendent of the new sugar factory. The gravel street had no curbs, like most streets in Garden City at the time.

The previous owners of the house were Blanche and Phil Darby, a popular family with three teenage sons. Their home had been a gathering place for many. Ralph Hope described Mrs. Darby, his Sunday School teacher, as a "charming and beautiful lady." For some 50 years after the Darby family occupied the house, old-timers in Garden City still referred to it as "the old Darby place."

Little did Clifford know in 1920 that the old Darby place would be the residence for three generations of Hopes and would still be the home of Clifford, Jr., and Dolores Hope in 1995. Early on, some residents of the street, with delusions of grandeur, had brick pillars inscribed "Gillespie Place, Private Drive" erected at both ends of the drive. The street was not then and never has been a "private drive."

Clifford and Pauline's wedding was a simple one, apparently arranged to suit Clifford's busy schedule. It took place on a weekend (three days before the 1921 legislative session opened) in Martin and Laura Sanders' Topeka home, 1271 West Street. Dr. Henry E. Wolfe of Wichita, a Methodist minister whose daughters were close friends of Pauline, performed the ceremony. There were 40 guests, mostly family. An undocumented clipping from a Garden City newspaper, after reprinting a report from *The Topeka State Journal*, editorialized:

> This wedding is of particular interest to the people of Garden City. The groom grew up to manhood here, received his early training in the city schools, and afterwards went through college and law school mostly by his own efforts. At all times he so conducted himself that he secured and kept the confidence of the people, and last fall when they were looking around for a man to represent the county in the legislature Mr. Hope became the unanimous choice. Since his return from the war he has been associated with Judge Hutchison in the practice of law. He and his bride will receive a cordial welcome when they return home.

Clifford could not have written a more compelling political ad.

In the spring Pauline conscientiously tried to adjust to western Kansas ways in general and to Garden City and Gillespie Place in particular. By far the youngest wife on Gillespie, she was sensitive to perceived criticism by the older matrons on the block. She joined Fortnightly Club, an afternoon social group, where she began a lifelong friendship with Mae McAllister, wife of a successful local lumber man. She also established a good relationship with Clifford's parents and his sisters, Mary and Mildred.

The 1921 legislative session marked the beginning of Governor Henry J. Allen's second term. An accomplished orator, he was described as having a vigorous, almost combative style in dealing with the crises of his office. Clifford admired the Governor's outspoken opposition to the Ku Klux Klan, which had commenced organization in Kansas by mid-1921. Overall, the session was one of mediocre accomplishments, but it did authorize submitting a World War I veterans bonus proposal to the voters, and it gave married women the right to recover damages for personal injuries. But it failed to pass a statewide hard-surfaced road program, which Hope strongly supported. Opponents argued that roads were a local responsibility. It was not until 1928 that a constitutional amendment was adopted authorizing a state highway system.

Clifford made many friends during the legislative session. Though on the opposite side of the "Good Roads" debate, Will P. Lambertson of Brown County, who would later serve in Congress, wrote the young legislator on April 16, 1921: "I liked the way you swung into things." Clifford also had a special friendship with Thomas County Representative A. A. Gillispie, editor and owner of the *The Rexford News*, who later told him, "Mrs. Gillispie will never forget" that she and Pauline "were the brides of the House at our first session."

Clifford became a joiner: the Masonic orders (undoubtedly at the urging of Judge Hutchison), the Odd Fellows, Woodmen of the World, American Legion, Salvation Army, and later Kiwanis Club. He was most active in the Legion, frequently traveling to meetings around the state, a plus for a rising, young political star. By 1921 there were 347 Legion posts in the state, and the veterans organization was a powerful political force in Kansas and the nation throughout the decade.

Hope was involved in many political campaigns in 1922. He supported W. Y. Morgan, publisher of *The Hutchinson Herald*, in a seven-man GOP primary for governor. Morgan won with only 29 percent of the vote; because of his political scars and a fractured party, though, he lost the governorship by 19,000 votes to Jonathan M. Davis, the Democratic candidate. There was a spirited campaign for Speaker of the Kansas House. Clifford's first choice was Ezra Beard of Sedgwick, but he was also a good friend of the winner, Charles Mann, Osborne County newspaper editor.

Hope's correspondence in 1922 shows that in the late summer and fall he was actively soliciting support for his candidacy for speaker pro tem, not a powerful position, but one useful to his climb up the political ladder. Phil Zimmerman, a Spanish-American War veteran and a busy GOP operator, was a strong supporter. In his many letters seeking support from House members, Clifford made neither promises nor threats. Time after time he noted that if the member could not vote for him, "there would be no sore spots" and "we will be good friends just as we have always been." This attitude of never making political threats nor seeking revenge became Hope's hallmark during his career in Congress.

Clifford spent much time seeking to establish a game preserve in Finney County, an unsuccessful effort until some years later. But he did earn the

Judge William
Easton
Hutchison,
Clifford's law
partner, *ca.*
1920.
Finney County
Historical Society,
Garden City, KS

respect and admiration of Alva Clapp, fish and game warden, who wrote, "I would go a long way to please you. You have toted fair with me always."

There is no record of Hope's law firm correspondence, but in 1922 he did not sign up for a $10 life membership in the Kansas State Historical Society because he could not afford it. However, he was able to join the next year after his pay increased to $200 per month.

With the convening of the 1923 session in January, Charles Mann was elected speaker on the first ballot over Karl M. Geddes of Butler County in a close race, 49 to 43. Hope was then elected speaker pro tem over H. W. Shideler of Crawford County, 48 to 43. The maneuvering in the race was a stroke of luck for Hope. *The Topeka Daily Capital* of January 9, 1923, reported on its front page:

> It had been generally understood in lobbying circles that if neither of the seventh district candidates for speaker was nominated, Hope would seek the pro tem place. The withdrawal of J. M. Whitman, of Pratt, and Charles A. Mosher, of Ford, in the agreement to boost Geddes, left the field open for Hope. Up to that time it appeared that Shideler had clear sailing.

Governor Davis's one term in office was stormy. He had a penchant for removing appointed officials from office. He forced the resignation of Dr. Samuel J. Crumbine, popular secretary of the State Board of Health, and the removal of E. H. Lindley as chancellor of Kansas University. However, Ben Paulen, Davis's successor as governor, immediately had Lindley reinstated. The Legislature overrode 34 of Davis's 38 vetoes. In an April 1923 letter, Hope stated that Governor Davis lost prestige "by an arrogance in assuming to himself the right to dictate to the legislature in his autocratic manner."

Although an official state highway system had yet to be established, on April 10, 1923, L. R. Tillotson, a state highway engineer, wrote Clifford:

> I have always known that you were enthusiastic for roads, and I am in hopes that with your position in the Legislature, we can work again in the future on the road program and its final consummation as a fixed state and national program, which would be of benefit to all concerned.

Near the end of the 1923 session there was talk of J. N. Tincher, 7th District congressman, running for governor in 1924, but that did not materialize.

In June 1923, less than two months before his untimely death, President Harding, planning to run for reelection, spoke in Hutchinson and Dodge City; Hope attended those events.

In the meantime, Clifford and Pauline had started a family. Edward Sanders Hope was born on the evening of September 6, 1922, in the Gillespie Place residence. The healthy seven-pound, eight-ounce baby was delivered by Ronald M. Troup, M.D., Garden City's most popular family doctor. Edward was the first grandson of Harry and Mitta Hope and, of course, the only grandchild of Laura and Martin Sanders.

Martin had purchased a lot at 1600 Lincoln Street in Topeka in 1922 and built a three-bedroom home. Its distinctive feature was a concrete exterior finish in which pebble-like rocks were embedded. On visits to Topeka when I was growing up, it was great fun to chip the rocks out of the concrete and play with them. Clifford and Pauline stayed at this residence with her parents during the 1923 and 1925 legislative sessions.

In the early morning on February 16, 1923, the five-month-old Edward seemed restless, with flu-like symptoms. At 5 a.m., Pauline noticed a small blood blister on his body. Blisters spread rapidly, accompanied by internal bleeding. Dr. Belnap, Martin and Laura's physician, was summoned, and later, Dr. Charles Van Horn. They were helpless to stop the bleeding from purpura, a rare blood disease. Edward died early that afternoon.

When word of Edward's death was received at the House session, a delegation of two senators and three representatives, including Nellie Cline, one of only three women in the 1923 Legislature, was appointed to accompany Clifford and Pauline to Garden City. The House adjourned out of respect at noon the next day. Cline, a distinguished lawyer from Larned, was especially helpful to Pauline on the long train ride to Garden City. Edward was the first to be buried in the family plot in Valley View Cemetery, years before his grandparents were put to rest there.

Clifford and Pauline were grief-stricken, but their grief was assuaged by my birth ten months later. Clifford appears to have tried to forget as soon as possible. In his 1923 correspondence file, a telegram from Judge Hutchison is the only reference to Edward's death. I don't recall that my father ever mentioned the death to me except in a letter written on my birthday during the Battle of the Bulge in 1944, when he did not know whether or not I was safe from the Germans' surprise attack. He stated simply how glad he and Pauline were on that day of my birth in 1923, "after losing our first boy." Some years later when Pauline had Edward's shoes bronzed, Clifford showed no interest in even looking at them. He was not one to grieve over what might have been — in family, politics, or life in general. He accepted tragedy and disappointment and got on with his life. Pauline accepted the tragedy also, but for the rest of her life she fondly and sadly remembered their first-born son. She completed Edward's baby book as best she could, pasting in clippings about the legislative delegation and his funeral and a poem which began:

> The baby has gone to the homeland bright,
> An angel in heaven fair;
> Safe from all sickness and sin's dreaded blight,
> Happy in God's gracious care.

On the page recording that Edward "arrived on September 6, 1922," she made a simple, poignant addition: "and left us on Friday, February 16th, 1923, at 2:30 o'clock PM."

When I was growing up, Pauline discussed Edward's birth and death with me periodically. She had thought at first that perhaps she and Clifford were being punished for Clifford's political successes, but she had soon rejected that thought. Years later her daughter, Martha, wrote: "By the time I first learned of Edward's birth and death, Mom spoke of it simply as something that happened. Either the pain of the loss was greatly diminished by then, or she chose not to show it." As for me, probably due to Mom's talking to me about Edward, at an early age I began to think about the mysteries of life and death — why some are taken and some are spared. On the one hand, I realized that but for Edward's death I wouldn't even have arrived, or at least not so soon. On the other hand, I thought how good it would have been to have had a big brother. As an introvert and a dreamer, I spent a lot of time with those thoughts and somehow reached the conclusion that I had an obligation to work doubly hard for Edward's sake and my own.

Pauline recollected my birth in a letter she wrote from Washington at the time of my 27th birthday, on December 21, 1950:

> I don't remember too many details but I do know that late on the night of the twentieth Dr. Troup, Daddy and I sat around the coal range in what is now your kitchen. Dr. Troup sat with a watch in hand with a glance at me then a look at the watch while he told one funny story (which he could do so well) after another. Then in the early morning, he said to me "You'd better go along to bed and have that baby." He didn't add "boy" but I knew so well I was going to have a boy for that's what Daddy and I wanted with all our hearts. You know, for you've been told

so many times, that you filled Edward's place as well as your own and that's why we've always loved you doubly.

In June 1924, Pauline, with her new baby son in tow, spent much time in Topeka and Valley Falls visiting her parents and numerous Sanders and Corkadel relatives. Clifford wrote Representative Elmer Euwer, a banker in Goodland, in July, and at the end of the otherwise strictly political letter, he added,

> I have forgotten whether your new baby is a boy or girl, and don't suppose it makes much difference, because whichever it is, it's worth a billion dollars or so, and probably pays dividends at about the rate of 100%. Our young son is getting quite grown up, over 6 months old now.

Hope ran for a third term in the November general election, defeating Ellsworth Sherman, an industrious and prosperous farmer, by an eight-to-five margin. But most of Hope's political activities in 1924 centered on his campaign for Speaker of the Kansas House. By late April he had begun writing the Republican members, announcing his candidacy and asking for support. A number indicated they might also be candidates: Charles F. Johnson of Leonardville (who was defeated in the primary); Benjamin F. Endres of Leavenworth; F. L. Martin, a former judge, of Hutchinson; Douglas Hudson of Fort Scott; H. W. Shideler of Girard (whom Hope had defeated for speaker pro tem); J. A. Farell of Clay Center; George W. Plummer of Perry; and Clyde W. Coffman of Overbrook. In replies to Hope's letters, many complimented him on his performance as speaker pro tem. Following his usual practice, he referred to his prospective opponents as "good men." For J. H. Glotfelter of Emporia, whose courage he greatly admired, he outlined his thoughts concerning the duties of a good speaker:

> My conception of the duty of the Speaker is that he should give every member an opportunity to be heard and secure a fair consideration of the matters in which he is interested, and that he should not, in any way, use the power of his position to put across any personal opinions which he may have or force through legislation in which he may be particularly interested.[1]

By the time of the Republican caucus in early January, the speakership race had been narrowed to two candidates and one issue: Clyde Coffman supported legislation to legalize the existence of the Ku Klux Klan in Kansas; Clifford Hope firmly opposed it. In the 1924 statewide election and the 1925 legislative session, legalizing the Klan was the most challenging and exciting issue. As Speaker of the House, Hope played a key role in defeating the Klan.

Much has been written concerning the revival of the Klan on a nationwide scale in the 1920s, and several excellent articles have been written by historians on the Klan in Kansas during this period. Little, however, has been written on Clifford Hope's part in the battle. Fortunately, Hope wrote four well-researched newspaper columns on the subject in 1965.[2] In addition, he spoke of the Klan in a wide-ranging taped interview in January 1970. This material is supplemented by my memories of what Clifford told me about the Klan and my own research on the Klan and on the Reverend Gerald B. Winrod, a prominent figure in Kansas from the 1920s to his death in 1957. Winrod believed in conspiracies against white, fundamentalist, Protestant America.

Hope started his series of Klan columns by giving a brief synopsis of the 20th-century Klan, telling how in 1915 a shrewd Alabaman, William J. Simmons, who had been engaged in fraternal organization work, conceived the idea of reorganizing the Klan. "With the help of some clever promoters who knew a good thing when they saw it, Simmons parlayed it into a national organization." Hope explained to his newspaper readers that to give it a wider field of operation, the new Klan, although claiming to be a reincarnation of the earlier organization, actually added anti-Semitic and anti-Catholic stands to its original racist agenda.

To gain a foothold in Kansas, Hope wrote, organizers going into communities directed their first efforts to members of Protestant churches and Masonic orders, where they emphasized what they called the high moral principles of the organization. "And, of course," Hope pointed out, "they appealed to the subconscious and conscious prejudices that most of us have as well as to the fact that Americans are natural-born joiners." He noted that by these tactics "they got many good people, including prominent citizens, as well as some not so good, in the organization." But from the beginning, he pointed out, the organization in Kansas and other northern states lacked the "cement" which held it together in the South, "namely the idea of keeping the Negro in his place." The plain fact that the

Kansas Klan was mostly a money-making project for its organizers and officers made its members the subject of considerable derision and ridicule, Hope wrote, recalling:

> In his campaign for Governor in 1924, William Allen White told the Klansmen they were suckers to pay $10 as a membership fee and buy a lot of paraphernalia in order to hate Negroes, Catholics and Jews when they could stay out of the organization and do it for nothing.

And he told about a song making the rounds about this time, "Daddy Stole Our Last Clean Sheet and Joined the Ku Klux Klan."

Even so, the Klan was an obvious presence in the state — strong enough, in fact, that in 1922 it prompted Governor Henry J. Allen, who was completing his second term, to bring forth a resounding challenge. Hope wrote:

> He ordered the attorney general to bring an action in the Supreme Court to oust the organization for the state on the ground that it was a Georgia corporation which had not obtained a permit to do business in Kansas.

The suit was filed in November 21, 1922. Allen did not stop there, Hope noted. "He took to the stump where he used his rare oratorical gifts to expose the organization and its purposes." In an October 28, 1922, speech at Coffeyville, a strong Klan center, Allen said the Klan and its programs were foreign to the ideals that had long prevailed in Kansas and the nation. In his column, Hope wrote:

> After pointing out how Americans of widely varying racial and religious backgrounds had given their lives on the battlefield of France, Allen concluded with these stirring words: "This is not a political issue. It is not a partisan issue. It transcends the obligations of partisanship and relates itself to the most sacred cause of free government — the cause of individual rights. No more grotesque abuse of the word 'Americanism' could be used than to call this Klan organization American.

Americanism is tolerant, and this is organized intolerance. Americanism is law abiding and this is organized outlawry. Americanism is kind and charitable and neighborly; this is organized cruelty and bigotry. Americanism is broad and big and open and brave; this is narrow and furtive and cowardly."[3]

Hope wrote that it was not clear what part, if any, the Klan had played in the 1922 gubernatorial election, but it had been active in municipal and local elections that year. In a column he stated:

The election returns for 1922 do not indicate that it played any important part as far as the state ticket was concerned. Jonathan M. Davis, the Democratic candidate for Governor, defeated W. Y. Morgan by a little over 18,000 votes. This was an upset, but there were other causes which could have brought it about. There had been a bitter seven-cornered fight for the nomination. In addition, Mr. Morgan had been in politics for many years and bore numerous scars from earlier battles. The remainder of the Republican state ticket was elected and the party had its normal majority in the legislature.

Organization-wise, the Klan's influence increased in 1923 and 1924, Hope noted.

By the latter year, it claimed 100,000 members in Kansas and was beginning to throw its weight around. Klan members elected a mayor in Emporia and in a number of other communities. They began to meddle in school affairs and to set themselves up as moral censors in their communities.

The Klan did not have clear sailing in the state. Some attempts — not always successful — were made to hinder it. Hope wrote:

The attorney general had ruled that Klansmen could not wear masks in their parades, but many local peace officers made no attempt to stop them. On July 31, 1923, 1,200 robed and hooded men paraded down Kansas Avenue in Topeka.

In 1924 and 1925, the Klan made its big play for political power, but although it appeared to be a thriving organization it was, in fact, fighting for its life, Hope wrote:

> It was a Georgia corporation which had not received permission from the State Charter Board to do business in Kansas. Hanging over its head was a suit brought by the attorney general in the State Supreme Court to oust it from doing business in the state, based on the fact it had not secured such permission.

The State Charter Board, Hope pointed out, was composed of three members — the attorney general who had brought the ouster suit; Secretary of State Frank J. Ryan, a Catholic who naturally took a dim view of the Klan and all its works; and the state banking commissioner, who was appointed by the governor. The attorney general and the secretary of state were first termers and candidates for reelection. Hope wrote:

> If both were re-elected and the ouster suit was successful, the position of the Klan would be precarious indeed. The only out then would be legislation to amend the law so as to exempt the Klan from its provisions.

This situation brought the Klan into the 1924 primaries and general election in a big way. The three positions they targeted were secretary of state and attorney general (because of their membership on the Charter Board) and governor (because of his leadership in the party and the fact that he appointed the state banking commissioner and would have to sign any bills to exempt the Klan from the provisions of law relating to foreign corporations). The race for governor in the Republican primary was a close one. There were four candidates. Lieutenant Governor Ben S. Paulen, who had the Klan endorsement, came out 8,000 votes ahead of Clyde M. Reed, who opposed the Klan. Former Governor W. R. Stubbs was the third man, 6,000 votes behind Reed; a fourth candidate received only a small vote. Hope added:

> Since Paulen received only 35 percent of the vote, it could not be considered a very impressive show of Klan strength but it gave the organization a victory which it badly needed at the

time. Ryan and Attorney General Griffith both had Klan-supported opponents in the primary but each won rather handily.

At the Republican Party council, efforts were made to insert an anti-Klan plank in the platform but it failed (according to Hope, principally because of the opposition of the nominee for governor). Hope believed this failure to take an anti-Klan position probably did more than anything else to get William Allen White into the governor's race as an independent, anti-Klan candidate. Hope wrote:

> While his entry did not affect the results as far as the governorship was concerned, it enlivened what was otherwise a dull campaign and drew nationwide attention to Kansas. White's was no front-porch campaign. For six weeks, he covered every quarter of the state in his Dodge and drew large crowds wherever he spoke.

It was a Republican year — in the state and in the nation. Coolidge carried Kansas by a tremendous vote. In the governor's race, Paulen received 323,403 votes, Davis 182,861, and White 149,811. Ryan and Griffith were elected, but ran far behind the rest of the ticket. In the legislative races, Republicans elected 90 of 125 members of the House and 32 of 40 members of the Senate.

On January 10, 1925, the Supreme Court announced its decision on the state's case to exclude the Klan from doing business in Kansas. Hope wrote:

> The decision was in favor of the state and the judgment of the court prohibited the Klan from organizing or controlling lodges of the Knights of the Ku Klux Klan in Kansas or exercising any corporate functions in the state.

The decision came three days before the opening of the Legislature, and the field of battle shifted immediately to the third floor of the State House. Hope noted:

> I got a pretty good idea of the Klan strength when they came

within two votes of defeating me for Speaker of the House in the Republican caucus.

He had thought he had the speakership locked up by eight to ten votes. Such was the power of the Klan at that time; it was living up to the name "the invisible empire."

The fight in the Legislature was on. Hope wrote that the first indication of Klan legislative activity was the introduction of Senate Bill 269 on February 6:

> This bill exempted foreign benevolent and charitable corporations (which the Klan claimed to be) from the requirement to secure approval of the State Charter Board before doing business in the State. This was the beginning of a series of legislative gyrations which is probably without parallel in the Kansas legislature.

The Committee on Corporations, to which the bill was referred, recommended that it be referred to the Committee on Judiciary. That committee reported it favorably on February 19. It came up in the Senate on February 25. Hope recalled:

> Opponents offered amendments to make the bill inapplicable to organizations whose members wore masks in public, or which incited mob violence or racial hatred or religious intolerance. These amendments were voted down by the bill's supporters who had previously been claiming it was an innocent little bill to help lodges like the Masons and the Odd Fellows.

The bill passed the Senate by a vote of 23 to 14 and reached the House on February 27. Hope wrote:

> The ease with which it passed the Senate made its proponents pretty cocky. This perhaps was their undoing. They stated publicly that Governor Paulen had promised to sign the bill and before it could be referred to a House Committee, a motion was made to declare an emergency, suspend the rules and advance the bill to a roll call. This motion, which requires

a two-thirds vote is usually reserved for bills relating to God, Home, and Mother — or to the Flag, or maybe Veterans.

The roll was called. The vote was 77 yeas and 40 nays. Hope observed:

> It was a surprising display of Klan strength, but it wasn't two-thirds, and the move failed. This was the beginning of a long series of parliamentary moves by proponents and opponents. In all, there were five roll call votes in the House with the opponents gaining as the issues were better understood. The bill was reported without recommendation by the Judiciary Committee. The final vote on March 6th was Yeas 57, Nays 65. This ended the Klan as a political force in Kansas and also got it off the back of Governor Paulen and the Republican Party.

What Hope's newspaper article did not mention was what happened to Senate Bill 269 from the time it passed the Senate on February 25 until its first vote in the House on February 27. The clerk of the House in the 1925 session was O. H. Hatfield, chosen by Hope. Hatfield had been a representative from Gray County in the 1921 and 1923 sessions. He ran for the state senate in 1924 but was defeated. He and Hope were good friends, so his appointment as chief clerk was a natural. At the time Senate Bill 269 passed the Senate, Hope was in Wichita, or on his way there, to give a speech to the Kansas Livestock Association annual meeting. He did not return via train until the early morning of February 27. The Klan supporters had deliberately waited until Hope was gone before rushing the bill through the Senate. The plan then was to ram it through the House under emergency procedures while Hope was absent. This was thwarted by Hatfield. When the original of the bill was delivered to him from the Senate, he temporarily "misplaced" or "lost" it. Hatfield met Hope at the train and informed him of the Klan supporters' maneuvers. After that, the bill was "found" and the February 27 vote proceeded.

Hope recited Hatfield's actions to me several times over the years, expressing gratitude to Hatfield for his quick thinking, and he spoke of it in the 1970 taped interview: "Really he [Hatfield] was trying to protect me." Why didn't Hope mention Hatfield's actions in the 1965 newspaper columns? That remains a mystery.[4] He probably considered the incident too difficult to explain in a short space. In the 1970 interview, Hope did

W. P. Lambertson, 1939.

explain that he had assured the Klan forces that he would not bury the bill at the bottom of the calendar and that it would be considered in the normal course of business, which indeed it was. He also explained that he was never threatened by Klan supporters, including Masons. They knew where he stood and apparently respected his position. Unlike the flamboyant and courageous Governor Allen and William Allen White and others, Hope did not go around making speeches and waving his arms against the Klan; he just stated his position firmly and clearly and let it go at that. In the winter of 1925 he was already thinking seriously of running for Congress the next year, and he had no idea what the Klan strength and opposition to him might be. Therefore, his position was a courageous one; it would have been easier and safer politically to have acted pleasant and resisted taking a decisive stand.

Hope's opposition to the Klan did not impair his ability to work with Governor Paulen. When the Legislature adjourned in mid-March, Hope was praised in *The Topeka Daily Capital* for his part in securing enactment of the Governor's program, which included establishing the Board of Regents to administer state colleges and universities, a new state banking board, and the Forestry, Fish and Game Commission. *The Topeka Daily Capital*'s front-page news story read like an editorial. It began:

> Thanks in part to the consistent and constant refusal of the house of representatives to pass the reactionary measures sent over from the state senate, the Kansas legislature which completed its work yesterday has to its credit the most constructive legislation in more than a decade.
>
> The house was free thruout the session from the "bell weather" type of leadership, the members doing their own thinking on most measures. Clifford Hope of Garden City, speaker, probably had more to do with the legislation passed in the house than any other one man, with Jackson of Comanche, Plummer of Jefferson, Hamilton of Shawnee, Walter of Hamilton, Martin of Reno, Archer of Brown, and Enders of Leavenworth among the outstanding figures on the majority side of the house. Sloan of Jackson, minority floor leader, and young Bennett of Washington, were leaders on the minority side.[5]

Quietly, but courageously, Hope had amassed an impressive record during his three terms in the Kansas House of Representatives and acquired some influential champions. By late September 1925, in answer to inquiries concerning his running for Congress, Hope replied that he had not yet made any definite political plans for 1926.

Chapter 4

The Great
Campaign of 1926

*N*O RECORD HAS BEEN FOUND *indicating when Hope first thought of running for Congress. He was never one to reveal his dreams. It is probable he did not seriously consider running until after being elected Speaker pro tem in the 1923 legislative session and possibly not until the incumbent congressman, J. N. Tincher (a Republican lawyer from Medicine Lodge), defeated Democrat Representative Nellie Cline of Larned by a slim 6-5 margin in the strong Republican year of 1924, indicating considerable dissatisfaction with Tincher. After a successful term as Speaker in the 1925 session, Hope received much encouragement to run.*

Political considerations did not deter Hope from giving his usual frank answers on legislative issues. In late November 1925 he wrote the American Bankers League in Washington:

I am in receipt of your favor of recent date as well as several previous letters requesting that I go on record as being opposed to federal inheritance tax. I have always been in favor of inheritance taxes, both state and federal, and do not see any reason for changing my opinion at this time.

By January 1925 Hope had decided to run for the 7th District congressional seat whether Tincher sought reelection or not. This southwest Kansas district had been represented by several distinguished and/or colorful representatives. Its first congressman, Samuel Ritter Peters, a lawyer from Newton, had been elected in 1884. At that time, the district consisted of 36 counties and included Wichita. The colorful Populist, Jeremiah "Sockless Jerry" Simpson (1891-1895, 1897-1899) of Medicine Lodge, succeeded Peters; Chester Isaiah Long, also from Medicine Lodge, battled Simpson for the seat repeatedly in the 1890s, serving from 1895-1897 and again from 1899-1903, when he resigned to become a U.S. senator. Victor Murdock of Wichita, managing editor of *The Wichita Eagle*, succeeded Long and served in Congress until 1915, first from the 7th District and from 1907 on from the newly created 8th District. (It included the four eastern-most counties of the old 7th.) Murdock became a national leader in Teddy Roosevelt's Progressive Party. Edmond Haggard Madison, a Dodge City lawyer and judge, followed Murdock and served until his death in September 1911; George Arthur Neeley, a lawyer from Hutchinson, was the first Democrat elected from the 7th District. Jouett Shouse, a Democrat businessman and farmer from Kinsley, succeeded Neeley in 1915 and served two terms. Shouse then became assistant secretary of the treasury and later a New York and Washington businessman.

J. N. Tincher defeated Shouse in 1918. Although his name appeared on the ballot as "J. N. Tincher," his full name was Jasper Napoleon Tincher. (When I was a small boy, I thought his name was Jeremiah Napoleon, confusing him with Jeremiah Simpson.) He was commonly known by the nickname "Poly," derived from "Napoleon." It also suited his considerable, roly-poly proportions. Years later Hope described Tincher as "having a build like Jackie Gleason, only more so." Poly's oratorical skills and other political talents, demonstrated in his eight-year congressional career, have been overlooked in large measure by historians.

Born in Missouri in 1878, Tincher moved to Medicine Lodge in 1892 and began practicing law there in 1899. After his election to Congress in 1918, he quickly established himself with the Republican leadership and became a drinking buddy (during the time of Prohibition) of Nicholas

Longworth of Cincinnati, husband of Alice Roosevelt, the former President's flamboyant daughter. Longworth became Majority Leader in 1923 and Speaker in 1925, serving in that post until ousted by the Democrats in 1931. Years later, Clifford Hope wrote to Poly's nephew, L. K. Cushenberry:

> Poly was a real power when he was in Congress. It was a period when political lines were drawn considerably closer than they are today. There wasn't too much legislation and certainly nothing like all the chores a congressman is expected to do for his constituents now. This left time for a lot of political debate and I don't suppose there was anyone in the House more adept at that than Poly. So the leadership usually called on Poly when a real fracas came up. At that time the two leading Democratic spellbinders were Alben Barkley and Tom Connally of Texas, both of whom later went to the Senate. You probably remember the Chautauqua tour that Poly and Alben Barkley made one summer. Outside of their political debates these fellows were all good friends, something that people who are not experienced in politics never could understand.

Once when his train from Washington was running late, goes one Poly story, he telegraphed the Santa Fe in Kansas City to hold the train to southwest Kansas for a "large Congressional delegation." Poly was the delegation.

Poly's last battle in Washington was witnessed by Hope in early 1927, just before his term expired on March 4. Later Hope wrote:

> At this same time there was another Kansas congressman named Jim Strong, not quite as big as Poly but about the same general shape. They didn't get along too well, although both were Republicans. They got into quite a hassle one day in the speaker's lobby of the House. The battle was bloodless, however, since they couldn't get close enough to deliver any real blows. The newspaper boys described it as a "navel engagement."

Despite his enjoyable years in Washington, Poly's heart was in Kansas.

Upon his retirement, he returned to Hutchinson, where he practiced law for 24 years before his death in 1951.

As a good old boy, Poly had built up an organization of postal appointees and other friends, but by early 1926 stories of his drinking activities and presumed carousing did not set well with many of his God-fearing, teetotaling constituents nor with disappointed office seekers. Poly probably wanted to run for a term or two more, if he could do so without primary opposition. In any event, he wished to pick his successor.

Against Judge Hutchison's advice, Hope announced his candidacy for Congress on February 18. The Judge thought it best to ascertain Poly's plans first. Newspaper reports of the announcement contain no statement from Hope other than that he was running. He made no promises of any kind. For the Garden City newspapers, he didn't need to. E. E. Kelley of *The Garden City Herald* ran a front-page editorial which stated in part:

> We have confidence in Clifford Hope and in the promise of his future, for he is sound of head and heart and soul. His ideals are high. He is clean in life. He is slow to make promises, but when once his word is passed it is good. He is not shifty, nor foxy, nor does he have his fingers crossed when he says yea, yea or nay, nay.
>
> More than seven years have gone by since the armistice. The boys came home from making the world safe for democracy, were hailed as heroes and given three rousing cheers. But up to date Kansas has not offered to send one of them to congress. This year the Seventh District has the chance to bestow that honor on an overseas man.
>
> The "Better wait a couple of years" of the politicians is beginning to grow stale. A number of the Legion boys heard that two years ago and four years ago. They are still waiting. This is a good year to decide whether or not the probationary period is over.[1]

The Garden City Telegram expressed similar thoughts, adding that the eastern section of the district had held the representative post almost continuously since the beginning, E. H. Madison of Dodge City being the only exception.

Poly's reaction was swift and surprising. Six days after Hope declared his candidacy, the congressman announced his retirement at the end of his term. *The Hutchinson Herald* stated that Tincher had wanted to retire two years earlier but had stayed to help make Nicholas Longworth Speaker of the House. It went on to explain:

> His purpose in making known his decision at this time is partly to give aspiring Republicans in the district an opportunity to announce for the nomination long enough in advance of the primary to be able to make a thoro [*sic*] campaign. Mr. Tincher naturally hopes to see some political friend of his become a candidate and win the nomination but if he has a favorite for the nomination he has not yet made that fact known.[2]

One thing was certain: Hope was not Poly's candidate.

But Poly's announcement gave a tremendous boost to Hope's campaign. Hope might have been able to beat Poly in a two-person race, but there was no assurance there would not be more candidates. Poly had had primary opposition in 1924. The Hope forces represented the new guard versus the old. Although five other candidates ended up filing by the June deadline, Hope was the only veteran of World War I and the youngest candidate by far. The Hope campaign developed into one in which almost everything went right. He could wage a positive campaign without mention of Tincher. At the same time, he received much of the anti-Tincher vote. The fervor of some of these voters is illustrated by a letter Hope received from Hutchinson, Kansas:

> I note in the papers, and with great satisfaction, that you are a candidate for the Republican congressional nomination in the 7th District. Feel like singing the Doxology. I was wondering when some representative man or woman would come forward and rid us of the incubus of this drunken, blatant, demagogic old political Frankenstein. The bunch of professional piecounter, thimble-riggers who have run Republican politics for a generation, on a mental and intellectual shoe-string, ought to be taught a lesson.

By starting early and out-campaigning his opponents, Clifford Hope received support from many former Tincher voters against the splintered opposition. Good fortune was with him, but good planning and hard work by the Hope forces helped create the good fortune. More than three decades later, southwest Kansas voters were still talking about that campaign.

The question of financing the campaign was easily solved. Hope borrowed $7,000 from the bank, with four substantial backers as cosigners. If Hope won, he would pay off the note; if he lost, the cosigners would pay. Clifford was still earning only $200 per month from Judge Hutchison. If he won, his congressional salary of $10,000 per annum would start March 4, 1927, although the first session of Congress would not begin until December. The cosigners were Judge Hutchison; E. Lester McCoy, chairman of the Finney County Republican Central Committee and prosperous Garden City Ford dealer; Joe Stewart, vice president and manager of The Garden City Company, which owned the sugar factory and thousands of acres of irrigated land in southwest Kansas; and Conrad Gabriel, then a city commissioner and theater owner.

After service in the Navy in World War I, Lester McCoy, one of the cosigners, had returned to Garden City and become active in Republican politics and the American Legion. In 1924 he became Finney County Republican chairman, and two years later, as Hope's choice, he was elected Republican district chairman. He served in both posts for almost three decades, a political sage whose advice was sought by aspiring candidates long after that. McCoy served on the state Board of Regents for more than 20 years. In addition to his crucial campaign work in 1926, Lester remained a loyal friend of Clifford throughout his congressional career and thereafter. Though always more conservative than Hope, he defended Clifford's views. (McCoy supported Eisenhower for President in 1952 at Hope's behest when his personal choice was Robert Taft. He was the elder sage of Garden City at the time of his death, when 94.)

As for the last two cosigners, Joe Stewart employed Judge Hutchison's firm as legal counsel for the company and, therefore, became well acquainted with Clifford. Conrad Gabriel, born in St. Louis, came to Garden City in 1919 when he purchased the Windsor Hotel. Successively, he became a theater owner and operator, president of the First National Bank, furniture store owner, and a real estate investor. When the First National Bank failed to reopen after the bank holiday in 1933, Gabriel sold his home and other assets voluntarily for the benefit of the bank's depositors.

Arthur Carruth, editor of *The Topeka State Journal*, for whom Clifford had worked during college days as baby sitter and newspaper carrier, dispatched his political reporter, A. L. "Dutch" Schultz, to Garden City for a lengthy interview with Clifford and many townspeople in March 1926. The resulting article was more a eulogy than a factual report, but it made for excellent campaign propaganda when reproduced and distributed throughout the district.

Judge Hutchison, then 66, served as Clifford's unofficial campaign manager with backup from A. M. Fleming, who handled mailings and "held down the fort" when the Judge was on the road. They, with McCoy, were Clifford's three campaign executives of sorts. The Finney County Hope for Congress Club's executive committee lists 49 prominent citizens as members. In addition to businessmen, farmers, bankers, lawyers, editors, doctors, and club women, its membership included the district judge, the superintendent of schools, and four ministers. These were working members; many of them hit the campaign trail in July, including Clifford's uncle, J. W. Hope.

Before Clifford owned a vehicle, he walked a mile back and forth to work twice a day and took the train or hired a livery vehicle when going out of town. In March, after purchasing his first automobile (a Model T Ford), he started on-the-road campaigning. Without a driving lesson of any kind, he took off on the highways, such as they were. A 90-mile trip from Kingman to Kinsley once took him 12 hours. For years afterward some of Hope's friends observed that he was "a mighty poor driver."

In a 1958 newspaper column, Clifford reminisced about the 1926 campaign:

> In some ways campaigning today is different — in other ways it hasn't changed a bit. The changes are more in the outer manifestations rather than in the fundamental basis of effort. Now, as then, the fundamental weapon of the campaigner is the handshake. People still like to see the candidates and size them up from their appearance and manner as well as on the basis of party affiliations, views, and records. Everything else being equal, people vote for the people they like, although of course other factors enter into it. Therefore now, as in 1926 — or 1856 for that matter — handshaking and visiting are the most formidable campaign weapons.
>
> Most of the other campaign manifestations, however, have

changed since I was first a candidate for Congress in 1926. There will never be another campaign like that for me. Never having sold books or anything else (except groceries) for that matter, it was my first experience in meeting and talking to thousands of people. I will always recall with gratitude how good and kind they were to me, even those who were supporting my opponents, of whom there were five in the primary race — all of them good men and formidable opposition.

First there was Senator John Whitman of Pratt, who had served in both the state House of Representatives and the Senate, and who was an influential and prominent member of the State Senate at the time he ran for Congress. Senator Whitman had many friends over the District and came out second in the race.

Then there was Judge F. L. Martin of Hutchinson, a former District Judge and a member of the Kansas House of Representatives from Reno County for several terms. Judge Martin was one of the most effective debaters on the floor of the House and one of the few men who had the oratorical ability and influence to change votes by speeches.

And there was Harry Hartshorn of Topeka (legal residence, Ford, Kansas), one of the most prominent agricultural leaders in the state and a very influential man in the cooperative movement which was making rapid strides at that time; Carl Newcomer, a banker born at Brownell, was another candidate, and the fifth one was W. L. Farquharson of Garden City.

I was the youngest of the lot, and I don't think there was any doubt but what I told my story to twice as many people as any of the other candidates. I always thought that another help was the natural desire of many people to help a young man get ahead. Also, I had a pretty fair acquaintance of the District formed during my service in the state House of Representatives. I think the fact that I was a World War veteran was of some help at that time, as veterans were just then beginning to be active in politics. There were no such organizations as Young Republicans and Young Democrats. They came later.

The primary race was the big race. When I won that, I was as good as in, although I had a worthy Democratic opponent in the person of Harry Brown, County Attorney of Reno County. But 1926 was in the middle of the nineteen twenties. No important questions were agitating the public. Most people were keeping cool with Coolidge and voting Republican.

I will always remember many little instances of the campaign and some big ones. With such a large number of candidates, the primary race was really in doubt until the last minute. I left Hutchinson for Garden City about 4 o'clock in the afternoon on the day before election. One of my strong supporters sped me on with the admonition that "if you can just keep yourself from getting killed between now and tomorrow, I think you are going to be nominated." With that ringing in my ears, about five miles east of Garden City I came up behind a car pulling a trailer with a calf in it and with no tail lights of any kind, and actually bumped into the trailer before I saw it. My first thought was, "This is it. I am going to get killed before I have a chance to be nominated." However, there really wasn't any damage done. Even the calf wasn't hurt, and I came on home without further incident.

Just after I crossed the Arkansas River bridge west of Hutchinson, I stopped at a house which I had not made before. I thought I could check up a little, and without disclosing my identity I asked the man I met there how he thought the Congressional race would come out. He said, "Well, it will either be Judge Martin or Senator Whitman. The folks down here don't think much of that young fellow out west." Since that checkup turned out so discouraging, I decided not to do any more of it since there wasn't anything that could be done about the matter anyway.[3]

Hope was the only candidate who filed by petition. The process of getting signatures on petitions helped increase enthusiasm among his supporters and made all petition carriers an important part of the campaign. Hope made a point of calling on all newspaper editors, especially weekly editors. Some of the friendships formed, such as those with the Herbert Cornwell family in St. John, lasted a lifetime.

Of all the candidates, Whitman seemed most reluctant, not really having his heart in the race. In early March he wrote Hope: "I will certainly speak a good word for you whenever I can." Whitman did not file until June 15, just before the deadline. It appears that he finally got into the race at the urging of Poly and his friends after their efforts to get others to file failed. Whitman was one of the first to pledge support to Hope after the primary.

W. L. Farquharson was the noisiest candidate, attacking most of the others at one time or another as a sort of loose cannon. At first Hope was concerned that Farquharson would split the west-end vote to Hope's detriment. This proved not to be the case. Farquharson didn't carry a single county and ran behind Hope in every county. In March Clifford surmised,

> Some of the fellows down east have framed up on me a little by trying to bring out a local candidate against me. That is, he [Farquharson] is posing as a local candidate although he spends more of his time in Wichita than in Garden City.

Farquharson's most prominent local supporter was L. E. Busenbark, the maverick publisher of *The Garden City News*. He took delight in defying the overwhelming support for Hope by the local establishment.

The campaign correspondence indicates that rumors abounded. Many were answered by Judge Hutchison in his usual meticulous manner. Poly claimed Clifford had lied to him, telling him he would not run against him; Clifford had made no such statement about the 1926 election. Poly also claimed Clifford was running because he, Poly, had not appointed Clifford's father, Harry Hope, to be Garden City postmaster. Harry, in fact, had no intention of giving up his civil service status as assistant postmaster. A rumor in Larned had it that Hope's wife, Pauline, was a political supporter of Nellie Cline, the Democrat who had run against Poly in 1924. Indeed, there was a personal friendship between Pauline and Nellie, developed at the time of Edward's death. Nellie had accompanied Pauline to Garden City for Edward's burial. Judge Hutchison explained, "Mrs. Hope has been consistent in her Republican record — just as consistent as the rest of us." Some residents of the Fort Dodge Soldiers Home, a remaining stronghold of the Klan, were worried that Clifford might be a Catholic. And George L. Reid, a Tribune lawyer and long-time friend of Judge Hutchison, had heard that Clifford favored repeal of the Kansas anticigarette law. The Judge assured Reid that Clifford did not favor repeal and that he did not use cigarettes or tobacco in any form. The Judge ended his letter, as he often did, saying of Clifford: "He is one of our kind and is true blue in every respect."

Clifford's campaign brochure stated his experience and qualifications in great detail. Pertinent portions of the E. E. Kelley endorsement editorial were set forth, including "He voted right on all questions." But neither the brochure nor Hope's newspaper ads took a stand for or against any legislative issues of the time. When asked, however, Hope made his positions clear. He favored further extension of the Sheppard-Towner Maternity and Infancy Act, the establishment of a Federal Department of Education, and strict enforcement of Prohibition. He opposed "any measure which would make the amendment of the Constitution more difficult." He would not commit himself to a position on the Equal Rights Amendment proposed by the National Woman's Party until he had time to study it further.

When a Hutchinson worker asked Hope's views on organized labor, Hope promised to "fairly and honestly represent everyone in the district, whatever his occupation or business." As for labor unions, he said,

> I have a high admiration for the great constructive work which has been done in recent years by labor organizations . . . in securing for their members the benefits of just compensation and better working and living conditions. . . . Labor questions and labor legislation will have a square deal in my hands.

Labor union membership in the 7th District was small in 1926. Most members of the railroad and craft unions were Republican. Later, with the rise of the CIO (Committee on Industrial Organization) in the 1930s, Hope's attitude shifted. He opposed militant organized labor and its attempts to woo farmers.

There were few black citizens in the district then or later but probably most were Republicans. A black lawyer and member of the American Legion, William D. Harrison, of Hutchinson, wrote to a friend, George Winters,

> I believe George that the time is not very far off when my people will have more than a janitor's job, and when fellows like you and Cliff get into office I know things will be better. Therefore you may rest assuredly I am doing everything in my power for Cliff.

On the same day, he wrote Cliff,

> I will do everything in my power for you, not only because
> you are an ex-serviceman, but a real white man. I think our only
> salvation lies in such men as you. You not only give your people
> a square deal but mine as well.

Clifford continued to speak well of his opponents, especially Judge Martin. When S. W. McComb of Zenith wrote he was committed to Martin, Clifford replied, "[Martin] is a splendid man in every way and will make an able Congressman, so I do not blame you in the least for supporting him."

Despite their almost daily contact, Judge Hutchison continued to address Clifford as either "Mr. Hope" or "Dear Sir," signing his letters "Wm. Easton Hutchison." Several supporters over the district had suggested the campaign slogan, "Here's Hopin' for Hope." The Judge may have been one of them; however, at first he worried over whether "hopin'" would be considered poor grammar. He concluded the slogan was catchy. And indeed it was. (In the final days of the campaign, Farquharson and his son reportedly were seen marking "Hopeless Hope" on Clifford's posters.)

Lester McCoy returned from a vacation in Green Mountain Falls to campaign throughout the district in the final days.

Correspondence indicates that Pauline didn't spend any time on the primary campaign trail. For much of May, June and probably early July, she visited her parents in Topeka. She and Clifford apparently had a tacit agreement that he would do the campaigning, and she would spend full time performing her duties as wife and mother.

In late July family tragedy struck. Pauline's father, Martin Sanders, suffered a severe stroke and died on July 25, nine days before the primary election. Pauline left for Topeka immediately upon learning of her father's condition, leaving her young son with the neighbors, Etta and Simeon Moss. Clifford left for Topeka also and was there when Martin died, but he did not stay for the funeral on the 28th. He felt an obligation to return to the campaign and his hard-working supporters even though Judge Hutchison and others presumed he would stay for the funeral. Pauline was distraught, and the fact that Clifford had left before her father was put to rest appalled her. For the rest of her life, she was frank about the matter. "I have never forgiven Clifford," she told family and friends. To my knowledge, they never argued about the matter. She was sure he had done wrong, and he was just as sure he had done what he thought was right. And that was that. This sad event graphically illustrated Clifford and Pauline's differing values. To her, family came first, above all else; to him, during his congressional term family was important, but public duties came first.

There was a heavy turnout for the August 3 primary election. When the votes were counted the tally read:

Hope	10,315
Whitman	5,878
Martin	5,551
Hartshorn	4,034
Newcomer	3,359
Farquharson	2,290

Hope received 29 percent of the total vote; indications were that he was the first or second choice of a substantial majority.

Congratulations came from many, including all primary opponents. Carl Newcomer wrote, "The battle is all over and I just want you to know that since it could not be me, that I am mighty glad that it was you." C. B. Griffith, Kansas attorney general who had battled the Klan, observed that Clifford was "under no obligation to the Ku Klux." (Griffith and Hope shared a mutual admiration for one another.) C. C. Scates, Dodge City banker, expressed the feelings of many when he wrote:

> While you had a broad and favorable acquaintance over the district and those who worked with you had confidence in your ability and your integrity, if any one man deserves credit for your nomination over and above all others, it is our mutual friend, Judge Hutchison. He has lived so long and so honorably in this section of Kansas, that people just felt that when he worked for you as he did, that you would fill the bill.

The people of Birmingham, Iowa, took pride in their native son. L. G. Boies, a real estate broker, wrote:

> I assure you that you are an important character in our talk these days, and trust that in your mind your promotion may not

obliterate our little hamlet in your esteem. Remember us to
your good Father and Mother.

In many letters, Clifford expressed the thought that as far as he could
tell there were "no sore spots around the district." He had a good visit with
Poly in Hutchinson on August 25, and Poly pledged his support. It was
customary for the nominee for Congress to select the Republican district
chairman. Hope, of course, selected Lester McCoy, despite McCoy's recommendation that the chairman should come from Hutchinson. McCoy's
election by the district committee at the party council in late August was
a formality. Estelle V. Ingels of Larned was elected district vice chairman.

After the hard-fought primary, the general election campaign in that
Republican year was a breeze. But the Hope organization took no chances.
A headquarters was set up in Hutchinson with Grant Chamberlain in
charge. Clifford's law school fellow students, Mabel Jones Shaffer and her
husband, Don, were strong supporters. Mabel's letters to Clifford reveal
her to have been a very shrewd politician. (In keeping with the times,
Mabel was listed only as an "associate" in Don's Hutchinson law firm.)
Mabel noted that Pauline had made a hit with groups in Hutchinson, so
Pauline apparently made some campaign appearances, despite her reluctance to do so.

Clifford campaigned with Senator Charles Curtis, who was up for reelection, as well as with Governor Paulen and Senator Capper, who set up
an extensive speaking schedule on behalf of the GOP ticket. Clifford wrote
of these travels in a newspaper column in 1958:

> Some of the most interesting trips in my early campaigning
> days were made with Charles Curtis and Arthur Capper, United
> States senators at the time. It would be hard to find two men
> with greater differences in their personalities than Senators
> Capper and Curtis, but they were both good campaigners and
> very popular with the people of Kansas, as shown by their long
> records in the Senate.
>
> During my first year of campaigning, I spent several days
> with Senator Curtis. We made a trip through Kingman, Pratt,
> Stafford, Barton and Rice Counties, possibly including another
> county or two. No one was a better campaigner than Charlie
> Curtis, and I marveled at the number of people he knew per-

sonally and how well he remembered his friends of former years. Whenever we went into a town there were always some of these friends down on the street to meet him and practically always he knew them and could readily recall their names. The trip was a real educational experience to me in the technique of campaigning.

I made a number of campaign trips in this District with Senator Capper. While he did not have the wide personal acquaintance of Senator Curtis, he was even more widely known because practically every family in the Seventh District was a subscriber to one or more of the Capper papers, so there always were a great many people out to see and talk to Senator Capper, and you could tell by the way they acted that they had a real affection for him, built up through the years.

Farmers especially were interested in talking to him, and many of them came to thank him for his part in farm legislation. There has probably never been a man whom more farmers knew by reputation or who had a greater following among the farmers of America than Arthur Capper. This was partly because of his work in Congress and partly because of the great influence of his farm papers.

While I admired Senator Capper in many ways, my strongest recollections of him will always be of his kindliness and his helpfulness, not only to me but to thousands of Kansans and Americans everywhere.[4]

Lee Kemper and Bert Daugherty of Garden City, who lived and breathed the American Legion, organized the Servicemen's Hope for Congress Club, which was active in the primary and general elections. They emphasized that Clifford was the only ex-serviceman running for Congress on either ticket, saying, "If we don't elect Hope this year, it may be a long time before we again have as good a chance to elect a serviceman."

Judge Hutchison hit the campaign trail again and spent time in the Hutchinson headquarters. Never one to waste a minute, he took along abstracts of title from his law office to examine in spare moments. And groups from Garden City campaigned as they had in the primary. J. R. Bosworth, Realtor, reported to Gladys Miller, the Judge's faithful, efficient secretary and office manager, "We worked thoroughly Rush and Ness Counties, both lines of the railroad and worked every town, big and little. Drove 328 miles. Met with wonderful success every place. Everybody in Ness and Rush County, including the Klans and Catholics are for him."

On election day, November 2, Hope's victory over Harry Brown, Reno County attorney, was a landslide — 49,072 to 27,374. Clifford carried every county.

No complete record of campaign expenses can be found. One list shows a total of about $2,200. In any event, total expenses in both elections came to considerably less than the $7,000 Clifford had borrowed.

Among congratulatory letters was one from C. S. Gibbens of Nickerson written the day after the election. Gibbens observed that Hope's youth should be of advantage to the 7th District, that he could be in Congress a long time. There was no adverse concern nor worry about the evils of seniority at that time. "I have a fatherly interest in you and your success, having lost my only son, near your age, in the army after the war was over," Gibbens wrote. "I, like many fathers, transfer my hopes to youthful friends."

Of all the other members of the Kansas congressional delegation, Homer Hoch of Marion was the most friendly and helpful in the days following the election. Hoch gave expert advice on committee assignments, recommending either agriculture or judiciary. With strong recommendations from Homer and Poly, Clifford was appointed to agriculture when his term began the following March.

Immediately Hope was besieged with requests and demands of constituents, the most persistent of which concerned postmaster and rural mail carrier vacancies. Poly ended up leaving at least seven vacancies for Clifford to fill. A Civil War widow asked for increased pensions for veterans and widows. To each, Clifford pointed out he could do nothing until his term commenced.

Hope wisely sought to disengage himself from Kansas government matters with one exception. His friend, John D. M. Hamilton of Topeka, who in 1936 would become Alf Landon's campaign manager and GOP national chairman, was a candidate for Speaker of the Kansas House. His principal opponent was Clyde Coffman, the Klan candidate who had run against Clifford in 1925. Although personally friendly with Coffman, Hope was determined to defeat the Klan once and for all. He vigorously solicited votes for Hamilton. An anecdote concerning the race circulated following a meeting for new Republican legislators held at Scott City. When Coffman was introduced to Simon Fishman, just elected from Greeley County, Simon remarked, "Vell, you are a Klansman and I am a Jew." Hamilton won the speakership in January.

The year 1926 had been a wonderful landmark for Clifford. When it ended, he was eager to get started on congressional duties.

Chapter 5

Early Days in Congress —
The First Year and
Family Life (1927-1934)

*O*N FEBRUARY 1927 the United States Supreme Court upheld the right of states to control the Ku Klux Klan, putting an end to the Klan as a national movement in the 1920s. Calvin Coolidge, from his Black Hills vacation retreat, in August issued his famous "I do not choose to run for President in 1928" statement. Later that month, Gutzon Borglum began work on his monumental sculpture on Mount Rushmore. In September, Gene Tunney again defeated Jack Dempsey for the world heavyweight boxing championship after surviving the "long count" in the seventh round. Eight days later, Babe Ruth hit his 60th home run for the season, setting a record. The next month **The Jazz Singer**, featuring Al Jolson was released; it was the first "talking" motion picture. The Holland Tunnel under the Hudson River, the first of its kind, was opened for traffic in November, and on December 1, Ford Motor Company announced its new Model A, replacing the famous "Tin Lizzie" Model T. Fifteen million Lizzies had been sold.

But the event which captured the heart of America and, indeed, of the world in 1927 was Charles A. Lindbergh's 33½-hour solo flight from New York to Paris in late May. President Coolidge sent a Navy cruiser to bring Lindbergh home to a hero's welcome in Washington and a ticker-tape parade in New York. A whirlwind 48-city tour in the *Spirit of St. Louis* followed. Clifford and Pauline Hope were among the many admirers of "Lucky Lindy." (They later admired Anne Morrow, whom Lindbergh married in 1929. In appearance Pauline resembled Anne, something which more than one constituent noted over the years.)

Back in Kansas in early 1927, Clifford was preparing to assume his congressional duties. He made a quick trip to Washington in late February to establish his office and attend the meeting of the House Republican Caucus, before returning to Garden City to await the start of real business in December. He hired John Walker Cross, a young secretary-manager of the Dodge City Chamber of Commerce, as his secretary and sole employee in Washington effective March 4, 1927, the date Hope's term began. (At this time, before passage of the Lame Duck amendment, Congress adjourned immediately after March 4 and did not reconvene until December 1927.) Hope also employed Miss Bernice Reed as his stenographer in Garden City. House members, with an annual salary of $10,000, were allowed $4,000 for clerk hire; not more than $3,300 could be paid to one employee. Hope was assigned Room 238 in what later became the Cannon House Office Building; it was then the only office building for House members.

Judge Hutchison, always one to do the proper thing, thought Clifford should remain in Washington until his term began on March 4, but Clifford found it unnecessary. While Cross held down the fort in Washington, Hope wound up his Garden City law practice about October 1. Although his name remained in the Judge's firm, he did not practice law and received no compensation from the firm thereafter.

During this time, Hope and Cross had no difficulty handling the congressional office work between them. Cross managed to attend law school night classes, as did a number of Capitol Hill employees. He and Hope soon learned a congressman was supposed to be able to answer myriad questions and solve any problem a constituent might have with the federal government. The one-man office in Washington frequently was left unattended for considerable periods as Cross made trips to government bureaus around Washington to gather information for Hope.

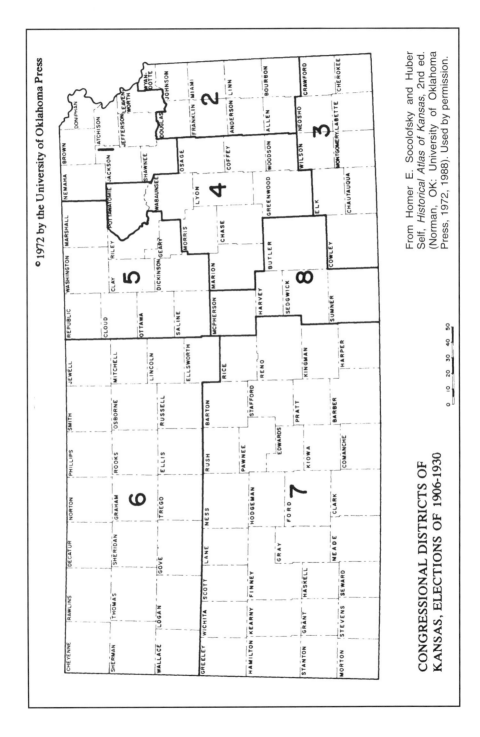

CONGRESSIONAL DISTRICTS OF
KANSAS, ELECTIONS OF 1906-1930

From Homer E. Socolofsky and Huber
Self, *Historical Atlas of Kansas*, 2nd ed.
(Norman, OK: University of Oklahoma
Press, 1972, 1988). Used by permission.

Clifford Hope (left) and his law partner, A. M. Fleming, in their Garden City, Kansas, office, *ca.* 1920s.

Edith Ann Lessenden

With no pressing or emotional national issues on the horizon, Hope and Cross occupied nearly all their time from March to December with personal requests from constituents. While often trivial, the matters were important to the persons concerned. Postal matters — the appointing of postmasters and rural mail carriers and attempting to arbitrate disputes between post office and patrons — were the most vexing to handle. In an early letter to Cross, Hope requested a copy of all postal rules and regulations, stating, "It will be necessary to become a walking encyclopedia of postal information."

In a 1969 newspaper column, Hope recalled that he had learned some of the disadvantages of dispensing political patronage soon after he was elected to Congress. Even before he was elected, he wrote, delegations from various towns were waiting to talk to him about post office appointments. Some would be for one candidate and some for others. After he was elected, he tried to explain he would not actually take office as a member of Congress until March 4 and until then recommendations for government positions in the district would have to be made by retiring Congressman J. N. Tincher. Hope wrote:

> I soon discovered that this was not a satisfactory reply to my future constituents, particularly in the case of seven post-offices where examinations had already been held and eligible lists established. The normal procedure would have been for Mr. Tincher to make his choice from the eligible lists and so advise the Postmaster General. Instead, he advised the interested parties and their friends that he thought the proper thing to do under the circumstances would be to let the new Congressman handle the matter.[1]

Tincher's reluctance to deal with the appointments was understandable. "Every one was a hot potato," explained Hope. "In one case the matter had been dragging along for three years and about everyone in town was on one side or the other." The situation was much the same in the other towns. Hope said:

> Frankly, I was no more anxious than Mr. Tincher to make these controversial appointments. I told him that while I appre-

ciated his generosity in waiving his rights in the matter I would not be offended at all if he went ahead and made them.

Hope became "reconciled to the fact that being a member of Congress was not all beer and skittles, as the old saying goes."

Correspondence between Cross in Washington and Hope back in his Kansas district indicates a developing warm friendship and a keen sense of humor on the part of both. They did, however, continue to address each other as "Mr." When Clifford requested speech material via Cross from the Library of Congress on the relationship of government to the plumbing profession, Walker replied: "It appears you have a splendid opportunity to make a contribution to 20th-century literature under the noble caption: 'The bathtub follows the flag.' As far as I have been able to ascertain it is almost a virgin field." In reporting on the postal situation at Plains, Hope joked that it was not getting any worse, "mainly for the reason that would be impossible." Cross kept Hope informed on the exchange of information and gossip among congressional staffers. In May he wrote,

> At least in the House Office Building the prospect for a special session (to deal with the flood situation on the Mississippi) has been thrust into the background by one of the offices receiving a letter from the father of triplets who demands government aid.

In July Cross wrote, "You will note an enclosure from an individual who desires to hire an honest man and a lawyer and seems to think it will be necessary for him to hire two people." Later that month, he reported three visitors to the office from the district in one day (an unusual occurrence). He commented, "It was really quite a pleasure to meet someone who talked United States and to assist in showing them the city."

Applications from young male constituents for appointment to Annapolis and West Point took considerable time but were much more pleasant to handle than postal appointments. One of Hope's first appointments to Annapolis was that of Robert Isely, son of C. C. Isely of Dodge City, a businessman with many interests and an enthusiastic supporter of Clifford in the 1926 campaign. Cross knew the Isely family well and highly recommended Robert, whom Cross called "a splinter off the old log." When Robert graduated from Annapolis, he chose the Naval Air Corps as his branch of service. His career had a heroic but tragic end when he was shot down over Saipan in World War II. The airfield there was named in his memory.

Lotus Van Huss, secretary to Representative Marvin Jones of Amarillo, asked Clifford about the employment of her 17-year-old daughter in his office during the coming year. Mrs. Van Huss's parents lived in Garden City, and Clifford had a high regard for her. (Marvin Jones's biographer, Irvin M. May, Jr., described her as "an efficient, strikingly beautiful woman."[2]) Clifford hired the daughter for the following school year.

During these early months, Hope set patterns of service for the people in his district which he was to continue for 30 years. For instance, in the first months his office was established, he was allocated 116,000 agricultural bulletins for distribution. He and Cross prepared a press release announcing a list of some 700 bulletins that would be sent to constituents upon request. Getting government publications out to his district became an office priority.

The first year of which I have clear memories is 1927, when I was three — most of them concerning Pauline rather than Clifford. Pauline, at 28, was not looking forward to life in Washington, especially the social activities, but she was determined to do her part as a loyal congressman's wife. As she repeatedly stated later, she made every effort "to hold [her] end up." She was not aware of the snickers this quaint phrase generated among family and friends. She hated leaving our pleasant home on Gillespie Place with its large yard and stately elm trees, where cooing turtle doves in spring and summer added to the sense of contentment and security.

Pauline was a conscientious, attentive mother who wanted me to be good, if not perfect, and desired for everything to go right for me. After her marriage she never worked outside the home, devoting all her time and energy to being a proper wife and mother in accordance with her strong moral beliefs and the trend of the times. She spent much time preparing meals on a coal range in winter and on a kerosene stove in summer. She loved to fix chicken, starting with a live bird. She tied the fowl's legs to the clothesline and neatly cut off the head with a butcher knife rather than wringing the neck and letting the headless chicken flop about over the yard. Then after plunging the bird in hot water, she plucked off the feathers, removed the innards, and cut it up piece by piece with the skill of a surgeon. She had me watch the latter operation, explaining in detail the chicken's digestive functions, including the purpose of the pebble-filled craw. Years later she confided to her grandchildren that she had wanted to be a doctor, possibly a surgeon.

I remember being terrified by the noise of the road grader on our gravel street and running inside at its approach. Pauline stopped the driver and asked him to talk to me to prove he was not driving a monster. After that, there was no problem.

Pauline ordered most of our groceries by phone. For years she delighted in telling about a delivery by Otto O. Baker, owner of East Side Grocery. Hearing the back door open and thinking it was Clifford coming in, she called, "Come on in, honey, I'm in the bedroom."

I have a few memories of Clifford that year. Often when he was in town we would all drive to the railroad station after supper to watch the evening train come through.

Pauline seldom went to Clifford's law office, but when she did she routinely removed the soiled handkerchiefs that were stuffed in the cubbyholes of his big rolltop desk. He had an annoying habit of hiding away the used handkerchiefs, especially during the hay fever season.

My mother and I spent much of 1927 in Topeka with her widowed mother, Laura. I also remember another trip — to a three-day Peace Treaty celebration in Medicine Lodge in October. Held every five years, it commemorated the 1867 signing of peace treaties with five tribes of Plains Indians. The re-enactment of the event was impressive for Clifford and Pauline and thrilling for me.

In November we left for Washington driving a new Nash via Topeka and Valley Falls to Clifford's birthplace in Birmingham, Iowa. Clifford had not been there since 1901. He was the first Birmingham native to be elected to Congress, so he was sort of a hero to the Hope relatives and to the townspeople who remembered his parents. My only memory of that visit related to a painful spanking I received on Aunt Annie Hope Moore's bitter cold front porch for misbehaving. We also visited Sanders cousins in Zanesville and Crooksville, Ohio, whom Pauline, ever friendly, was eager to meet.

During the long days on the road, Pauline insisted we play games to while away the hours. Clifford and I were not willing participants. He certainly had enough to think about, and I preferred to stand next to the windshield absorbing all the new scenery, thinking and daydreaming. We settled on counting white horses, which were then numerous and did not require too much interruption of thought.

We were headed for the Burlington Hotel in Washington — where Walker Cross was staying — upon the recommendation of former Dodge Citians, Lewis and Emma Pettyjohn, who had lived there for several years. Lewis was chairman of the Federal Farm Loan Board. (Their daughter, Juliet Denious, had married Jess Denious, publisher of *The Dodge City Globe* and prominent Republican politician.) Other Kansans lived there, including Clif Stratton of *The Topeka Daily Capital*, owned by Senator Arthur Capper. Stratton was a speech writer for the Senator.

For a going-on-four-year-old who had been thrilled by the evening train in Garden City, Kansas, the Burlington — on Vermont Avenue just south of Thomas Circle — seemed fabulous. We had a one-bedroom apartment on the fifth floor. Later, during the winter and early spring, my grandmother, Laura Sanders, lived in a room down the hall. The Burlington housed many elderly guests, most of whom were widows. Among other residents were Representative Eugene Cox and his family. A Georgia Democrat, Cox would later become a fiery opponent of the New Deal. He had a pretty little daughter, Jean, with whom I played in the small garden by the hotel dining room. Probably what impressed me most at the Burlington was the oval opening in the hallway on each floor, from which one could look down to the center of the lobby.

Washington, with a population of 450,000, was often described in the late 1920s as a sleepy, Southern city. This may have been true (except that it was filled with statues of Union generals!), but for our family, the city with its monuments, museums, parks, downtown shopping, and entertainment was a wondrous place. We decided to see as much of it as we could. In addition to visiting the usual sights — the White House, Washington Monument, Lincoln Memorial, Mt. Vernon, the Library of Congress, and the Smithsonian (there were then only three museums) — we explored Rock Creek Park and the Soldiers' Home, The National Cathedral, Meridian Park with its many statues, the Franciscan Monastery, and even the more obscure Adams monument at the grave of Marian Adams in Rock Creek Cemetery. Pauline escorted visitors from Kansas to various sights.

Early on we began taking long rides on Sunday afternoons to do much of our exploring. After an afternoon of "driving around," we returned home for a simple supper of bread and milk — it was Pauline's day off. In the years before the New Deal, Clifford had more spare time than he would ever have again in his years in Congress.

Often at Sunday noon we ate at the Allies Inn on New York Avenue, southwest of the State, War and Navy Building (now the Old Executive Office Building). The inn was named in honor of the World War I allies. Clifford gave me an overview of that war when we first ate there. Once there was a special exhibit of Joan of Arc paintings at the nearby Corcoran Gallery of Art, and Clifford told me the story of Joan of Arc's life. He appeared to have some knowledge of every great event in history (and many minor ones), or so it seemed to me. We explored the area around Thomas Circle, named in honor of Union Major General George H. Thomas, the Rock of Chickamauga. "Chickamauga" may have been the first multisyllable word I learned. Across Vermont Avenue was the Portland Hotel, the first luxury hotel in Washington. To the north of the circle was Luther Memorial Church, with its imposing statue of Martin Luther.

On up Vermont Avenue was the Vermont Avenue Christian Church. The 45-year-old building seemed ancient to me. Because Pauline had been a member of the Disciples of Christ denomination (or the Campbellite Church, as Clifford often referred to it) and because it was close by, she and Clifford began attending there. I was enrolled in Sunday school, which met in a row house north of the church. The house with its dark, dingy wallpaper seemed even older than the church. My most vivid memory is of singing "Faith of Our Fathers" there, especially the line "our fathers chained in prisons dark" on a rainy, dreary Sunday morning. In 1930 the National City Christian Church was built at Thomas Circle, and we attended services there until we moved to the Chevy Chase area in 1935.

In addition to sending me to Sunday school, Pauline often read me bedtime Bible stories from Hurlburt's *Stories from the Bible*, a book that even now sits on the shelves at my home, having served my children in their early years. Perhaps my interest in those stories helped compensate for the unpleasant disposition my mother said I had.

Pauline loved to shop in downtown Washington, within walking distance of the Burlington, and often took me with her. We walked through Franklin Square, past the imposing old Franklin School, and on to the Palais Royale, Woodward and Lothrop, Hechts, Lansburgh Bros., and Kanns, all large department stores. Sometimes we walked or took a street car on Pennsylvania Avenue out to the House Office Building for supper with Clifford. Pennsylvania Avenue from *The Washington Evening Star* building at Eleventh on east was rapidly degenerating. The old National Hotel, built in 1816, badly needed repairs. We usually ate in the block on B Street (now Independence Avenue) just east of the House Office Building, sometimes at the Capitol Hill Cafeteria (also known as the Greasy Spoon), or, if we had more time, at the Ugly Duckling. Then if we really wanted to make an evening of it, we would go to the brand new Fox Theater at 1328 F. Street. The ornate theater had three levels; we always sat in the mezzanine. For a modest sum we could see a movie, Fox Movietone News, and a lengthy stage show, complete with chorus line. The Fox was a magic place for me.

On other nights Clifford and I might roughhouse at home with sofa pillows. I do not remember ever playing games together after this.

I had a stuttering habit. My parents told me, "You can't become a congressman if you stutter," to which (I am told) I replied, "How about a senator?"

Although Clifford relished his work as a congressman and I was having a wonderful time, Pauline was concerned about me. She wanted me to be a "good boy," which required obeying parents' orders. I had a firm conviction also: I would not take orders from anyone, anywhere, anytime. (This attitude later got me into big trouble in the Army during World War II. Requests and suggestions were OK, but not orders.) Once Pauline told me to wash my hands before supper. I refused, and she ended up spanking me seven times before I agreed. After I completed washing, I looked up at her with an angelic smile and said, "I did it this time, but I won't do it again." Hard spankings were an accepted means of disciplining stubborn children back then, and I received my share, not only from my parents' hands but also from a small circus whip and a plywood board foot Clifford had received as a souvenir from a lumber company. He did not seem overly upset about me, figuring I would outgrow my antipathy toward parental orders, but Pauline was beside herself. She was always frank with me; she told me — and others — that I had an abominable disposition. ("Abominable" was the second big word I learned. I couldn't spell it but I could pronounce it.) That fall, when we were back in Garden City, I was expelled from kindergarten for yelling and screaming at the wrong times and for refusing to lie down on my rug and take a nap. Pauline was distressed, but when I entered first grade and had serious lessons to learn, I became a good student.

Another great source of anxiety for Pauline was her Washington social obligations. Protocol required that she call upon the First Lady, the Vice President's wife, and the wives of Supreme Court justices, ambassadors, and all members of Congress with seniority over Clifford. The "calling" at the White House consisted of taking a taxi (Pauline never drove in Washington) to the north entrance of the White House and giving three cards — two of Clifford's and one of her own — to the footman, who would pick them up at the taxi window. Other calls involved delivering cards to the respective residences, whether or not the wives were home. Of course, many were out making their calls. One afternoon Pauline made 13 calls, finding no one in; she came home and cried. Several years later she was astounded when the Belgian ambassador's wife returned a call in person; that dear lady had not forgotten American assistance to Belgium during World War I.

Mrs. Homer Hoch, wife of Kansas's 4th District congressman, was of great help to Pauline concerning social matters, including appropriate apparel. Pauline joined the Congressional Club at Sixteenth and New Hampshire Avenue, N.W., a social club for the families of members and former members of Congress.[3]

In addition to its various social functions, the club had a Red Cross day once a week, when members gathered for six hours to make surgical dressings. Pauline attended many of these sessions, especially when I was overseas during World War II.

Clifford and Pauline soon learned personally of the provincialism of many Washingtonians and Eastern members of Congress. Years later Clifford wrote:

> I can recall Members of Congress from the eastern states referring to Kansas when they meant Nebraska and Nebraska when they meant Kansas, and when confronted with their error, saying directly or by implication, "Oh well, what's the difference anyway? Who cares what goes on in either state?"

An elderly resident at the Burlington told Pauline that she spent her summers in the West. When Pauline asked where, the woman replied, "Cleveland." (Another version of this story has her answering "Buffalo.")

In March 1928 Clifford wrote Uncle Wilson Ragsdale: "Our four year old, Clifford Jr., and myself had a fine ride with Lindbergh this morning." According to Joyce Milton, President Coolidge had just presented the Medal of Honor, authorized by Congress the previous December, to Lindbergh. In appreciation, Lindbergh offered free airplane rides to members of Congress. Although flying in a plane was still considered an act of daring by many, the congressmen turned out in great numbers with their wives, children, and — in a few cases — their mistresses, a total of 835 people.[4] I regret I have absolutely no recollection of our flight. I am certain that Pauline was afraid to fly and had refused the offer.

In addition to our Washington-area sightseeing, Pauline insisted on our visiting relatives and friends who lived nearby: Cousins Willis and Joie Gregg and Lizzie Swift in Coatesville and Aunt Mary Corkadel in Oxford, Pennsylvania; and even an old school friend from Topeka, Shelby Rhodes Keith, who had returned to her hometown of Middletown, Virginia, many years before.

Soon after our return to Washington in December 1928, I contracted nephritis (a disease in which the kidneys stop functioning), possibly from an infection acquired at a sleazy hotel in Indiana. For a week or more, Clifford and Pauline thought they might again lose their only child. This was long before the advent of antibiotics. The only way to extract liquid wastes was to wrap me in scalding blankets several times a day to sweat them out. This process pained Pauline more than it did me. By Christmas Eve I was well enough for a visit from Santa Claus, who told me I could have one stocking filled with goodies but not two. I remained in bed at our apartment much of the next two months.

In the spring of 1929, Pauline became pregnant with my sister Martha, so she and I stayed in Garden City when Clifford returned to Washington in November. He was in Washington when Martha was born on December 4, much to Pauline's distress. She noted in Martha's baby book, "No Daddy present." Clifford did rush home immediately upon learning of Martha's birth, as reported in *The Garden City Telegram*:

CONGRESSMAN HOPE ARRIVES HOME
BY UNIVERSAL AIRPLANE

Trains traveling 50 to 60 miles an hour or more, as they do today, are plenty fast enough for a congressman when there is nothing more important to attend to than pass a tariff bill, give farmers relief, reduce income taxes, or declare war on Haiti.

But when a daughter is born and Daddy wants to get home to see her, that's different. So when Congressman Hope received word this week that a new daughter had arrived at his home in

Garden City he jumped on the first train leaving Washington for Chicago, where he boarded one of the big fast Fokker planes on the Universal line for Garden City. It took him just seven hours to get here from the Chicago airport, and he made the trip from Garden City airport to his home, a distance of a mile and a half, in a minute and a half less than nothing.

If congress pulls any boners while Congressman Hope is away it will be just too bad, that's all.[5]

The Chicago-Garden City air route was part of the recently established coast-to-coast air-rail service. Clifford left for Washington after Christmas, but Pauline, Martha, and I did not join him until the end of February. Our departure was particularly sad. Since returning to Garden City in the summer of 1929, we had acquired a part German Shepherd and part mixed-breed dog. Jumbo was playful, friendly, and faithful. We attempted to find a new home for him on a farm close to Garden City; but he repeatedly returned to our Gillespie Place home. The day before our scheduled departure, he was taken to a farm eight miles from Garden City and tied up. When Harry Hope came to take us to the train at 6 a.m. the next day, Jumbo was on our front steps with a gnawed-off rope around his neck. Later Gillespie Place friends told us he returned time after time to our home before finally disappearing.

This time we lived in the Capitol Towers Apartments, just east of Union Station on Massachusetts Avenue, N.E. Pauline enrolled me in the nearby Peabody Public School on Stanton Square. Clifford probably chose our apartment because of the proximity to both the school and the House Office Building. He could walk to work.

The family returned to Garden City in the summer, where Pauline and the children remained through 1931 while Clifford attended the congressional sessions. He did return early enough in 1931 to be at home during the blizzard which swept the Great Plains in March. Years later Martha made some insightful observations about Pauline's life during these times:

Looking back on Mom's life now from the vantage point of motherhood and grandmotherhood, I am aware of how it must have been for her during the times when Pop was in Washington and she was alone with us kids to care for in Garden City. She was so social a person I wonder how she coped with being tied down with kids to raise alone. Not to mention traveling alone with us by train to Washington.

She was outspoken about the aspects of Washington life she disliked. She hated the demands of propriety, the formal customs which recognized rank and prevented meaningful contact with other women whose husbands were in government service. The expectations on wives were much greater in the days before World War II than they were to be later on. But she dutifully did all she was told was necessary, to be a credit to Pop, I'm sure and because she believed she had no choice. But she lacked confidence in her ability to carry it all off properly. She spoke of herself as "a small town girl," out of her depth in the Washington social whirl. Some women thrived on it, but it was not Mom's style.

She did make friends though and was cherished as a confidante. She was a good listener and took to heart the troubles her friends shared with her. She was a worrier and sometimes felt overwhelmed by the difficulties of her friends and family members. Yet she wished she had more family and deeply regretted she was an only child. She always hoped Cliff Jr. and I would be close, a hope not easily realized when we were children with six years between us.

Mom had done quite a bit of singing as a young woman in Kansas, entertaining with popular ballads of the day at club meetings and such. But Washington was not a place for that, so she sang in the church choir instead.

By the early 1930s, Clifford had selected the best and fastest route for driving between Garden City and Washington. We took U.S. Highway 50 to Hutchinson, then angled up to Highway 81 at McPherson, then north to Salina and Highway 40 east to Topeka. Sometimes we stopped in Topeka and Valley Falls to visit Pauline's relatives, but more often we made those visits on the return trip. Occasionally we stopped in Atchison to see Uncle Frank Corkadel, a kind man. He was the janitor at the First Christian Church, living in a small house north of it. From Atchison we took Highway 59 to St. Joseph, Missouri.

From St. Joe we headed directly east on Highway 36 to Hannibal, Springfield, and Decatur, Illinois, and on to Indianapolis. It usually took an hour to drive straight through the center of that spread-out city. From Indy we continued straight east on Highway 40, the route of the old National Road, also known as the National Pike. The Pike was authorized by Congress in 1806 and was eventually extended to Vandalia, Illinois. Some of the Pike's metal mile markers could still be seen alongside new Highway 40. We drove through Springfield, Columbus, and Zanesville (with its Y-shaped bridge), Ohio; Wheeling, West Virginia; to Washington, Pennsylvania (home of Washington and Jefferson College, whose president was Ralph Hutchison, son of Judge Hutchison). From there 40 turned southeasterly across southwestern Pennsylvania to Cumberland and Frederick, Maryland, and from that point on we went south on Highway 240 to Washington.

In all the years we traversed that route, we never stopped to see a single historical or tourist site. Those sites included the Mark Twain attractions in Hannibal; the Lincoln shrines in Springfield; the birthplace of James Whitcomb Riley (then a well-remembered Hoosier poet) right on the highway in Greenfield, Indiana; and Fort Necessity, Pennsylvania, where George Washington fought the French and Indians. Our trips were always rush, rush, rush, or so it seemed to me. We did, however, remember and search out favorite cafes for repeated visits, such as the Red Cardinal Inn in Pittsfield, Illinois (which was still in business in 1995).

We did the trip of about 1,500 miles easily in four days, with Clifford doing all the driving until I became 16. At first we stayed in rooms for tourists and then cabin camps (the forerunner of motels), with hotels as a last resort. Pauline had an aversion to entering hotel lobbies and registering, a procedure she referred to as "having the whole tribe (all of four people) traipsing across the lobby." Ohio in the early days had a 45-mile-an-hour speed limit on its neat brick highways, rigorously enforced by motorcycle patrolmen. Once when stopped for speeding, Clifford cited the constitutional provision that no member of Congress shall be arrested going to or from sessions of Congress, except for treason, felony, or breach of the peace. Although the officer appeared not to have heard of this provision, Clifford, at his persuasive best, convinced him, and we proceeded on.

We had no prearranged places to spend the nights. The only exception was the White Swan Hotel in downtown Uniontown, Pennsylvania, where we always stayed on our trips back to Kansas. Uniontown was a drive of only a half day or so. Clifford liked to work at the office until mid-afternoon; then we headed north and west, often arriving after dark. The hotel had white swan designs on the wallpaper and bedspreads. In fact, white swans appeared all over the place. It was a pleasant place to stay, and Pauline made it an exception to her "no hotel" rule. The White Swan was a new hotel built on the site of the 1805 White House Tavern. I later learned that General George C. Marshall had been born in a modest home a block or two away.

For some reason I have special memories of the late winter and spring of 1932. We arrived in Washington sometime after Christmas and moved into an apartment on the second floor of South Cathedral Mansions, across the street from the Washington Zoo. The first neighbors we saw were several mafia-looking types across the hall. They left and returned each day with large suitcases; we assumed they were bootleggers.

Pauline enrolled me in the third grade at James F. Oyster Public School at 29th and Calvert Streets. Years later I learned Oyster had been a prominent District of Columbia commissioner, and the school's name had nothing to do with the oyster shells used to fill in the playground. There was no school lunch program, so I made a fast trip home for lunch. I could have taken my lunch, but I was lonesome for my friends in Garden City and Pauline knew it. Once when she had a luncheon engagement, Clifford came home to eat lunch with me.

The bicentennial of George Washington's birth, 1932, was duly celebrated at Oyster School. Miss Chamberlain's third-grade class presented a pageant, for which Pauline spent hours and days sewing a George Washington suit for me. Pictures of costumed class members appeared in *The Washington Evening Star*; it was a big deal, I thought.

In the early mornings, Clifford and I took hikes near the Washington Zoo, which did not then have a security fence. Most afternoons I hiked by myself through the zoo and ended it by scaling a 50-foot cliff just for the heck of it.

Promptly at 6 p.m. each weekday in the late spring and early summer, one could hear the *Amos 'n Andy* radio program blaring from a dozen radios through the open windows of our apartment. It was the number one, favorite radio program that year.

Most middle-class families in Washington in 1932 — and for some years before — employed black maids who worked five or six days a week, often for $10 a week plus meals. That winter Gertrude Green came to work for us. She became a lifelong friend of Pauline and Clifford.

Gertrude was not our first maid, however. Bernice Lacey, a pleasant person, had been our maid when we lived at Capitol Towers, but we lost contact with her when we returned to Kansas in the summer. When we came to South Cathedral Mansions, we first had a maid named Mildred who, I believe, had worked for the previous tenants. Pauline usually worked right along with whoever was working for her in performing household tasks. Mildred was not accustomed to this. One day Pauline told her, "We are going to wash windows today." Mildred indicated that washing windows was not part of her duties, to which Pauline replied with a most unfortunate choice of words: "Mildred, I've never asked you to do any niggardly work." Mildred's reply could have been expected. "I'se no nigger!" she responded angrily. And quit.

Gertrude Green, 16, was Mildred's successor. Pauline taught her to cook and do housework as well as to take care of Martha and me. Years later Martha recalled, "Mom recounted to me, and in later years to Gertrude, how she sent Gertrude out with me to the Washington Zoo and then followed at a discreet distance to see how Gertrude treated me. She was quickly reassured." Gertrude had a calm disposition, spoke in a soft voice, and was a joy to have around. Pauline, as usual, encouraged Gertrude to tell of her personal problems and sympathized with her, adding those problems to her list of perpetual worries. Gertrude worked for us until the beginning of World War II when she, like many other maids, found much better-paying employment with the federal government as a clerk. Clifford and Pauline stayed in touch with her.

To the best of my recollection, Pauline and Clifford — although they did not believe, in theory, in segregation in schools and public accommodations — accepted Washington's legal segregation laws of the time without giving the matter much thought. This was the view of most white people then. The only federal civil rights proposal at that time was a federal anti-lynching law. Clifford supported that measure, but it was defeated each year in Congress for some time.

In the fall of 1932, we were back in Garden City where I was in the fourth grade at Hutchison Grade School. On Frances Willard Day, a day designated by Kansas law to promote the virtues of temperance, several ladies from the Women's Christian Temperance Union (WCTU) appeared before our class to lecture against smoking. They brought with them a white rabbit and a dropper filled with nicotine, informing the class if drops of nicotine were given to the rabbit they would immediately kill him. Then

Clifford Hope's parents, Harry and Armitta, on a 1934 visit to the family at Mount Vernon, together with Cliff, Jr., Martha, and Clifford.

Martha, Pauline, Cliff, Jr., and Clifford R., in front of their Oliver Street home, *ca.* 1940.

the ladies offered to give the bunny to a member of the class. I was selected to receive him. Pauline was not as happy about my good fortune as I was, but we kept and cared for the rabbit until leaving for Washington that winter.

Long before 1932 Clifford had fit confidently into the ways of Washington and become totally absorbed in governmental affairs there and in the concerns of his constituents back home. As for members of his family, we were gradually, if somewhat tenuously, adapting to life in the nation's capital for part of each year.

Chapter 6

Early Days in Congress — Politics (1928-1932)

*C*LIFFORD'S FIRST SESSION OF *Congress began in
early December 1927. Thanks to the recommendation of
Poly Tincher and especially to the good offices of Homer
Hoch, Kansas's 4th District congressman, Clifford
became a member of the Committee on Agriculture, where he
served during his entire tenure in Congress. Kansas then had
eight representatives in the House — all Republicans, save one.
Daniel Anthony, in poor health at the time, was a newspaper
editor and lawyer from Leavenworth. Ulysses Samuel Guyer was
a lawyer from Kansas City and former mayor of that city.
William Henry Sproul, a lawyer from Sedan, had succeeded in
defeating Phil Campbell, veteran chairman of the House Rules
Committee in 1922. Homer Hoch of Marion, an editor and
lawyer, later served as Kansas Supreme Court justice. James
George Strong, Poly Tincher's opponent in the previously mentioned "navel engagement," was a lawyer from Blue Rapids.
Hays Baxter White, a farmer and teacher, came from Mankato.*

The lone Democrat, William Augustus Ayres, a Wichita lawyer, later became a member of the Federal Trade Commission.

In 1927 Kansas's senior senator was Charles Curtis. Then Majority Leader of the Senate, he would be elected Herbert Hoover's vice president in 1928. Much was made of the fact that he was part Kaw Indian. His congressional career began as a representative in 1893, and he served continuously in Congress from that time except for a two-year absence as a result of the Republican-Bull Moose split in 1912. A staunch conservative, he could be considered Kansas's most successful politician up to that time, but historians in recent years have not dealt with him kindly. (A biographer of Alice Roosevelt Longworth even related that Curtis cheated at cards.)

Clifford's memory of Charlie Curtis as a veteran campaigner with a wide acquaintanceship was expressed in a previous chapter. Pauline had even more personal memories of him. At a party given by Curtis's sister, Dolly Gann, in his home, Pauline discovered to her horror that she was wearing a three-quarter-length dress while all the other ladies had come in full-length gowns. Clearly uncomfortable in her "too short" skirt, she sat alone on a side row of chairs wondering what to do next. Senator Curtis, sensing her anxiety, came over to sit beside her and visit for quite some time. Pauline never forgot his kindness and told about it frequently over the years.

For two decades Clifford was associated in Congress with Kansas's other Senator, Arthur Capper. He greatly admired Capper's business career. Born a poor boy, Capper was a young man when he built a publishing empire around the flagship *The Topeka Daily Capital*. Progressive by nature, Capper lost the race for governor in 1912 by only 29 votes. He graciously accepted defeat, then was elected in 1914. Four years later he won a U.S. Senate seat, which he held for 30 years. When the bipartisan Senate Farm Bloc consisting of 12 farm-state senators was organized in 1921, he became an enthusiastic leader, sponsoring much legislation to benefit agriculture.

Unfortunately for his place in history, Capper stayed in the Senate one or two terms too long, finally retiring under pressure at the age of 83 in 1948. A Kansas curmudgeon political writer, W. G. Clugston, referred to him as "Capper, the Christ-like statesman."[1] In the 1940s, a Great Bend editorial writer called him "Old Zero."[2] But the greatest damage to the Senator's reputation was caused by his "hands-on" approach to women; he loved to touch and pat one and all, and that — many years before sexual harassment became a hot issue — came to overshadow all his accomplishments as a public servant. Forty years after Capper's retirement, David Brinkley wrote in *Washington Goes to War* that Capper was "widely known among women staff members as the Senate's most tireless fanny patter."[3] My wife can verify Capper's propensities in this regard. In January 1949 Dolores was helping put me through law school by working for the Associated Press in Topeka. Assigned to do a story on the retired senator on his birthday, she remembers how he firmly grasped her knee throughout the interview.

My only personal memory of Senator Capper was having him show me his recently removed appendix in 1937. He kept the thing in a jar on his desk.

Professor Homer Socolofsky, Capper's conscientious biographer, says Capper was not widely known as a statesman, "due partly to his expert ability to discover the ebb and flow of Kansas opinion and to shift with the tide."[4] I believe Clifford would have gone along with that, but he probably would have added that Arthur Capper should be remembered for his many years of kindly service to all Kansans, especially farm families.

In 1927 the most-remembered Kansas Representative in the House was one who was no longer there — Philip P. Campbell of Pittsburg, in what was then the 3rd District. Born in Nova Scotia, Campbell came to Kansas in 1867 at the age of five. In the 1960s Clifford wrote a column about Campbell, calling him a "man of ability, who, during 20 years in Congress, attained a high place among Republican leaders in the House."[5] He remembered one of Campbell's "foibles" was wearing a lock of hair on his forehead "a la Napoleon."

In 1922 Campbell was chairman of the Rules Committee, then, as now, a position of great power. "He was in line for higher responsibilities," according to Clifford, and had he been reelected in 1922, would probably have been chosen Republican floor leader in the 68th Congress and Speaker in the 69th instead of Nicholas Longworth.

But alas, he made a mistake which turned out to be as disastrous to his fortunes as Napoleon's invasion of Russia was to his. He bought a house across the Potomac in Virginia, a colonial mansion with a long history of illustrious occupants and a magnificent view of Washington. This brought him an opponent in the primary who was rude enough to tell the citizenry of the district that their congressman had left Kansas and moved to Virginia. Result: William Henry Sproul, nominated; Philip Pitt Campbell defeated.

What Clifford did not mention were the final days of the 1922 primary campaign when, at a political rally, Sproul bribed Campbell's band to play "Carry Me Back to Old Virginny." (I saw Campbell and his Virginia home not long after we arrived in Washington and can attest to both his Napoleonic lock of hair and his palatial mansion.)

As in the case of Arthur Capper, the memory of Phil Campbell's conduct and demise lived on. David Brinkley mentioned Campbell in *Washington Goes to War* as an outstanding example of what can happen to a congressman who forgets the people back home;[6] and Tip O'Neill, in his autobiography, *Man of the House*, cited Campbell for his dictatorial manner and arbitrariness in the House Rules Committee.[7]

When Clifford arrived in Washington, many up-and-coming leaders of the House were already serving, including Democrats John Nance Garner, Sam Rayburn, and John McCormack, and Republican Joe Martin. Clifford became friends with all of them, even making friends with some of the more eccentric members. Probably his favorite among the latter was Representative George Holden Tinkham.

Hope wrote in a 1968 column:

> During my time in Congress I served with more than two thousand members of the House and Senate. Some of them were brilliant, most of them were able and a few were rather stupid. Some of them stand out in my memory mainly because they were different from the average run of members.[8]

Congressman Tinkham, who represented a Boston district, was one who "stood out." In the column Hope noted that Tinkham was

> a blueblood whose ancestors came over on the Mayflower, and as befitted one with such antecedents, a graduate of Harvard. He was a man of independent means, a bachelor, a lawyer and a Republican. He was elected to the House of Representatives in 1914 and retired after 28 years of continuous service. Earlier he had served as a councilman in Boston and the state Senate.

Tinkham's chief claim to fame at the time Hope came to Congress was being a congressman who never visited his district. Hope explained to his readers:

> This was in an era when Congress was in session only about half of the time. Then, as now, most members of Congress hurried home after adjournment to mingle with their constituents and to mend their political fence.

That was not for Tinkham. The Boston congressman was a big game hunter, and for him the adjournment of Congress meant the beginning of hunting season. As soon as possible he set sail for Africa, Asia, South America, or any place where the hunting was good.

According to Hope, this did not mean Tinkham completely neglected his district. Hope recalled that the congressman

> maintained a well-staffed office in Boston to take care of his constituents and to conduct his campaigns. . . . I remember asking him if his continued absence didn't cause some dissatisfaction among his constituents. Tinkham replied, "Oh, I'm just a myth in my district now and the only way to preserve a myth is to never let the reality catch up with it."

Hope also reported:

> [Tinkham] was not one to lie awake at night agonizing over how to vote on a controversial bill. He simply voted the party line, said little during floor debate, and introduced few bills. . . . He broke his usual silence by delivering anti-prohibition speeches once or twice a year.

In 1942 Tinkham retired from Congress, leaving (according to Hope) "with the good wishes of his colleagues and a record of no hits, no runs and no errors."

When Hope became a member of the Committee on Agriculture, American farmers — especially wheat farmers — were suffering from the lack of control over the prices received for their products and over prices of products they had to buy. These problems had plagued farmers for years.

When they took their wheat to the grain elevator, farmers had two choices: take the price offered or keep the wheat. When they went to buy fertilizer, machinery, or any other items for farming operations or family living, farmers had to pay the price asked by the retailer. Farmers sold at wholesale and bought at retail. Furthermore, individual production goals could be changed by droughts, floods, insects, and other natural disasters, so farmers could not control output as could manufacturers.

The Department of Agriculture, after much study, had determined that from 1909 to 1914 farm product prices had been at parity with the prices of non-farm commodities. This fair price relationship was designated as 100 percent of parity. The 1909-1914 period became known as the golden era of American agriculture. (Some historians have extended this era to 1918.) George Peek, a Moline, Illinois, businessman, led the fight for parity prices in the 1920s, and a mighty fight it was. A series of bills, each designated as the McNary-Haugen Bill (named after Senator Charles McNary of Oregon and Representative Gilbert Haugen of Iowa, chairmen, respectively, of the Senate and House Committees on Agriculture), were considered by Congress in the 1924, 1927, and 1928 sessions. The provisions of each bill were complex and varied, but the purpose was to make the tariff effective, by way of an equalization fee on domestic consumption, with the excess production to be sold at the world price. The idea was to give the farmer a parity price for that part of the crop consumed in the United States. The bills were vigorously opposed by President Calvin Coolidge, Secretary of Commerce Herbert Hoover, and Secretary of the Treasury Andrew Mellon; they saw the bills as government interference with the free enterprise system, then effectively controlled by big business.

Poly Tincher supported the McNary-Haugen Bill in 1924 when it was defeated in Congress, but after Coolidge carried Kansas and other farm states that year, Tincher switched positions — much to the dismay of Kansas farm leaders, especially Ralph Snyder, president of the Kansas Farm Bureau. Tincher's "no" vote in February 1927 precipitated his famous "navel engagement" with Representative Jim Strong. (Tincher was the only Kansas member who did not then support the bill.) Snyder, therefore, welcomed Hope as Tincher's replacement and was surprised when Hope did not immediately endorse the McNary-Haugen legislation.

Hope, in his usual forthright manner, wrote Snyder in August that he was not convinced the legislation would accomplish its purpose; however, conferences with Snyder and others convinced him that it was worth a try. In the spring of 1928, Hope voted for the bill in committee and on the floor. Coolidge again vetoed it, with an even sharper veto message than in his 14,000-word veto explanation in 1927. Thus ended the McNary-Haugen attempts to improve the lot of farmers.

In the meantime, Hope resolved to learn all he could about proposed solutions for agricultural problems. Early on he established a reputation as the most serious student of agriculture in the House. Unlike Poly Tincher, when there was a conflict between the Republican Party position and what Hope perceived to be in the best interests of farmers, he chose the latter position.

Despite farmer opposition, Herbert Hoover was easily nominated for President in 1928. With Charlie Curtis as his running mate (nominated by none other than Poly Tincher!), Hoover received additional support in Kansas. He called a special session of Congress in early 1929, which resulted in enactment of the Agricultural Marketing Act. The act's purpose was to place agriculture "on a basis of economic equality with other industries." It established a Federal Farm Board, which set up government-financed stabilization corporations designed to keep surpluses from depressing farm prices. The board had no authority to control production.

The stock market crash in October and the resulting panic caused farm prices to tumble. By 1931 the board had lost $356 million attempting to support prices. With low prices, farmers raised even more crops in an attempt to make ends meet.

Years later Hope wrote to his friend, agricultural economist Walter W. Wilcox:

> The Agricultural Marketing Act of 1929 was purely an Administration Bill, with little or no farm organization support, although there was a grudging acceptance of the fact that it was that legislation or nothing. Even at that, it was pretty much log-rolled through Congress. I recall that two members of the committee of five appointed by the Chairman of the Agricultural Committee to draft the legislation, received appointments to federal judgeships not too long afterwards.

By 1931 farm leaders such as Hope realized that other legislative remedies were needed. Of the various plans and panaceas being circulated, the one receiving the most support was the Domestic Allotment Plan, originally written by USDA economist W. J. Spillman and modified and promoted by John D. Black of Harvard and M. L. Wilson of Montana State College. In the spring of 1932, Wilson visited Hope in his office. He was impressed when Hope told him he was aware of the Domestic Allotment Plan and pulled a copy of Dr. Black's book, *Agricultural Reform in the United States*, from his desk drawer. Hope and Senator Pete Norbeck of South Dakota introduced bills embodying the plan for the purpose of publicizing it, but Congress adjourned for the summer and the elections without taking action on them. Although Hope supported Hoover for reelection (despite the President's farm policies) and Wilson was a strong booster of Franklin D. Roosevelt, they kept in touch concerning the Domestic Allotment Plan during the summer and fall.

In newspaper columns written in 1966, Hope summarized the various congressional hearings of 1932 that culminated in December after the election.

> The hearings held by the House Committee on Agriculture, beginning on December 14, 1932, demonstrated that the farm organizations had indeed gotten together on a program. This applied not only to the Farm Bureau, Grange, and Farmers Union, but to a large number of important commodity organizations as well. In all, 13 groups were represented at the hearing. Never before or since have farm organizations shown as great a degree of unanimity as this occasion.

> The proposal which they submitted was based on the domestic allotment plan of M. L. Wilson and his associates. In brief, it provided for a voluntary program of production control on wheat and certain other farm commodities of which there were exportable surpluses. It called for payments by the Federal Government to farmers who complied with the program. These payments were to be made on that part of a farmer's production which was consumed domestically for food.

> Funds to make these payments were to come from a tax levied on the processing of the commodity, and were based on the difference between the lower buying power of current prices for the commodity as compared with the buying power of prices

for the commodity during the base period of 1909-1914 when a more favorable relationship existed as far as farm prices were concerned.

The hearings lasted several days following which Representative Marvin Jones of Texas introduced a bill covering wheat and several other commodities. The bill passed the House, but no action was taken in the Senate prior to the end of the Congressional session on March 3rd.

Although Hope regretted loss of Republican control of the House as a result of the 1930 election and follow-up special elections, he was pleased that his friend Jones, a Democrat from Amarillo, had become chairman of the House Agricultural Committee. Jones's and Hope's districts were separated by only a 30-mile strip of the Oklahoma panhandle. They worked together closely until Jones left Congress in 1940. Hope was also pleased by the election of Edward A. O'Neal of Alabama as president of the American Farm Bureau Federation in 1931. O'Neal and Hope worked well together until O'Neal's retirement in 1947.

Agricultural problems and proposed legislative solutions consumed much of Hope's time from 1928 to 1932, but he also took time, by working increasingly longer hours, to establish himself as a hard-working, respected congressman. Hope, who did not wish to be considered a one-issue or one-area representative, studied all major issues carefully.

From the beginning he promptly answered letters from his 325,000 constituents, stating exactly what he thought on various issues rather than just telling letter writers what they wanted to hear. His letters were often long ones — especially those written to people with whom he disagreed. To them, he explained his views in great detail. He never took polls; the letters, wires (telegrams), and telephone calls (few in number and expensive at that time) were his polls. Years later a friend of mine in Liberal observed, "If you'd write ol' Cliff and say 'Hello,' he'd write back immediately and say 'Hi.'"

In December 1944 Clifford's youngest brother Ralph, just elected to the Kansas Legislature from Atchison County, sought his advice on how to be an effective legislator. In addition to advising Ralph to "study all important bills carefully and be prepared to express your views on them" and to "become the master of some field of legislation," he gave his opinion on party loyalty.

While I believe in Party government and Party responsibility, I think a man ought to be reasonably independent and that in the long run it will help him rather than hurt him to follow that course. If you feel it should be necessary to follow a course which may be different from that of the majority in the Party, it ought to be a case where you have a good reason for doing what you do and where you can justify it to your own conscience and in such a way as to appeal logically to fair-minded people.

Clifford also advised Ralph to familiarize himself with the rules

either before the session begins or early in the session. Most members are too lazy to study them or don't think it is worthwhile. A member who is familiar with the general principles of parliamentary law, not only can take care of himself in better shape on the floor, but he also will invariably gain the respect and confidence of other members who are not familiar with the rules of legislative procedure.

He cautioned Ralph to be "more or less careful" in his association with lobbyists. "There is nothing wrong with lobbyists," wrote Clifford "and they can be of great help to members of a legislative body." But Ralph was warned to avoid getting tagged as a representative of any special-interest group. Clifford advised:

At the same time, there isn't any reason why you shouldn't give every consideration to the problems of these groups and some of their legislative representatives are good men with whom to advise and counsel, providing you can give the proper weight to any bias or prejudice or self interest which naturally exists.

He suggested maintaining "friendly and pleasant relations with the newspapermen without making an effort . . . to seek publicity." It was Hope's opinion that publicity was "more often a liability than an asset."

Hope also believed that he should pay his own campaign expenses. In a rural district, before the time of television advertising, this was much easier to do than it would be today. Although after his first several elections he accepted donations from friends, Hope did not solicit them; he customarily borrowed from the bank to pay expenses, then made repayments during his next two-year term. Late in his career Pauline announced happily, "This is the first campaign in which Daddy hasn't had to borrow money."

From the beginning, Hope was interested in soil-and-water conservation. Next to farm surplus and price support problems, he probably spent more time on conservation matters than on any other subject. In a letter to the National Association of Soil and Water Conservation Districts in December 1969, he recalled that the first bill he got through Congress was a wild fowl refuge bill which established the Cheyenne Bottoms Game Preserve near Great Bend, Kansas, in 1928. "The discovery of oil in the area increased land prices tremendously and it was impossible to go ahead with the project," he said, adding that later, after the oil excitement subsided, the State Fish and Game Commission "took over the project and with the aid of Federal Fish and Wildlife Funds set up a very fine preserve." In the same letter, he observed, "As I look back upon my years in Washington I get more satisfaction out of the time and effort I gave to conservation matters than any other subject."

During most of 1928 Clifford's office force consisted of Walker Cross, secretary (a position which would later be designated "administrative assistant" or "AA"), and Miss Van Huss, stenographer. The latter left in September. She was succeeded by M. C. Schrader, son of a prominent physician and Republican of Kinsley, who arranged for young Schrader's employment, at $150 per month, without his knowledge. Young Schrader immediately enrolled as a night school student at George Washington Law School. When Hope and Cross were in Kansas during the spring and summer of 1929, Schrader held down the office alone. Years later he recalled there were few visitors and the telephone did not ring for long periods of time, so he spent much of the summer playing bridge with other secretaries. Schrader's most vivid recollection of his employment with Hope concerned New Year's Day 1929. Hope, who did not customarily welcome in the new year, announced that the office would be open on New Year's Day. Schrader spent the eve celebrating at the Wardman Park Hotel and got his tux off just in time to get to work. Cross had celebrated at another party. After about five minutes spent looking at the two celebrants and trying to talk with them, Hope decided, "We'll just not work today." In the same interview Schrader recalled that Hope "had the reputation of being a hard worker in comparison with other congressmen of that time."

During the latter part of 1929, Cross and Schrader left to pursue their legal careers. Cross became a prominent Washington lawyer and Schrader returned to Kansas after graduating from law school; later he became probate judge of Finney County for 28 years. Replacing them were George L. Reid, Jr., and his wife, Ilene, as secretary and stenographer respectively. George, who had worked in the Kansas Insurance Commissioner's office, had become acquainted with Clifford through American Legion projects. He was the son of George L. Reid, Sr., a Tribune lawyer who had written Judge Hutchison in 1926, concerned that Clifford might favor repealing the Kansas anti-cigarette law. George did not take after his father. He was not a lawyer; he was also a chain smoker. But above all, he was loyal to Hope. He was a shrewd, skilled organizer and negotiator — and a keen judge of human nature. In both Washington and Kansas he knew when to praise and when to needle people. He became a true friend to Clifford, keeping close contact during Hope's entire career in Congress. As for Ilene, she was the most talented, competent stenographer Clifford ever had. She became his secretary when George served in the Army during World War II.

Meanwhile, Kansas politics, sometimes dull, had again become exciting. In 1928, Clyde M. Reed, Parsons publisher — backed by fellow publishers William Allen White, Victor Murdock, and Henry J. Allen — won the Republican primary for governor, defeating John D. M. Hamilton (Speaker of the Kansas House), and four other opponents. Hamilton was backed by Dave Mulvane and W. Y. Morgan and others in the Old Guard, but he was also supported by younger voters and veterans, including his good friend, Clifford Hope. Hamilton had supported Hope on the Klan issue in 1925; Hope had supported Hamilton for Speaker in 1927. Reed defeated Democrat Chauncey B. Little in the 1928 Republican landslide, and Herbert Hoover beat Al Smith in Kansas by more than two to one (513,672 to 193,003).

In the 1930 GOP primary, Clyde Reed was defeated by Frank "Chief" Haucke of Council Grove, a former commander of the American Legion, star athlete, and a hale fellow well met. Hope was Haucke's enthusiastic supporter and lifelong friend. Years later Hope remembered their campaigning together in the rain over muddy roads in southwest Kansas. Harry H. Woodring, a Neodesha banker, won the Democratic nomina-

Clyde Reed in the back seat (right) during his gubernatorial primary campaign, *ca.* 1928. Alf Landon is seated up front (left).
Kansas State Historical Society, Topeka

tion. (He was also a former state Legion commander and a friend of Haucke.)

What could have been a rather colorless election battle was changed completely by the entry of a write-in, independent candidate, Dr. John Romulus Brinkley, who had achieved fame and fortune for his goat-gland operations, claimed to restore masculine virility. By 1930 the Milford doctor's medical license had been revoked, but he continued to operate a powerful radio station. He commenced a colorful campaign, promising almost everything to everybody. The result was a Woodring victory over Haucke by only 251 votes (217,171 to 216,920). Brinkley amassed 183,000 write-in votes. Some people claimed that if all ballots of persons intending to vote for Brinkley had been counted, he would have won. It was alleged that Republicans and Democrats on election boards cooperated in throwing out all ballots on which Brinkley's name was misspelled or were otherwise not technically correct according to law. In any event, the size of his counted vote astounded many politicians. In October the old pro, Poly Tincher, wrote Hope that he thought Dr. Brinkley might get 50,000 votes; Hope responded with a forecast of 30,000 to 40,000. After the election Hope wrote to a number of constituents, "If I had known beforehand just how weird the election was going to be, I probably would have been scared to death." He never forgot that election. In his presidential address to the Kansas State Historical Society in October 1969, Hope described Brinkley as a "quack doctor," "a crook and a scoundrel of the first order," and "a thoroughly bad man." That was strong language for the 7th District congressman.

Brinkley tried again in two years with his name on the ballot as an independent. This time his campaign was much better organized. When I was eight, I saw Brinkley's medicine-show-type entourage at Stevens Park in Garden City. It came complete with a band and introductions of Mrs. Brinkley and their son, Johnny boy.

Woodring, running for re-election, was edged out by the Republican harmony candidate, Alfred M. Landon (278,581 to 272,944); Brinkley received 244,607 votes. Landon was one of only five Republican governors elected in 1932. Brinkley's race undoubtedly took votes from Woodring and gave the election to Landon.

In 1932, at the height of the Depression, the Hoover-Curtis ticket lost badly in Kansas as well as in the nation. On a cold November day after the election, President Hoover and his wife, Lou Henry Hoover, were returning to Washington from California in their special train on the Rock Island Railroad. The train entered Kansas at Liberal, and the Hoovers made rear-platform appearances at Liberal and later at Pratt and Hutchinson in the 7th District. They invited Clifford and Pauline to ride with them through Hope's district. A saddened Hoover asked Clifford, "By how much did I lose Kansas?" The answer was by 75,000 votes; Hoover carried only three counties in the 32-county 7th District. At the Pratt stop in the evening, the President asked Hope to introduce him to the crowd. In response to the introduction, Hoover said, "I'm afraid your congressman's voice came through the campaign better than mine." There were large crowds wherever the train stopped; although most hadn't voted for him, Hoover *was* still the President and people felt sorry for him. Clifford and Pauline also were genuinely sorry for him, Pauline perhaps more than Clifford.

In 1937 Clifford wrote to his friend, Iowa editor Don Berry:

> I have a very high regard for Herbert Hoover's achievements along some lines, but he is a man who has absolutely no aptitude for political life and utterly lacks the ability to get along with people which is the first requisite of anyone occupying the position of President. No one could ever discuss anything with Hoover while he was President because he very distinctly gave the impression that his mind was already made up. . . . While history may deal very kindly with Mr. Hoover, it isn't going to help right now when we are trying to build up the party.

Hope won his general election races in 1928 and 1930 by large majorities, but in 1932 he was faced with a primary opponent, courtesy of his old off-again-on-again friend, Poly Tincher. Poly, upset because Hope had not reappointed the Hutchinson postmaster originally appointed by Poly, persuaded State Representative O. W. (Orrie) Dawson of Great Bend to enter the race. Hope was handicapped in campaigning because Congress did not adjourn until July 16; the primary was August 2. He knew voters were down on Hoover and incumbents in general. Fortunately for him, Dawson did not wage an aggressive campaign. Hope's supporters spread the word that Dawson was Poly's candidate and that Dawson, a four-term state representative, had a mediocre record. During the primary campaign, a Hope supporter, R. L. Wilson of Richfield, wrote Hope that Dawson would "promise anything from cancellation of all taxes to a golden harp in Heaven." Hope won the primary by a two-to-one margin.

Aaron Coleman, Hutchinson businessman, was the Democrat candidate. In early October *The Hutchinson Herald* predicted Hope would be swept out in a Democratic landslide. Again Hope was lucky — his opponent did not mount an aggressive campaign. Coleman agreed with Hope on many issues. Both opposed repeal of the 18th (Prohibition) Amendment. For the most part, Coleman remained silent on issues of taxation. Hope, in his customary forthright manner, advocated taxes based upon ability to pay — that is, income and inheritance taxes. He opposed taxes on gasoline, electric current, and checks; and he opposed an increase in postal rates. He favored reduction in non-essential government spending. In short, he advocated pragmatic solutions to the problems of taxation and government spending. Waging an intense campaign and telling it like it was, paid off on election day. Hope defeated Coleman by an almost 12,000-vote majority (59,269 to 47,418), carrying every county except Reno, Coleman's home. Clifford wrote his law school classmate, Mabel Jones Shaffer:

> It always leaves a better feeling afterward for a candidate to get a good vote in his own county and anyway Aaron made a nice clean campaign in every way so I was pleased that he could get the satisfaction which naturally comes from carrying one's own county.

Early in the campaign Mabel had written Clifford, "You have that personality that inspires faith and belief even if you are not spectacular."

From 1926 through his 1932 campaign, Hope had a policy of neither soliciting nor accepting campaign contributions. After the 1932 election, he wrote J. C. Butler, M.D., of Hutchinson, returning the doctor's unsolicited contribution because "I have always refrained from asking or accepting campaign contributions from friends." As previously stated, in later campaigns Hope did accept contributions, but I have not found any evidence that he ever made any mass appeal for campaign funds.

Nationally the 1932 election was a Republican disaster. Democrats carried the House elections 313 to 117. Kansas Democrats captured three of the state's seven congressional seats and held onto one of the two senatorial positions.[9]

The Kansas delegation to the U.S. House of Representatives, 1935-1936. From left to right: John M. (Jack) Houston, 5th District; W. P. Lambertson, 1st District; Clifford R. Hope, 7th District; U.S. Guyer, 2nd District; E. W. Patterson, 3rd District; Frank Carlson, 6th District; Randolph Carpenter, 4th District. H. J. MacDonald, 1935

Of all the Kansans who entered Congress from 1929 to 1933, the most interesting and fascinating — at least to Clifford — was W. P. Lambertson, of the 1st District. Clifford wrote two newspaper columns about him in 1968. The first one began, "William Purnell Lambertson, usually known as Bill, was one of the most independent, controversial and durable figures in the history of Kansas politics. He was frequently an extremist, sometimes of the right and sometimes of the left." Hope continued:

> At the Republican National Convention in Kansas City that year, [Lambertson] was one of the leaders of a delegation of farmers who picketed the Convention, demanding the defeat of Hoover and a platform plank endorsing the McNary-Haugen bill. They failed in both efforts.
>
> Bill was elected in November but continued his bitter criticism of Hoover after he went to Washington. For this, he lost patronage, consisting mostly of postoffice appointments. That didn't seem to hurt Bill, however, and he was triumphantly elected to the next seven Congresses. . . .
>
> After the Roosevelt administration took over in March 1933, Bill went all out for the New Deal. However, as time went on his basic conservatism and natural inclination to "be agin" the government began to assert themselves. Never one to do things by halves, he swung all the way to the right and became the standpatter of standpatters. . . .
>
> Bill always strove to maintain an image as a plain Kansas farmer. In Washington, he lived in a small apartment in an unfashionable area near the Capitol. He refused to attend official functions where formal dress was required.

Hope's columns did not include reference to Bill's foibles. For instance, he customarily played golf at the public courses in Washington in his bare feet, leaving his shoes at the first tee. Once a caddy made off with his shoes. This habit of Bill's was reported nationwide, and "Barefoot Bill" was compared to "Sockless Jerry" Simpson.

Upon Lambertson's death in 1957, his eulogy read in part:

> For well onto half a century he provided the political life of his state and nation with variety. He was a nonconformist.

Without sacrificing in any degree his ideals of personal and public morality and justice, he simply did not fit into the common mold in which the general run of public servants are shaped.[10]

By comparison, Hope's political life was more orderly. While he, like Lambertson, did not sacrifice his ideals of morality and justice, Hope was more of a conformist, choosing a directed, steadier path — then, perhaps, fate played its part too. Before the 1932 congressional elections, Hope ranked ninth out of 11 Republican members on the Committee of Agriculture. As a result of the defeat of many Republican members (including former chairman Gilbert N. Haugen), Hope advanced to second place, behind John D. Clarke of New York; Clarke was killed in a car accident in November 1933. Hope would not have then become the top-ranking Republican on the committee except for another quirk of political fate: August Andresen of Minnesota, first elected in 1924 (a term ahead of Hope), was defeated in the 1932 debacle; he was elected again in 1934 and served on the committee until his death in January 1958. But for his defeat in 1932, Andresen would have outranked Hope on the committee during Hope's entire remaining terms in Congress (until January 1957). Thus by the vicissitudes of politics and an act of God, Hope, at the age of 40, became the top-ranking Republican on the committee, a position he held until he retired. These events determined the course of the rest of Hope's congressional career.

Chapter 7

Dust Bowl and Depression — The Dirty Thirties (1933-1939)

*I*MMEDIATELY AFTER HIS *inauguration on March 4, 1933, President Franklin D. Roosevelt called a special session of the new Democrat Congress. On March 16 a bill similar to one introduced by Representative Marvin Jones (D, Texas) during the previous lame duck session was sent to Capitol Hill by the President. Things moved swiftly during the spring of 1933, and by May 12 the bill that became the Agricultural Adjustment Act of 1933 had passed both houses and was on the President's desk. Although Congressman Hope had some reservation about this landmark legislation, he put all partisanship aside in the interest of the nation's farmers and worked diligently during the Depression decade to make the administration's agricultural program a success.*

The AAA bill was one relatively small part of the package of emergency legislation passed by the 73rd Congress with little debate during the famous first "Hundred Days" of the New Deal. The main purpose of the bill was to raise farm prices to parity, defined as bringing "prices to farmers at a level that will give agricultural commodities a purchasing power with respect to articles farmers buy, equivalent to the purchasing power of articles in the base period, August 1909 to July 1914." This was a long-range, not immediate, objective; in the short run, the emphasis was on acreage reduction. The Secretary of Agriculture was given broad powers to reduce output to bring production in line with demand. Cash payments were made by the government to farmers agreeing to reduce their acres devoted to the production of the so-called basic commodities: wheat, cotton, rice, tobacco, corn, hogs, and dairy products. The program was financed by a tax on processors of farm commodities, who would pass the tax on to consumers.

When this bill reached the floor of the House, debate was limited to four hours; no amendments were allowed. Hope was in a dilemma: Although the bill allowed the secretary to put a voluntary wheat allotment plan into effect, it also gave him dictatorial powers, so Hope decided he could not support the measure in that form. The bill passed the House the next day by a vote of 315 to 98. The only members of the Kansas delegation to vote against the AAA were U. S. Guyer from the Kansas City area and Hope. After the Senate passed a different version of the bill, Hope served as a member of the conference committee which, in Hope's opinion, improved the bill; the House approved the conference report by voice vote, with Hope voting "yea." However, the original vote was the only roll-call vote, and Hope's recorded "no" vote would come back to haunt him in the 1934 elections. Once the bill became law, Hope worked hard to help implement it. He, Secretary of Agriculture Henry A. Wallace, and Governor Alf Landon toured Kansas in late June to explain the Act's provisions, and Hope and his office force worked diligently to expedite benefits for individual farmers.

The year 1933 and the years immediately following brought additional federal aid to farmers and their families. The Commodity Credit Corporation was established to make nonrecourse loans to producers of storable commodities who complied with AAA programs. If prices rose, the loans could be paid off; if they fell, the CCC took the mortgaged crop in payment, and the indebtedness was discharged in full. The Farm Credit Administration provided loans to farmers at lower interest rates than banks offered. Some banks would not lend at all, considering such loans too risky. In 1935 the Rural Electrification Administration was set up to provide loans to rural electric cooperatives and local government entities. The great majority of farms had been without electricity up to that time.

The AAA proved helpful to farmers in raising prices and stabilizing production, but on January 6, 1936, the AAA was declared unconstitutional by the U.S. Supreme Court on the grounds that Congress had no power to control agricultural production and that processing taxes were unlawful. In February Congress passed the Soil Conservation and Domestic Allotment Act as a replacement for the AAA. The act (which Hope fully supported) provided benefit payments based on soil conservation practices, thereby reducing acreage and production. Two years later the Agricultural Adjustment Act of 1938 consolidated previous price-support programs. As agricultural historian Michael W. Schuyler stated, "The philosophy and programs embodied in the legislation [Second AAA] would structure American farm policy for the next half century."[1]

The volume of correspondence between Hope and his constituents from 1933 to 1939 reveals some of his thoughts during those tumultuous times. In early 1935 Claude M. Cave, a former member of the Kansas Legislature from Haskell County, wrote Hope asking questions about eight pending issues. In a six-page reply Hope answered his questions in detail, ending with:

> All of this sounds as if we might as well abolish Congress, which I think is about correct, as long as the present situation continues. I mean there is no particular use in having a Congress which finally follows whatever suggestions that come from the White House. It is not so bad in the Senate of course but here in the House of Representatives, practically all important legislation is becoming, and will be, brought up for consideration under gag rules which permit no opportunity for amendment and little for debate. There is nothing which Republican members of Congress can do about the matter, but as long as individual Democratic members (many of whom I know do not personally favor much of the legislation which is being passed) continue to vote gag rules upon themselves and tie their own hands, there is no likelihood that the situation will be changed.

Soon after the Supreme Court declared the AAA of 1933 unconstitutional, Arthur E. Taylor of Great Bend, upset by that decision, wrote that Supreme Court decisions should be required to be unanimous. Hope replied that he understood that divided decisions of the court were distressing to many people and that a unanimous decision is always more satisfactory and conclusive; but he explained that since the law was not an exact science but a "living, growing, progressive thing," differences of opinion were inevitable. It seemed to Hope "that the only basis to go on is to take the views of the majority just as we do in other matters, even in the political or business world." Hope wrote:

> This doesn't mean that the people are without a remedy in the matter, because our constitution was written with the idea that it should be a growing document and not a rigid declaration. Therefore, methods were provided for amending it, and the fact that twenty-two amendments have been adopted and many more than that submitted by Congress shows the practicability of that method of procedure.
>
> After all, the Supreme Court was set up as a tribunal to prevent the usurpation of the rights of the people and of the states by the legislative and executive branches of the Government. The men who drew that document knew all too well from practical experience what executives and legislators were capable of unless restrained in some way. The main purpose of the constitution is to protect the rights of minorities and to make sure that the rights given the people and the states under the constitution are not taken away from them by Congress or the President. As long as our Constitution is in effect we are in no danger of Fascism or Communism, because governments of that type can only be established by taking away the rights and privileges of the people and vesting them in the state. Of course, if the people themselves wish to surrender their rights and put them in the hands of a central government, they can do that by amending the constitution, but neither Congress nor the executive [President] can take those rights away simply by asserting the power when it does not exist.

During the House floor debate in late February on the stopgap bill replacing the unconstitutional AAA (the bill that became the Soil Conservation and Domestic Allotment Act), Hope denounced both the Republican and Democrat leadership for switching positions on farm legislation since 1932, depending upon which party was in power. Over a lengthy report by Clif Stratton in *The Topeka Capital* on February 21, 1936, headlines told the story:

HOPE LAUGHS, BUT
GRIMLY, AT FARM
RELIEF POLITICS

In Unusual Speech in House
Supporting Administra-
tion Measure, He De-
mands End of Horseplay.

G.O.P. SIRED IT AND AAA IDEA

But Democrats Denounced
Both, Then Took Them up
As Own, to See Both Con-
demned by Republicans.

Hope was referring to the 1932 GOP platform advocating government action to reduce and control production while the Democrats opposed control or reduction in production, but favored some efforts to control crop surpluses after they were produced. Once the Democrats were in power, both parties switched their official positions. Hope observed:

> Now any reasonable person would naturally suppose that after the Democrats adopted the Republican farm policy the Republicans would feel pretty good about it and would proceed to lend their co-operation and even say "I told you so."
>
> That would have happened everywhere except in politics. The question being in politics, it seems the only thing some Republicans could do was to decide the policy they had previously approved had immediately become a bad policy, when the Democrats put it into effect. We have heard up and down the land Republican orators denouncing the Republican policy of

1932 and condemning the Democratic party for putting it into
effect . . . as being an economic monstrosity, a program of
scarcity, and something that no decent nation in its senses ought
ever to have done.

Whatever the final vote on this bill may be, I hope no Democrat will vote for it because it is a Democratic measure and that
no Republican will vote against it because it is a Democratic
measure.

The farmers are getting tired of that sort of thing. They feel
their problems are of enough importance to be considered from
a non-partisan and economic viewpoint, and they are not going
to put much confidence in any political party which considers
them on any other basis.

In addition to the woes of the Depression, western Kansas and the Great
Plains area suffered drought and dust storms during much of the 1930s.
Literally, black clouds hung over the area for a number of years. Much has
been written about the Dust Bowl, especially in the years since Hope's
death in 1970. The drought began in January 1932, and by the end of 1934
it had affected three-fourths of the United States.

The Dust Bowl area was confined to parts of five states in the southern
High Plains. Professor R. Douglas Hurt wrote:

Although the boundaries of the Dust Bowl were never
precise, its general location encompassed that part of the southern Plains where the drought and wind erosion were the worst
— a 97 million acre section of southeastern Colorado and
northeastern New Mexico, western Kansas, and the panhandles
of Texas and Oklahoma. This area extended roughly four hundred miles from north to south and three hundred miles from
east to west with the approximate center at Liberal, near the
southwestern corner of Kansas. Wind erosion was most severe
within a hundred-mile radius of that town. The outline of the
Dust Bowl changed from year to year, depending upon the
amount of annual precipitation; however, the "blow area" never
covered the entire 97 million acres which were potentially subject to severe wind erosion. Instead, the Dust Bowl reached its
greatest extent from 1935 to 1936 when it covered about 50

The Dust Bowl.

million acres and was concentrated largely in southwestern Kansas.[2]

Hope's presidential address to the Kansas State Historical Society in October 1969 titled "Kansas in the 1930s" centered on the Dust Bowl. Starting his talk with a review of the turbulent history of the state from the time of "bleeding Kansas" in abolition times, he observed "none of these calamity periods can compare from the standpoint of financial loss, long-lasting distress, suffering, and discouragement with the decade of the 1930s." He elaborated:

> The great depression which began in the fall of 1929 affected Kansas just as it did every other part of the country, but on top of it there was superimposed almost a decade of drought and dust storms. In other words, Kansas and neighboring Great Plains states got a double dose of misery and calamity.
>
> During the decade in question agriculture was relatively a more important industry in Kansas than it is today. The decrease in agricultural income which came as a result of drought and low prices was a serious blow to the entire economy.
>
> Farmers in the 1930s suffered from both short crops and low

prices. While the 1931 wheat crop of 251 million bushels was the largest grown up to that time, the average farm price was only 33 cents per bushel, and less than that in western Kansas. Toward the middle of the decade prices were higher but yields were low. Very much the same thing happened in the case of corn. Toward the end of the decade yields were somewhat better for both crops, but prices were down again.

Hope said the great 1931 crop brought a wave of optimism to many Kansans, he among them. Some attributed the high yields to climatic changes, and others gave new machinery and improved methods the credit. "A sort of madness pervaded," Hope said. "I bragged about that crop to everyone who would listen, in Washington and elsewhere." But the big crop proved to be more of a disaster than anything else. For one thing, he pointed out, it increased the supply of wheat when there already was a surplus and a declining export market. The price was driven below the cost of production. Even worse, the big crop encouraged farmers and others to believe that "the reckless and haphazard type of farming which brought about this expansion could continue without a day of reckoning."

Even the drought and blowing dust of 1933 did not overly alarm Plains people, Hope said. These were people used to dry years, to waiting for rains to come "next year." Instead, in 1934 the winds started early, and loose, unprotected top soil began to move in a wide area that involved much of the Great Plains.

The storm which originated in the Southwest on May 10, 1934, is commonly spoken of as the worst. Evidence of it reached points on the East Coast on May 12. Hope recalled:

> It showered dust on the Capitol and the White House. Some was said to have settled on the President's desk. When I left the Capitol that evening, I found my car covered with a film of familiar-looking Kansas soil.

Blowing dust reached its peak in 1935. By 1936 the drought area had expanded to include most of the states between the Appalachians and the Rockies. But in Kansas, Hope noted, blowing dust was less severe that year and gradually receded during the next four years.

Something that is not always understood about this period, Hope pointed out, is that the soil blowing could have been stopped much earlier than it was if there had been better organization and more cooperation. "Soil scientists and conservationists knew what needed to be done but this required a united effort on the part of land owners and operators."

Cooperation of this sort was hard to obtain, however, in part, Hope explained, because much land was operated by nonresident owners — "suitcase farmers" — who were on the land only during planting and harvesting seasons. The rest of the time they were busy farming "back east." (By "back east," Hope meant eastern Kansas or beyond.) Other land owned by nonresidents was farmed by tenants, some of whom lacked the interest and experience to do a good job. And then, Hope added, there were those who didn't have the implements or resources to do a good job. Some resident owners lacked the capital and/or the inclination to farm right.

During the worst years — when the wind blew for days at a time — Dust Bowl dwellers "lived very much as they always had, but with considerable adjustment to the changed conditions," Hope said. Meetings often had to be postponed; schools were closed for a day or two after long, hard storms to clean out the dust. But school and church activities went on, women's clubs held forth as best they could, and chambers of commerce and service clubs persevered. He continued:

> Frequently the storms were so bad that travelers had to pull off the roads and wait them out. There were stories of people who got lost in their own farmyards and there were a few instances where school children as well as adults lost their lives.

Hope said he and his family missed most of the big storms since they were in Washington during the winter and spring months. He saw some during short trips home, however, and their Garden City home gave them ample proof of the dust storms. In fact, my mother and sister and I were in Garden City from the fall of 1935 until the winter of 1937, but by that time the worst of the storms was over.

The house was closed tightly with weather stripping and similar devices, Hope said, but when the family came back in the summer, the attic and to some extent the rooms on the lower floor "were covered with fine dust a quarter to a half-inch or more in thickness." One year, probably

1935, 15 truckloads of dirt were hauled off the lawn and yard. (In another speech, Hope said "twenty-four loads" were removed.)

Hope's speech told about Kansas's way of making light of hard times by telling tall tales. Dust Bowl jokes were "a dime a dozen," he said. For instance:

> The dust was so thick a prairie dog burrowed 10 feet in the air.
> A man hit by a raindrop was revived by having a bucket of sand thrown in his face.
> Crows flew backward to keep the dust out of their eyes.

Strangers who thought the wind was blowing pretty hard were told, "This ain't nothin'. See that log chain hanging out there? When it stands straight out you can figure the wind is really blowing."

To him, Hope said, one of the most remarkable aspects of the Dust Bowl years was the reluctance of people to leave. Some did leave, of course, and the state as a whole lost population. The surprising thing was that the emigration from the strictly agricultural counties in the western half of the state was no greater than the average for the farming counties in the eastern half.

Hope quoted from a 1941 *Kansas Magazine* article by Ada Buell Norris to explain why many people stayed through the years of dust and drought. In "Black Blizzard," Norris described the horror of the dust storms, her anxiety for her family's safety, and asked the question which must have been in the minds of many western Kansans: "Why do we stay?" She answered:

> In part because we hope for the coming of moisture, which would change conditions so that we again would have bountiful harvests. And in great part, because it is home. We have reared our family here and have many precious memories of the past. We have our memories. We have faith in the future, we are here to stay.[3]

As if drought, massive crop failures, and dust storms were not enough, grasshoppers and jackrabbits invaded parts of the Great Plains area during the 1930s. They often devoured the few crops that had survived everything else. R. Douglas Hurt wrote that the jackrabbit population "proliferated beyond imagination." It was not determined, he said, whether the Dust Bowl provided improved breeding conditions or whether the rabbits migrated into the area in search of grass. But hundreds of thousands of jackrabbits competed for the sparse grass available, and Dust Bowlers were forced to exterminate them. "Almost every Sunday," Hurt wrote, "people gathered on selected farms outside their local communities to take part in a rabbit drive." They formed a large circle, sometimes more than a mile in diameter, and walked to the center with rabbits running ahead of them. "No guns were allowed — only clubs," he explained. As the circle closed in, the rabbits were driven into snow fence pens and clubbed to death. "Everyone who has a club of any kind is invited to participate in the drive," editors urged in announcing the drives in local newspapers. Hurt cited a Dust Bowl newspaper that called for "a grand and glorious" rabbit drive on April 14, 1935, "unless the dust is too terrific." As it turned out, the rabbits were spared by the dust that day.[4]

Thousands of letters to Hope described the trying conditions. The county commissioners of Gray County wrote him in 1935 that the farmers in their county

> are not able to receive further credit from the stores for groceries; their children are, in various instances, no longer able to attend school because of insufficient clothing to keep them warm going to and from school. . . . Many of the families are on the verge of starvation.

Hope attended scores of meetings in the Dust Bowl area and in Washington that sought short-term relief and long-term solutions. Although he had a reputation for being a mild-mannered person, he raised his voice often in frustration at what he felt were inexcusable delays by government agencies.

In a 1968 speech Hope spoke of the many inquiries and complaints he had received about the several governmental agencies operating in the Dust Bowl. "Some of these," he explained, "were quite urgent and even pitiful and I used to get pretty well steamed up over them." One such 1936 letter prompted him to write the regional director of the Resettlement Administration in Amarillo. "I guess I must have made it pretty strong," Hope recalled, "because a few days later I heard that my letter had put him

to bed for a week." A year later he wrote to the regional manager of the
Emergency Crop Loan Office in Wichita to protest strict loan requirements
for farmers who could not get loans from any other source, saying:

> This is not a matter which alone concerns the individual
> farmers whose applications are rejected. In the Wichita District
> it is a matter of public concern because of the serious condition
> existing in the Dust Bowl. The crying need in that area is that
> the land now blowing be worked and put in a cover crop of
> some sort.

He pointed out that every acre that could be treated was a step toward a
cure and that every loan refusal kept a farmer from putting out a crop, thus
adding to the acreage that was "abandoned and blowing."

Hope charged, "The Crop Loan Office is the only governmental agency
with which I am acquainted which is not cooperating in the work of reha-
bilitating this area." It would not do to pass the buck in these matters by
saying the rejected applications had been turned down by local committees or by loan office supervisors. "Supervisors and committees are working under instructions from your office and their attitude is simply a reflec-
tion of your position." Hope pulled no punches in accusing the organization of refusing to carry out the intent of Congress in making crop loans.
Of all the governmental agencies operating in the territory, he said, only
the Wichita office "failed to realize its responsibility in meeting the dust
menace."

Among long-term solutions were proposals for the government to lease
or buy marginal land and return it to grass. In Kansas this project never
really got off the ground except in Morton County in the southwest corner,
where acreage was purchased to form the Cimarron National Grasslands.

The most interesting proposal designed to retard wind erosion originated with Franklin D. Roosevelt in his 1932 campaign: the creation of
"shelterbelts" of trees. On this, R. Douglas Hurt wrote:

> Certainly, the Shelterbelt Project was never the panacea for
> ending the dust storms that many had hoped it would become.
> Forest Service experts realized from the inception of the project
> that the treebelts would not end the dust storms. Rather, the pri-
> mary purpose of the Prairie States Forestry Project was to grow

trees in order to reduce wind erosion, stabilize the land, and make the Plains "a better and more profitable place to live." The Forest Service did not intend to withdraw large blocks of land from agricultural production or to transform the Plains into a forest. Instead, the project was designed to help increase agricultural productivity of the protected lands. In this respect, then, the shelterbelts were only part of a larger conservation program. Still, when the Shelterbelt Project was combined with the work of other government agencies which fostered land retirement, controlled grazing, farm pond construction, strip cropping, terracing, and agricultural diversification, it made a major contribution to the physical and psychological fight against the wind erosion menace.[5]

This program was especially popular in Kansas, but the advent of World War II, with demand for greatly increased crop production, terminated it.

The myriad government programs and Hope's unflagging efforts inspired one wag (probably a Methodist) to exclaim that during the Dirty Thirties the people of southwest Kansas survived on "Methodist faith, Clifford Hope, and government charity!"

In the meantime, important elections were occurring in Kansas. Three new representatives were elected in 1934. Edward White Patterson, a Democrat lawyer from Pittsburg, defeated the flamboyant Harold McGugin in the 3rd District, and in the 5th District John Mills Houston, a Democrat lumber man from Newton, succeeded William Ayres who had resigned in August 1934 to accept appointment to the Federal Trade Commission. Although McGugin served only two terms (1931-1935), he was much in the news, mainly as a fiery opponent of the New Deal. I remember my father mentioning him often. Frequently he disagreed with McGugin, but Hope held the same sort of affection for him as he did for the erratic Bill Lambertson.

Probably the greatest surprise in the 1934 Kansas congressional elections was the defeat of Kathryn O'Loughlin McCarthy by Frank Carlson, Republican farmer from Cloud County. Carlson wrote to Hope soon after the election: "In my own district we had a very hard fight and to the surprise of most everyone, I won it." (Carlson won by a vote of 62,824 to 60,028.) Carlson would go on to become the only Kansan to serve as congressman (1935-1947), governor (1947-1950), and senator (1950-1969).

He became Hope's best friend in Congress during the years they served together.

Born in 1893, the same year as Hope, Carlson was a 35-year-old farmer in 1928 when he became involved in politics. Unlike Hope's deliberate start in politics, Carlson's start was unintentional. He often recalled the story about the day he was working on his farm when a car pulled into the field. Four local businessmen emerged. He said:

> I was disturbed because I was busy cutting wheat at the time. They told me there was an election coming up and they wanted me to file for the Kansas House of Representatives. I told them I would run, I just couldn't be bothered with campaigning be- cause from January to April I was busy feeding cattle. As they left, they said, "Don't worry, you won't win anyway."

But he did. And after two terms in the legislature and a stint as GOP state chairman, Carlson ran for Congress.

Another member of our family remembers Carlson's first campaign for Congress. In a newspaper column years later my wife, Dolores, recalled that her tap dance team had provided entertainment for Carlson's 1934 campaign in her hometown. Each member of the team had received a per- sonal letter of thanks from Carlson, asking "to be remembered" to the par- ents. Dolores thinks that her Democratic parents were so impressed that they voted for him.

In spite of the fact that the New Deal was riding high when the 1934 fil- ing deadline approached, Hope thought he would be easily reelected. Democrat Walter Huxman, a Hutchinson lawyer who had been expected to challenge Hope in the 7th District, announced in May that he would not run. He would have been a formidable opponent. (Huxman was elected governor in 1936 and later served as a federal appellate judge.) There was not an announced Democrat candidate until the last day before the June deadline, when four candidates filed, perhaps each without the knowledge of the others. The easy winner in the primary was L. E. Webb, a farm lob- byist from Dodge City with whom Hope was well acquainted. They had worked together in implementing the AAA and other farm legislation.

In early June 1934 Lester McCoy told Hope that some people were say- ing Hope had not been for the AAA until he saw it would pass, and then he switched sides. That charge became the basis for Webb's campaign. He held that in the early roll call vote Hope had voted against the bill because he was a tool of the Eastern GOP (who were against all farm programs) and that, in addition, he was a big corporation railroad lawyer. Hope, who by this time probably was regretting his "no" roll call vote, painstakingly explained he was initially against the bill because it contained no specific provisions for a domestic allotment plan for wheat. When he received assurance that the plan would be implemented, as indeed it was, he went all out to implement its provisions once the bill passed. Democrat big guns, including Senator George McGill, were mobilized in the attempt to unseat Hope on this single issue. But, as Hope later observed, Webb's campaign peaked too early, giving the Hope forces time to explain his reasoning. Webb challenged him to a last-minute radio debate and then failed to show up when they could not agree on the subject matter. Meanwhile, the Hope campaign pointed out that in the 1925 Legislature, Webb, a representative from Hodgeman County, had supported the Ku Klux Klan. On election day, November 6, Hope won by a vote of 63,952 to 53,104. That was his closest race. He never again was seriously challenged.

In late January 1970, three weeks before the severe stroke which resulted in his death the following May, Hope was interviewed by Professor James Duram of Wichita State University. This was a broad-ranging, taped interview, and Hope had no advance knowledge of the questions that would be asked. In response to Duram's question as to why he had voted against the original AAA bill, Hope replied,

> Well, as a matter of fact that — my vote against the legislation was — I don't know — I had worked on it myself; I had done as much work on that as anybody, but in the study of the matter and the — I guess maybe my innate conservatism sort of got the better of me at that time, and so I was a little skeptical about it — I had been for it, in fact I had introduced a bill in 1932 that had most of the basic provisions of this legislation, but it just kind of caught me on the rebound I guess because I wasn't opposed to most of the provisions in that bill; I mean the theory of it was all right as far as I was concerned.

This unclear response could be interpreted to mean that Hope, because he had some doubts about the bill, was simply voting the Republican Party position. However, that interpretation contradicts all of Hope's statements

Alf Landon speaking from the observation platform of the Sunflower Special at Canton, Ohio, August 22, 1936, during his campaign for the presidency. Kansas State Historical Society, Topeka

A 1936 photo of Alfred Landon (left), Kansas Senator Arthur Capper (center), and John D. Hamilton (right), Republican National Chairman and Landon's campaign manager for the presidency. Kansas State Historical Society, Topeka

to constituents during the 1933-1934 period and, indeed, his statements to our family at that time and afterward.

Although Kansas still had a 4-3 GOP margin in the House as a result of the 1934 election, overall the Democrats picked up an additional 14 seats, reducing the GOP membership to only 103 out of 435. This was a discouraging prospect to Hope and his colleagues.

In the 1934 governor's race, Dr. J. R. Brinkley challenged Alf Landon in the Republican primary but was badly beaten. Landon went on to defeat Topeka Mayor Omar B. Ketchum 422,030 to 359,877. Landon was the only Republican governor in the nation to be reelected in 1934, making him a logical contender for President in 1936.

Early on Hope was actively involved in the Landon presidential campaign, attending numerous meetings and making at least one scouting trip to New York. He was Landon's chief agricultural adviser before and after the latter's nomination on the first ballot at the Cleveland GOP National Convention. Hope became director of the farm division of the Republican National Committee, headquartered in Chicago. Don L. Berry, newspaper publisher and politician from Indianola, Iowa, was assistant director. This association was the beginning of a lifelong friendship. Hope and Berry frequently exchanged political news for the next three decades.

The extent of Landon's defeat by FDR is well-known. He received only about 38 percent of the vote and lost every state except Maine and Vermont, thereby coining a new political axiom, "As Maine goes, so goes Vermont." FDR carried Kansas with about 54 percent of the vote and carried 73 of the state's 105 counties, including almost all in western Kansas. Landon had been a good governor, but farmers did not want to risk losing New Deal farm benefits. FDR's coattails helped elect Walter Huxman as governor and nearly defeated Senator Capper; challenger Omar Ketchum won 49 percent of the popular vote. However, Edward Rees, lawyer and state senator from Emporia, defeated Randolph Carpenter for Congress, thereby giving Kansas Republicans five seats out of seven in the House, an increase of one.

Nationally the election was another real disaster for Hope's party. In the House, Republican membership was reduced to 89 out of 435 and in the Senate to a mere 16 out of 96. A week after election day, Hope wrote a long letter to Don Berry. After suggesting Republicans might need to change the party name in order to make inroads into the rural South, he said:

The term Republican is in bad order or a bad odor in a lot of places on account of its past connections. Of course, those older reactionaries are all going to die off some day, but I doubt if we want to wait until it happens. Even if it was the same party under another name, we could shake them off a lot easier, I believe, than continuing with the Republican name.

On the other hand, Hope continued, the name Republican still meant a lot to millions of people, and he was not sure if it should be given up lightly. One thing that impressed him, he confided to Berry, was the great number of Republicans who had come to his office and were ready to start the 1940 campaign right away. The same was true, he understood, in other states.

I think the feeling is a little more intense here in Kansas than elsewhere because there is quite a feeling of remorse over the shameful way this state treated Landon. Even some of those who voted for Roosevelt are going around now saying it was a great mistake for Kansas to turn Landon down.

Hope's own opponent was Thomas A. Ralston, an educator from Pratt County. Ralston was the first of those who ran against Hope in the next several elections to endorse the Townsend Plan. The plan originated with Dr. Francis E. Townsend, a California physician who proposed that every person over 65 receive a $200 per month pension, with the provision that this amount be spent within 30 days. The idea was to get the proceeds into circulation and hence boost recovery from the Depression. Townsend Clubs were organized throughout the nation, especially in the Midwest. (Some clubs also advocated maintaining traditional morality, inveighing against wearing lipstick, necking, and smoking cigarettes!)

Hope, remembering his 1934 campaign, did not want to take any chances in his 1936 race. On August 31 he wrote to Lester McCoy — who as usual was spending the summer in Green Mountain Falls, Colorado — encouraging him to raise some money for the campaign. This was a most unusual action on Hope's part. (I was not able to find any written evidence that Hope ever made such a request during any other campaign.) His 1936 campaign financial report showed $500 contributions from both Joe Stewart of The Garden City Company and Wiley Blair, president of Holly

Sugar Company in Colorado Springs. My guess is that McCoy saw or
called Joe Stewart, and Stewart called his friend and business acquaintance, Wiley Blair. These two contributions are the largest from individuals that I have found in any of Hope's reports.

Hope staged a rigorous campaign, giving six to ten speeches a day. In
every speech, he strongly urged the election of Alf Landon. He was concerned about all the federal money being poured into the district in the
weeks before the elections — to farmers, WPA employees, and others. On
November 3, however, most 7th District voters went for FDR and Hope,
the two elected officials credited with having "saved" them from the rav-
ages of the Depression and the Dust Bowl. Roosevelt carried all but
Greeley County in his 28,000 majority over Landon in the southwestern
Kansas district. Hope's majority over Ralston was only 14,000, due in part
to his having campaigned so hard for Landon. Ralston carried only Ford
County.

The session of Congress which convened in January 1937 seemingly
assured a continuation of New Deal reforms and experiments in government. Such was not to be, however. In February FDR, impatient because
the conservative Supreme Court had held certain New Deal acts unconstitutional, prepared a court reform act whereby the court would be increased
from 9 to 15 members. This proposal would have enabled FDR to appoint
6 new members with his way of thinking. Reaction was immediate and
astounding. Democrats, Republicans, and "plug" citizens from every
walk of life rose up in spontaneous opposition. ("Plug" at that time was
common parlance for "average" or "ordinary.") The greatest fear was
presidential dictatorship, then and under future Presidents. I remember
watching newsreels in movie theaters at the time. White-bearded Chief
Justice Charles Evan Hughes was vigorously applauded while FDR was
sometimes booed, a thing almost unheard of up to that time.

James C. and Eleanor A. Duram of Wichita State University have written an excellent and informative article titled "Congressman Clifford
Hope's Correspondence With His Constituents: A Conservative View of
the Court-Packing Plan of 1937."[6] The article covers much more than its
title indicates, analyzing conservative opposition to the New Deal and
providing a summary of Hope's career up to 1937.

The people of the 7th District reacted to the President's proposal in
accord with the rest of the nation. Hope was bombarded with letters, but
he answered every letter in considerable detail. His responses to those

favoring the plan were longer than his responses to those agreeing with him. He wrote seven pages to Herman Nelgen, president of the Hugoton Chamber of Commerce, who, although a Republican, favored FDR's plan because he thought the Supreme Court was usurping Congress's powers.

A summary of Hope's observations showed he felt that determination of the issue was directly up to the people and that there was need for continued protest to Congress. Democrats, he indicated, should lead the fight against the plan (as indeed they did), but opposition should be nonpartisan. The plan, he said, was a threat to the basic character of government — "an independent judiciary is the last safeguard against dictatorship." The way to change unpopular court decisions, he insisted, is by constitutional amendment.

He wrote specifically to Nelgen concerning FDR's claim that he couldn't go ahead with a flood control program or efforts to control blowing in the Dust Bowl unless something was done about the Supreme Court. "That is just purely 100 percent, unadulterated bunk," Hope said.

By July overwhelming opposition forced the Senate to vote to recommit the bill to the judiciary committee. Hope and others were disappointed that the bill was not killed outright. He thought the bill might "pop up again." That did not happen, however, in part due to retirement by conservative court members over the next several years, which enabled FDR to make his own appointments, beginning with Senator Hugo Black in August 1937.

In 1938 Senator George McGill was up for reelection, and many people urged Hope to enter the Senate race. On a Sunday afternoon in November 1937, Lester McCoy met in Topeka with Alf Landon and Lacy Haynes, Kansas correspondent for *The Kansas City Star* and a backroom power in Kansas GOP politics for many years. (Haynes was William Allen White's brother-in-law.) Both men told McCoy that Hope would be the best candidate to beat McGill. The controversial Clyde Reed, former governor, was planning to run as was Reverend Gerald Winrod, anti-Semitic and anti-Catholic preacher from Wichita. The party leaders hoped to field a better candidate. Hope replied to McCoy's report of the Topeka meeting:

> It is rather hard to know what to say in response to your letter. Although a few people have previously suggested to me that this might be a good time for me to run for the Senate, yet as you know, I haven't up to this time given any serious thought at

all to the proposition. I appreciate the interest which Alf and Lacy expressed in my possible candidacy and, of course, it would be a fine thing to get into any race with their support. Furthermore, I am guilty of having the same ambition that nearly every member of the House has and that is to go to the Senate some time. I realize also that a member of the House or anyone in active political life usually has only one or two good chances to make a senatorial race.

However, I just can't get up any particular enthusiasm about getting into the race at this time. Perhaps I play politics too much by instinct or hunches, but the way things look now, I just have a feeling that this isn't the right time for me to get into the senatorial race. If the Clyde Reed factor were out of it, it would be somewhat different. I think I could probably go into a campaign against Clyde Reed and arouse as little feeling and animosity among his supporters as anyone, however, knowing Clyde and his political history as we all do, I am sure that no one could feel that he could count on Clyde's support in the senatorial campaign for anyone who might defeat him in the primary. How far down that would go among Clyde's supporters, I don't know. In fact, I don't have much information or judgment as to what support Clyde may have or can expect to get. I do feel, however, that a nomination this year won't be worth a great deal unless one can command the united support of the party.

Later Landon visited with Hope in Washington, and William Allen White urged that Hope (or Homer Hoch or Frank Carlson) enter the race against Reed and Winrod, whom White feared, all to no avail. Hope simply did not have enough fire to make the race. Clyde Reed went on to defeat Winrod at the primary and the then-unpopular McGill in the general election. That was the first and last time Hope thought seriously of running for the Senate. He had found his niche in the House of Representatives.

Hope's opponent for Congress in 1938 was probably the most interesting and fascinating he had ever faced. Claude E. Main described himself as a farmer and actor who had been "identified with the theatre" in New York. Main rented a large tent and toured from town to town presenting vaudeville acts, including a magic act and a three-act play written by himself and performed by the Wallace Bruce Players, a theatrical group that toured Kansas for many years afterward. Main claimed to draw crowds of a thousand or more in every town. Some proper Republicans were quite critical, describing his performances as "dog and pony shows" and the actor as "the man with the Charlie Chaplin moustache." In addition to supporting the Townsend Plan, Main claimed "100% support for the New Deal." That was the wrong platform for anyone to run on in Kansas in 1938.

Clifford Hope and Payne Ratner, Republican candidate for governor, campaigned together in some towns. In Cimarron 1,200 turned out to hear them. Hope wrote the crowds were greater than for any candidate he had campaigned with before. His newspaper advertising stated he stood for "Keeping America Out of Other People's Wars" (Hitler had annexed Austria and the Sudetenland of Czechoslovakia that year) and "Pensions which will care for the aged in genuine decency and comfort." One ad read, "Hope is not a publicity seeker and does not accompany his efforts with a loud noise, but is a worker and a doer." On election day, the vote was Hope 72,893; Main 38,357.

In other Kansas races, Tom Winter, Republican lawyer from Girard, defeated Ed Patterson for congressman in the 3rd District, leaving Jack Houston the sole Democrat from the state. Payne Ratner, Parsons lawyer, easily defeated Walter Huxman in the latter's bid for reelection. Kansas Republicans had regained their virtual monopoly on the state's elective offices, and nationally the GOP had picked up 80 seats in the House. But apparently Hope believed his party could have done better, and he worried about 1940. In post-election correspondence, referring to Herbert Hoover's continued participation in GOP politics, Hope wrote to W. B. Wise in December that he wished Mr. Hoover would "take a four-year trip around the world."

Examination of Hope's correspondence files from the 1930s and 1940s indicates that probably his heaviest exchange of letters was with the previously mentioned C. C. (Charles Christian) Isely of Dodge City. For three decades Isely was a mover and shaker in almost every civic enterprise in the Dodge City area and a political leader in Kansas. Born in Brown County in northeast Kansas in 1875, he graduated from Fairmount College (now Wichita State University) in 1902 and soon moved to southwest Kansas, where he established the C. C. Isely Lumber company in 1908.

An inscribed photograph from U.S. Court of Claims Judge Marvin Jones, 1952. Jones, a Texas Democrat, had been head of the U.S. House Committee on Agriculture in the 1930s when Clifford Hope was the ranking Republican member.

Moving to Dodge City in 1919, he became involved in banking and organized the Dodge City Terminal Elevator in 1929. Later he promoted federal housing projects and almost all the farm legislation enacted in the 1930s. He also was a correspondent for *The Wall Street Journal* and other national publications. A Progressive ("Bull Moose") from 1912 to 1916, Isely campaigned for William Allen White against the Klan in 1924. Throughout his life he was a progressive Republican; he ran for the U.S. Senate in 1932 and 1942 but lost to Ben Paulen and Arthur Capper in the primaries.

I remember back in the 1930s going with my father for visits with C. C. in his cluttered office at the lumber company in south Dodge City. He talked a mile a minute, and it all made pretty good sense. Once he wrote Hope that he agreed with him "about 98 percent of the time," which was "a very high grade."

Gilbert Fite, the agricultural historian greatly admired by Hope, wrote in *American Farmer*: "Never before and never again would farmers exert as much political influence in Washington as they did between 1933 and the early 1940s." This was due in part to the bipartisan cooperation among members of the House Committee on Agriculture, led by Marvin Jones as chairman and Hope as the ranking Republican member. On the occasion of his retirement from Congress in 1940 to accept appointment to the U.S. Court of Claims, Jones gave a splendid speech titled "Sidelights on Congress." Hope was the first member to respond, praising Jones for possessing and exercising the rare art of getting people to work for him and with him. Jones and Hope kept in touch periodically until Hope's death in 1970. In the early 1970s, I had occasion to be in Amarillo on legal business. My clients took me to lunch at a downtown club and there introduced me to "Judge Jones." He was then in his nineties. Stooped and wizened as he was, he grasped my hand like I was a long-lost friend. It was as if he were again greeting his old friend Hope. Tears were in his eyes and in mine.

Although Hope still had doubts about many of the New Deal programs ("too much theory and too many professors"), by the end of the 1930s he was convinced of the continued necessity for federal government farm programs supported more or less by both political parties. These views were expressed in a letter to Cal Ward of the Kansas Farmers Union in 1935:

As far as I am able, I am going to try to keep the Republican

Party committed to a sound, sympathetic agricultural policy, but if the party does not see fit to go along that line, I will simply have to part company with it, as far as that issue is concerned.

He wrote in the same vein to his Republican friend, Don Berry, in 1939. Whatever might be said for or against farm subsidies, his judgment, he said, was

as long as we follow the present policy of spending for everything that comes along as passing legislation to enable labor and industry to increase the price of things the farmer has to buy, we are going to have to continue farm subsidies, probably in an increased amount.

In the 1930s, members of Congress did not suffer financially from the effects of the Depression in their personal lives, except to a limited extent. They took a 15 percent pay cut (reducing their annual salaries to $8,500) for a year or two at the beginning of the New Deal when all government salaries were cut by that amount. Their salaries were not raised above $10,000 until the Reorganization Act of 1946 became effective, increasing salaries to $15,000 and establishing a retirement system.[7]

Since the Hopes subsisted almost solely on his congressional salary, Clifford was in debt to his banker, Bob Downie, back in Garden City most of the time, usually to pay campaign expenses from the previous election. He never owned a credit card. In recent years I was asked if he ever overdrew his account at the House Sergeant at Arms Office (it was not called a "bank" then). I truly doubt he was ever overdrawn. Pauline was careful about keeping all family checkbooks balanced each month. However, she had several cousins who were small-time crooks during the Depression who were not so dependable. I distinctly remember the time Cousin Alphonse (not his real name) Sanders visited and asked Clifford to cash a $15 check, not an insignificant sum at the time. It was a hot check, and we never again heard from Alphonse. This did not bother Clifford but Pauline was — to use her words — "fit to be tied."

Private offices for ordinary members of Congress were provided for the first time when the New House Office Building (later named the Longworth House Office Building) was opened in 1933. Hope's office was moved to Room 1026 on the ground floor; then in 1935 he moved to Room

1314. This two-room office, with a private restroom for the congressman, was at the southeast corner of the building, adjacent to the elevator. It was a handy location, and I have fond memories of the office. The outer office was occupied by George and Ilene Reid and one or two stenographers.

Around 1937 I began working in the office regularly on Saturdays and sometimes after school. My only pay was my allowance received from my father, but that job and the excitement of working in a congressional office was fun. My main duties were reading the weekly newspapers from the 7th District (about a hundred of them) and clipping items of interest — especially birth announcements. Clifford sent all new parents a copy of the government publication titled *Infant Care*. It was a useful, popular item. When I had time, I would read some of the syndicated boilerplate continued stories that ran on the inside pages of many weekly papers. *The Zenda Headlight* was a memorable experience. It consisted of six boilerplate pages plus a front and back page of local news. The paper was wrapped for mailing before the ink dried, so the local news was often smeared beyond legibility. I always had to wash my hands before proceeding with the next paper.

Years later my sister Martha — six years younger than I — recalled those times:

> Being in his [Clifford's] office was always a special treat. Besides getting pushed around on one of the typists' chairs or playing with paper clips or drawing, there was friendly banter with the staff members. Especially with George Reid, who would tease me by calling me Martha Soap. I would counter by calling him George Seed. As I grew older, I came to sense that although the staff members might sometimes experience some friction among themselves they always pulled together to do what Pop needed. This personal respect and loyalty was a powerful thing. I surmised that it was a big factor in Pop's ability to work out differences with other legislators as well. My sense is that he did nothing consciously to cultivate such respect and loyalty, but that it was a response to the integrity and fair-mindedness that characterized all his dealings with people.
>
> I especially liked the times when Clifford Jr., Mom and I would meet Pop at day's end at his office to go out to dinner together. I especially liked going to the seafood restaurant on

the Potomac waterfront or to a movie. There was always a wait until Pop had finished going over all the letters he had dictated that day and signed each one personally. Only as I grew older did I realize that not all Congressmen gave their personal attention to all the correspondence with their constituents.

Perks available to congressional families and employees included haircuts at the House barbershop for 25 cents. Of more importance were books and research materials available from the Library of Congress for school assignments.

On returning to Washington in the winter of 1933, we moved to the Center Cathedral Mansions building at 3000 Connecticut Ave., N.W., where we lived for the next two years. I again attended James F. Oyster Grade School, but no longer did I hike alone in Rock Creek Park after school. My parents discovered an after-school activities organization named the Nelson Play School for Boys. It operated a small private school, first at a former country club in Silver Spring and later at a large house between 16th Street and Rock Creek Park. Pauline was eager to get me off the streets and into a "wholesome" (one of her favorite words) association with other boys. Each school day afternoon William Nelson Smith, the proprietor, picked up boys at Oyster and other schools, piled us into his new Chrysler Airflow (the first U.S. "streamlined" car), and took us to Rock Creek Park or elsewhere for two hours of fun and games.[8] On Saturdays we went to the school's headquarters. We didn't have enough players for two full baseball teams, so we played with only one base and home plate. I was the permanent first baseman. This turned out to be the high point of my athletic career.

Our family had the opportunity to enjoy professional baseball on occasion. Clifford was a fan of the Washington Senators even though they had a long run of dismal seasons after winning the American League pennant in 1933. In the 1930s Arch McDonald, a popular radio sports announcer, reported the Senators' out-of-town games from ticker tape, with the aid of a tabletop gong. When a single was hit, he struck the gong once, twice for a double, and so on. Most exciting was Arch's reporting, ". . . and Goose Goslin BONG! BONG! BONG! BONG! hits a home run!" Pauline joined in the fun of any game she attended but knew little of current league standings or sports history. One of my classmates at Alice Deal Junior High was James Naismith, grandson and namesake of the founder of basketball and the first basketball coach at Kansas University. I knew my mother had never heard of the original Naismith when she said to me one day, "Why don't you invite Nai over to supper sometime?" She thought his name was Nai Smith.

One night in the early spring of 1934 there was a knock at our apartment door. To our great surprise, there stood Harry and Armitta, Clifford's parents. Without much ado, they had put their suitcases into their 1930 Essex and headed for Washington to visit their congressman son on site. Harry had just retired from the post office in Garden City. He was not one to waste words by announcing their visit in advance. It was their first visit to Washington.

Other memorable events occurred the spring of my grandparents' unannounced visit. Old Gold cigarettes sponsored a $100,000 (then a tremendous sum) puzzle contest. Pauline and I were interested in entering, so Clifford obligingly purchased umpteen cartons of Old Golds. Sending in labels from the packs was a contest requirement. No one in our family smoked, so we threw away the cigarettes — perhaps thereby saving someone's health or life. That might be considered our consolation prize. We didn't win any others.

Clifford and Pauline lived by a set of what might now be considered conservative or "traditional values." Neither of them cursed or swore, and both used good grammar except for the Middle Western colloquialism of he, she, and it *don't*. Like most women of her time, Pauline believed a married woman's place was in the home. She frowned on most of Eleanor Roosevelt's activities, and she disliked Amelia Earhart's casual hairdo. My parents thought no one should "make money" on the Sabbath, a belief from their early childhood; and during the 1930s they did not believe in buying anything or going to the movies on Sundays. The prohibition did not, however, apply to the occasional weekend outing.

For several weeks during the spring of 1934, Clifford was more worried than I had ever seen him. One Sunday we drove our 1934 Ford on the Chesapeake Bay ferry across the eastern shore of Maryland to Rehoboth Beach, Delaware. None of us swam at the time, so all we did was walk up and down the beach once or twice. When we were returning to Washington in the late afternoon, our car was broadsided in the main intersection of an eastern shore village. I was dozing in the back seat, but was awakened by Pauline screaming, "What do you mean running into us, you crazy fool!" Her words were spoken more in fear than anger. Fortunately, no one was hurt — or so we thought — but within a few minutes the driver of the other car, who was eating an ice cream cone at the time of the accident, developed a backache. He was identified as the village horseshoe pitcher. The parties adjourned to the office of the local magistrate, an amiable fellow. The other driver insisted on a trial for his alleged injuries. It was agreed the trial date would be set for sometime after Congress adjourned. The driver inquired, "How will we know when Congress adjourns?"

Clifford was concerned. Although he had collision insurance, he had no liability coverage. He visualized really getting stuck by a small-town jury. He and Pauline discussed the problem all the way home and by the time we reached our apartment they were arguing. It was the most violent exchange I had ever heard between them, and I thought they would come to blows. Pauline was trying to give helpful advice, and Clifford did not want any. As it turned out, the problem was resolved within several weeks when George Reid, the master negotiator, volunteered his services. He returned to the village and settled the case for fifty dollars in cash. I am sure that during that Depression year the horseshoe pitcher put the then-sizeable sum to good use.

In 1935 we rented a house for the first time. It was in the Chevy Chase area of Washington, at 3902 Legation Street, N.W. We started attending the Chevy Chase Presbyterian Church, where Pauline sang in the choir and made many friends. I was in sixth grade and Martha in kindergarten at E. V. Brown School near Chevy Chase Circle.

For some reason, that school semester and the following summer were the worst times of my life. I was a real loner at the time and as nerdy as I ever was, before or after. I had few friends and all of them were strange. My "abominable disposition" (my mother's exact words) was at its worst. For one thing, I talked too much. More than once my father ordered, "Young man, stop that chattering." Once during the summer, when I had done something to arouse his ire (I don't remember what it was), he slapped me hard and I fell to the floor. Then he said, "And a good swift kick to go with it." Then I became really scared, but by the time his foot reached me, his anger had subsided. I received only a hesitant, light tap from his foot.

While my father surmised I would outgrow my problems, whatever they were, my mother was consumed with concern about me. She told me that I had "inherited the worst qualities of both [my] parents." She said this not in criticism but with sympathy. I was reluctant to ask her what those "worst qualities" were. I imagine she was including her propensity for worrying about everything under the sun and Clifford's excessive interest in politics, sometimes to the exclusion of all else. In addition, she was probably thinking of my selfishness and, on occasion, anti-social behavior, qualities which could not be attributed to either her or Clifford. Much later — after I was grown, married, and involved in politics — she wondered aloud, "What will ever become of Clifford Junior?" She asked the same question concerning other relatives and friends. She became a determined, constant worrier despite Clifford's efforts to allay her fears.

Pauline, Martha, and I spent the entire school year of 1935-1936 in Garden City. Those months of separation were hard on Pauline from time to time, but — her continuous worrying aside — she did not complain.

When we returned to Washington in the winter of 1937, we rented a more spacious, comfortable two-story home at 3221 Oliver Street, again in the Chevy Chase area. We lived there most of the time until January 1941. The owner was Ella Waldron Schumann, whom Clifford and Pauline had known at Washburn College in Topeka. (Ella's first husband was Edwin Menninger, son of Dr. Charles and Flo Menninger and brother of Drs. Karl and Will Menninger.) Ella's two daughters, Barbara Menninger and Suzanne Schumann, lived with her. She was deeply involved in the Oxford Movement, a religious organization. Ella made Clifford promise he would look after her small rose garden. Thus began his interest in rose gardening, a hobby which he pursued after he and Pauline bought a home in Washington in 1941 and continued for the rest of his life. A fresh rose in his lapel buttonhole during the rose-blooming season became his trademark.

About this time, Clifford began early morning golfing with Frank Carlson, Bill Lambertson, Clif Stratton and sometimes others at the public courses in Rock Creek and East Potomac Park. During non-golfing weather he played paddleball in the late afternoon at the House gymnasium, behind a large door marked "Bathroom" in the basement of the New (Longworth) House Office Building.[9]

Martha attended second grade (and subsequent grades) at Lafayette School close to our home, and I started Alice Deal Junior High in a splendid, new, Georgian-style building in the Fort Reno area, a mile or so away. Nearby was the new, equally splendid looking Woodrow Wilson High School, which I later attended. Between these magnificent buildings were several rows of 19th-century dwellings that had been occupied by black Washingtonians since before white settlement in the area. Grade school children of these families attended school in a dilapidated building next to the Alice Deal building (but on a lower level of terrain) even though the white Ben Murch Grade School was only a few blocks away. Black children who might be able to attend junior and senior high school had to travel for miles across town. It was not until then that I began to think seriously about segregated schools and segregation in general.[10]

The house on Oliver Street had a large guest bedroom for Pauline's mother, Laura Sanders, who stayed with us during the winter months until her death at age 61 in 1938. She was a pleasant, unassuming person to have around. Not so was Clifford's Aunt Coe who visited us at least once a year after the death of her husband in 1931. She went out of her way to criticize Pauline. Perhaps it was her way of making the statement that Pauline was not good enough for Clifford who, after all, was of "Ragsdale blood." On one visit she checked over a sock which Martha, then eight or ten years old, had tried to darn. Without asking any questions, she chastised Pauline for not knowing how to darn. Aunt Coe insisted that Clifford drive her to some of the Civil War monuments and battlefields around Washington. Because her father in the Union Army had been a prisoner of war, she delighted in badmouthing Robert E. Lee at every opportunity. The black-topped, two-lane highways around the battle sites had narrow shoulders, but whenever a roadside marker came into view, Aunt Coe yelled "Stop!" She was commanding, not asking.

As an only child, Pauline made special efforts to keep in touch with her aunts, uncles, and cousins. There were many Sanders cousins on her father's side, and she knew almost all of them and was especially fond of Eunice and Ruth McDonald. Her mother, Laura, had only two brothers, Frank in Atchison and Perry, who had taken over George Corkadel's 80-acre homestead three miles northeast of Valley Falls. Perry raised corn, oats, and hogs and had a small dairy herd. He and his good wife, May, barely made a living until the World War II years. Pauline, who had spent much time on the old home place while growing up in Topeka, made frequent visits, often on the return trip from Washington, especially after her mother died. Perry, May, and their son, Clarence, were dear to her.

Our most memorable Kansas visit during this period, however, came on a summer afternoon in 1938 when we went to see the famous William Allen White and his wife, Sally, in Emporia. White looked just like his

Clifford (left) and Pauline Hope and Representative Joseph W. Martin, Jr. (Massachusetts) on a trip to Hawaii, in the fall of 1937 at the invitation of the Hawaiian territorial government.

pictures: rotund, dressed in white shirt and slacks, reclining in a hammock and looking much like a well-dressed walrus.

The family took only hurried vacation trips — to Yellowstone in 1938, to the 1939 New York World's Fair, and to New England. This, of course, was more vacationing than most people were privileged to do in the 1930s. In the fall of 1937 Clifford and Pauline, with other congressional couples, visited Hawaii at the expense of the territorial government, then lobbying for statehood. That was the only time Pauline left the continental United States. She enjoyed that trip but had no desire to travel abroad. Her worry in getting ready for any trip exceeded its pleasures.

One year as the decade drew to a close, a national magazine (perhaps *The Ladies' Home Journal*) was running a series of illustrated articles on families in America. To be included was a typical congressional family. Upon recommendation of Clifford's colleagues, our family was chosen. Clifford and Pauline agonized for several weeks about accepting the invitation. They wanted to make certain our family would be portrayed just as it was — no frills or glamour. Finally, when they learned that various props would be used, such as a sumptuously-set dining room table, they politely declined. I, on the other hand, thought it was a great idea and was disappointed at their decision.

Chapter 8

The War Years
(1939-1945)

*W*HEN GERMANY INVADED POLAND, on Septem-*
ber 1, 1939, Clifford and I were in Garden City for
a brief visit. Pauline and Martha had remained in
Washington. We were staying with my grandparents,
Harry and Mitta Hope, and their unmarried daughters, Mary
and Mildred, at 621 Garden City Avenue.

Most of their radio news (no television then) came via KOA, a
powerful Denver station. Almost immediately that day, it and
other stations started playing martial music. "Why," asked
Mary, who usually had little to say, "are they playing those
marches? We're not at war." Clifford considered it an example of
war hysteria.

Honoring their treaty obligations to Poland, Britain and
France declared war on Germany on September 3. World War II
had officially begun.

Three days later Art Fleming, Clifford's old law partner,
closed his letter with:

We are immensely interested in the debate concerning neutrality measures and in the world war speculation but no one
seems to know just what ought to be done to assure the desired
result, that is, that we stay out of the boundary wars of Europe.

His comments pretty well reflected the feelings of the majority in the
country, especially in the Middle West, at that time.

From 1935 to 1941 Hope spent more time studying national defense
and foreign policy issues than any other. He was deeply concerned and
often in a quandary as to the right course of action. Although his views
generally were in accord with those of a majority of his constituents, they
were, in retrospect, dead wrong: He greatly misjudged the ambition and
power of Hitler and of the Japanese Empire. Later he would unabashedly
admit that these were his greatest errors of judgment in his entire congressional career.

In his book *Isolationism in America 1935-1941*, Professor Manfred
Jones lists three bases for isolationist belief during this period:

(1) The fear that U.S. involvement in a new war would bring a permanent dictatorship to the nation. (2) The need to preserve U.S. independence in the conduct of foreign affairs. (3) The belief that a war in either
Europe or Asia, regardless of its outcome, would not threaten the most
vital interests of the United States.[1]

This latter belief, Jones asserts, sprang from what some called the
"lessons of World War I" — the idea that the U.S. was tricked into the war
by selfish allies and that the war had failed to "make the world safe for
democracy."[2] Hope's views and those of his constituents probably were
based on the very things the professor outlined.

In 1935, by general agreement of the President and Congress, the first
Neutrality Act was enacted. It placed an embargo on the shipment of arms
and ammunition to belligerents upon the declaration of the President that
a state of war existed. In late January 1936 Hope wrote to Lena Carl of
Garden City:

It is most difficult to write a neutrality bill which will be
effective where world conditions change as rapidly as they are
now. What it is attempted to do in the measures which Congress
is considering is to remove all possible incentive for us to
become entangled in European politics and possible warfare. I

think it is the general opinion of everyone that we drifted into
the last war simply because we allowed ourselves to become so
entangled commercially with the belligerent nations that there
was no other avenue out. I think everyone wants to prevent that
happening again.

A month later he wrote Ray Bressler of Sitka that he did not think there
was much danger of the United States

getting involved in any wars during the lifetime of the present
generation. We have too many people who have gone through
the horrors of war, a great many of whom are now in positions
of leadership, to prevent anyone from getting a glorified idea of
war.

For the future Hope favored a "campaign of education . . . rather than trying to keep out of war by mandatory legislation." He placed his hope in
"an enlightened citizenship which will not be carried away by every little
war scare of international complication or hope of commercial gain." The
third Neutrality Act, signed on May 1, 1937, continued the main provisions of the first and second and implemented a "cash and carry" system
for belligerents who wished to purchase nonembargoed items in the U.S.
That summer, however, Japan invaded China, and FDR refused to invoke
the Neutrality Act in the war, stating that enforcement would hurt China
more than Japan. Although sympathetic to China, Hope argued that the act
should be strictly enforced.

Hope endorsed the proposed constitutional amendment introduced by
Representative Louis Ludlow of Indiana, requiring a vote of the people to
declare war except in case of attack. In November he wrote to Anna
Hauschild of Sterling:

I think this might prevent us from sticking our noses into a
lot of controversies in which our country has no real interest
and from getting the idea in our heads that it is up to us to see
that the whole world behaves itself.

Hope thought that was the real issue and that it accounted for "the
immense popularity of the proposal among the people" in general. He

sensed that the people felt the country had been drawn into controversies that were "none of our business." That is, he explained,

> [they] feel that there are still a good many men in high places in this country who think that it is the mission of the U.S. to take up the cause of the underdog in any controversy which may develop among world powers.

Because of that, he wrote Hauschild, people feel

> the safest way to assure that nothing of this kind will be done is to let the people who are going to fight the war and buy the liberty bonds decide whether or not there will be a war.

In March 1938 Hope expressed opposition to the proposed naval expansion program in a letter to the Reverend and Mrs. F. G. Smith of McCracken, writing that he felt the country already had an "adequate national defense."

> Without this program we have one of the two largest and possibly the largest navy in the world. I think that it is entirely adequate for national defense purposes and it seems to me that any addition at this time would mean a change in our foreign policy and could only be justified on the theory that we expect to either singly or with other nations engage in an effort to police the world. I am opposed to a policy of this kind. Irrespective of our motives in greatly expanding our navy at this time, it seems to me the policy can only result either in a world-wide armament race or war, possibly both. For that reason, I expect to oppose this program although, frankly, I don't believe that it can be defeated in the House.

By the time of the Munich crisis in September, my father and I (then a high school sophomore) had begun having frequent serious discussions about foreign policy. Had I known then I would be doing research for a book about him and his contemporaries years later, I would have kept a detailed diary. I do remember I did not share many of his moderate isolationist views. Perhaps it was because I was religiously reading *The Wash-*

ington Post, including Dorothy Thompson's columns, and had not then lived through a war. My father wanted to believe that giving the Sudetenland (German area of Czechoslovakia) to Hitler would, as Neville Chamberlain (Great Britain's Prime Minister) believed, bring "peace in our time." When Hitler swallowed up the rest of Czechoslovakia in March 1939, my father was amazed. He hadn't read *Mein Kampf*. He had believed Hitler's proclamation at Munich that he was seeking only to unite with the Germans of Austria and the Sudetenland and had no further territorial claims in Europe.

In letters to constituents in early 1939, Hope continued to urge that in order to stay out of war the best policy "is absolute neutrality in all conflicts" and that the people must maintain "an attitude and spirit of neutrality." Hope expressed doubt as to "whether the people can do that or not." In February he wrote to his longtime friend, W. A. Long of Fowler, who favored sending arms for cash to Britain and France, a concern that some radicals in the administration favored "a strong war policy so they can completely control the government in the event of war." Hope confessed, "I certainly don't want to set myself up as one who knows all the answers, because I feel sometimes as if I don't know anything about the question."

He spoke against harbor improvements on Guam which would likely lead to fortification. Hope feared this would be construed as an unfriendly act and give the Japanese militarist group an excuse for expanding their defenses.

In late September 1939 Hope wrote to his good friend C. C. Isely of Dodge City that of the people in the district with whom he had visited in early September, about 50 percent favored repealing the Neutrality Act, but his mail was running 20 to 1 against it. S. S. Vaughn of Larned wrote in October to urge repeal, and Hope responded in a long letter. The congressman said he believed the U.S. was the last stronghold of democracy and that the war was "just another phase of the battle of power politics that [had] been going on in Europe for the last thousand years." He was convinced that England and France "should win the war; if not, a stalemate would be the most that [could] possibly happen." He thought the Russo-German alliance was the greatest mistake Hitler had made, placing him "absolutely in Stalin's power." If Hitler "would achieve the impossible and defeat France and England decisively," Hope said, "it would take him 20 years to get over that struggle and be in shape to carry any attacks to this continent." In a conciliatory manner, as was his wont, Hope closed the letter by urging that the U.S. should be neither pro-British nor pro-German, but pro-American.

(The arms embargo was repealed and "cash and carry" legislation was enacted in November.)

One refreshing note in Hope's views at that time was his belief in "pay-as-we-go-defense." In April 1940 he wrote to Floyd W. Ross of Sterling:

> One thing I think we ought to do if we appropriate another billion dollars for defense is to bring in a tax bill to pay for the same. We are either going to have to do that or increase the debt limit, and it seems to me that that has gotten to a dangerously high point already.

Levying a tax to pay for additional expenditures, Hope suggested, might "bring about a further understanding of our problems among the people generally."

For some months after the war began, there was little action on the border between France and Germany. Some called it a "phony war." Those people were rudely awakened when Germany invaded Denmark and Norway in April 1940. During this time at our Oliver Street residence, it was my habit to arise before anyone else in the family and run down to get *The Washington Post* and *The Times-Herald*, mainly to read the war news. I remember well the morning of May 10. The headlines blazed "Germans Invade Holland, Belgium and Luxembourg." I ran upstairs to show the headlines to Clifford and Pauline, still in bed. That was the day World War II really began. Most Americans, including Clifford, were not really surprised. It was just that they were still hoping the war would, somehow, go away.

By September the great debate was about peacetime conscription — the first in U.S. history. Hope wrote to Mahlon Ely of Hutchinson:

> My personal position, which I have reached after giving the matter as much thought and study as I have ever given any public question, is that peacetime conscription would be resorted to only under the most unusual and urgent conditions and that those conditions do not exist at this time.

A few days later he delivered a statement which was printed as an Extension of Remarks in the *Congressional Record*. He questioned the need for one million new conscriptees when we already had 900,000 in the Armed Forces, a powerful Navy, and new bases in the Atlantic and when we were in the process of building the world's greatest air fleet. He called for a small, mobile army, stating we would need conscription only if Hitler conquered England, captured the British fleet, and attacked the U.S. within a few months. The only reason for a conscripted army, he said, would be for offensive use. Although the bill (Burke-Wadsworth) passed both houses by decisive margins, all the nine-member Kansas delegation voted against it except for the only Democrat, John Houston.

Hope wrote to Frank Russell of Hutchinson sometime in September after the vote was taken:

> During the past three years we have progressed step by step toward war; and if Roosevelt is reelected, there is no question whatever in my mind but what we will be at war within a year. This will not be a war to defend our own shores but will be a war in which we will be joined with England in attempting to destroy Germany and Italy. . . . I have not been able to persuade myself that that is the thing for us to do.

Hope said it looked like the present European struggle would end in a stalemate, "at least as far as the invasion of England [was] concerned." He thought England could hold off Germany but not win the war. He told Russell:

> A tremendous amount of propaganda already is being turned loose in this country in an effort to make us believe it is our duty to join with the British Empire in utterly destroying Germany and Italy. As time goes on that propaganda will increase, and the first thing we know we will take this new conscript army and send it overseas. I know Roosevelt has said that will not be done; but I have on my desk a list of almost a hundred promises which have been made by Mr. Roosevelt at one time or another since he began running for the Presidency in 1932, every one of which has been broken. Therefore, I do not feel we can rely too strongly upon his statement in this regard. I am not

The charismatic Wendell Willkie (center) and Clifford Hope during Willkie's 1940 campaign for President.

Finney County Historical Society, Garden City, KS

accusing the President of insincerity at all, but I do think he has
a way of changing his mind and he does it to an extent it is
unsafe to rely upon his position of today as being his position
of tomorrow.

Meanwhile there was a presidential campaign and an election in the off-
ing. In the spring of 1940, the two leading Republican candidates were
Thomas E. Dewey and Senator Robert A. Taft. Dewey, 38, had won fame
as a crusading New York district attorney, but had lost his race for governor in 1938. Taft, elected to the Senate from Ohio in 1938, was only a two-
year freshman senator. Neither had the personal following they later
acquired. Rank-and-file Republicans and others who disliked the New
Deal and the thought of an unprecedented third term for FDR were looking for a new face. They found their man in Wendell L. Willkie, an Indiana farm boy who had become a Wall Street lawyer and utility tycoon. He
had a common touch and a charismatic personality. Hope became one of
Willkie's early supporters among members of Congress.

Clifford and I attended the Republican National Convention in Philadelphia. It was my first political convention, and it was an exciting experience
for me. On the night of the balloting, I joined those in the north gallery
shouting, "We want Willkie! We want Willkie!" At the time, I claimed I
shouted louder than anyone else. Ballot after ballot, Willkie's strength
increased. A big breakthrough came with Kansas switching its 18 votes to
Willkie on the fifth ballot before he won in the sixth. The next day, prior
to the balloting for Vice President, I overheard a woman on the elevator
exclaiming, "So it's Clifford Hope for Vice President." I hurried to our
hotel room and lay down on the bed. That was the closest I had ever come
to fainting. Soon George Reid told me my father was being seriously considered in the event Senator McNary of Oregon, Republican leader of the
Senate, would not accept the nomination. McNary ended up accepting,
and that was the end of the Hope vice-presidential boomlet.

At Willkie's specific request, Hope was active in the campaign. In a column written for publication in 1968, he recalled:

> I had never met Willkie until a few days before the conven-
> tion, but like many others I was greatly impressed by him. Rep-
> resentative Joe Martin of Massachusetts, the Republican leader
> of the House of Representatives, was elected as party chairman

and he and Mr. Willkie asked me to serve as Director of the campaign activities relating to Agriculture. . . .

The Willkie campaign of 1940 was one of the most bizarre enterprises of its kind in history. Few men are able to start in politics at the top. Most of those who have done so like Grant and Eisenhower were popular heroes who realized that they knew little about the practical aspects of politics and depended upon experienced political leaders for guidance in that field.

. . . Having been so successful in his first effort [Willkie] had little idea of the tremendous amount of work, organization, patience and yes, drudgery which is a part of campaigning at any level of politics. . . . He scorned suggestions of his advisors that he get a good rest before officially opening his campaign.

After a strenuous speaking trip in Chicago . . . Willkie spent Sunday in Kansas City . . . mostly recuperating and taking treatments from a noted Hollywood specialist for his badly shattered voice.

The formal opening of the campaign was scheduled to be made at Coffeyville, Kansas, where Willkie had taught school in his earlier years, on the next afternoon; with a major speech at Tulsa in the evening. Thanks to the Hollywood doctor and to Willkie's natural vigor, his voice, while not up to par, was equal to the demands of the day and evening. . . .

The presidential campaign train is a thing of the past but . . . in its heyday (1928-1952) was a great institution. . . . Such a train was a self-contained unit consisting of sleepers, diners, lounge cars, press cars and private cars for the candidate, his staff, speech writers and others. . . .

Willkie made a speech from the rear of the train at every stop. His staff went to a lot of work to prepare background material on the area, its interests and problems. This he frequently stuffed in his pocket without looking at it and would end up by talking agriculture in an industrial community or the other way around as the notion struck him.

In spite of all the confusion, Willkie made a good impression. He liked people and people liked him. I've always felt that he made as good a race as anyone could have. President Roosevelt shrewdly took domestic issues out of the campaign by making most of his trips to defense installations and talking about his efforts to keep the country at peace in a wartorn world, even going so far as to assure the country in a speech in Boston that no American soldier would have to fight on foreign soil. Attacks on Willkie were left to Harold Ickes and other administration sharpshooters. In spite of this, Willkie made a good showing in the election, better than any Republican since 1928, and carried a number of midwestern states, including Kansas, where his majority was almost 125,000.

With his usual modesty, Hope did not mention his vice-presidential moment although it was widely reported by the Kansas press. Nor did he mention that he was Willkie's designated choice for Secretary of Agriculture, in the event of a GOP victory. In December 1959 Philip Willkie, Wendell's son, wrote Hope:

> I remember one day on the porch of our home in Rushville, Indiana, my father being asked who should be in the cabinet. When he came to the Secretary of Agriculture, he said, "There is just one man in the Republican party who knows the answers to the farm questions and that is Cliff Hope."

In response, Hope said he appreciated such a comment coming from a man whom he held in high regard. He wrote:

> I have been in a position to know something of the agricultural viewpoints of the last four Republican candidates for the presidency and have no hesitancy in saying that your father displayed more sincere interest in the farm problem than any of the others. The attitude of most of them, and I don't think I am being unkind in saying this, was "Why do I have to be bothered with this problem?" as if by ignoring it, it might go away.

Hope's correspondence during the Willkie campaign illustrates his disdain for big businessmen and other affluent people, who, because of their business success and wealth, fancied themselves to be political experts. In September Ray Garvey, a prominent Wichita businessman with whom most politicians would not have wished to tangle, wrote Hope complain-

Clifford R. Hope in his Washington, D.C., office at number 1314 New House Office Building (now Longworth), *ca.* 1940.

ing that Willkie was not asking FDR embarrassing questions and in general was running a poor campaign. The letter referred to "Roosevelt's chief chums, the international communists and international Jewish financiers." Hope was angered and did not mince words in his reply:

> What I would like to know is what are you doing for Willkie outside of doing a lot of crabbing because he isn't running a campaign just like you would run it? I think your suggestions are punk; and if I wasn't so busy working for Willkie and trying to overcome the defeatist attitude of "experts" like yourself, I could point out specifically just how many millions of votes would be lost by following your suggestions. If Willkie is beaten, it will be because people like yourself who ought to be out there working are standing on the side lines and crabbing. Just because he doesn't take time to give publicity to some of your pet ideas is no reason why he won't make a good President.
>
> This may seem like I am irritated and I am. No political party has ever had a candidate with the courage and the heart and the fighting ability of Wendell Willkie. Maybe he won't win. Maybe no one can win, but he's making a great campaign and presenting the real issues in an amazingly effective way. Whether he wins or loses is going to depend on fellows like yourself; and if you insist on crabbing instead of cheering and working, he will probably lose and you can have your four more years of Roosevelt.

Hope's blast at Garvey did not end their correspondence. In 1942 Garvey sent a handwritten note of congratulations to Hope upon his reelection.

In the 1940 Kansas election there was no Senate race, and all incumbent representatives were reelected. Hope again defeated Claude E. Main, who lacked funds for another tent show campaign. Governor Payne Ratner was reelected but by a margin of only 430 votes out of 850,000. Hope's files indicate he and Ratner did not have much contact with one another during the latter's administration.

On the home front during that summer and fall, I spent much time working at Willkie headquarters in Washington. I also took driving lessons from a private instructor (who later had a nervous breakdown), obtained my license, and began driving in the city traffic. This enabled me to take visiting Kansans on sightseeing tours of the capital city. I had been doing this for several years but not as a driver. My driving got me into big trouble one night that fall. I was visiting a girlfriend across town and was not watching the clock. It was about 7:30 p.m. Clifford and Pauline were scheduled to attend a reception that evening. When I arrived home, they were standing on the curb in their formal evening clothes as mad as I had ever seen them, probably as angry as they had ever been with me. I do not recall what my punishment was, but I never again was late getting the family car home. (I did, however, have some interesting high school escapades in that car, but they are beyond the scope of this story.)

After 13 years of renting apartments and houses, in January 1941 Clifford and Pauline bought a house at 3541 Brandywine, N.W., just off Connecticut Avenue and a mile or two closer to downtown and the Capitol than previous residences had been. The purchase price was $16,050, with monthly payments of $63.30.

In a 1966 column Clifford explained that for a number of years furnished apartments and homes were readily available for rent on reasonable terms. It was common, he said, for members of Congress to live in residential hotels. This changed by the late 1930s as expanding government agencies brought in more and more employees, making housing scarce and prompting him to buy the house the Hope family would occupy until they left at the close of the 1956 congressional session. Clifford recalled it as a "modest but comfortable house, just completed, in a pleasant neighborhood and handy to transportation and shopping centers." An important consideration from his standpoint was the opportunity to do some gardening. Upon discovering that the soil was very poor, he had it removed from the garden plots and replaced with good top soil. After a slow beginning and considerable work and experimentation, he succeeded in developing a rose garden of about 135 bushes and climbers, along with a number of flowering shrubs and some perennials. The garden became an important part of his Washington life. He wrote:

> In the early mornings and over weekends, it not only gave me needed exercise but also the opportunity for contemplation and reflection. It was my refuge when the worries and the problems of the office threatened to get me down. Although none of the other members of our family turned out to be working garden-

ers, they enjoyed the end result and gave me plenty of moral support, to say nothing of advice.

With our move, Martha transferred from Lafayette to Ben Murch Grade School, several blocks to the north. I continued to attend Woodrow Wilson High School, now just a few blocks away. My most memorable experience there was high school debate. The debate question for 1941 was "Resolved, that the power of the federal government should be increased." The affirmative was not a popular position, but I seized upon the idea of urging that federal government power should be increased in order to aid agriculture, bearing in mind the 1936 Supreme Court decision holding the original Agricultural Adjustment Act unconstitutional. Of course, most of our opponents knew nothing about agriculture, so using this argument was generally quite successful. My debate partner, Erma Fuchs, was a forceful personality and speaker. All this helped our team place second in a tournament at George Washington University. Clifford was quite pleased.

In June a family reunion was held in Garden City in celebration of Harry and Mitta's 50th wedding anniversary. Numerous relatives attended, and many of them stayed at our Gillespie Place home, Aunt Coe included. As she packed to leave, she could not locate her corset. That stern undergarment was found by cousin Dale Hope in his luggage when he reached Kansas City. Aunt Coe was out of shape in more ways than one over the incident.

Although I was looking forward to attending a college with some intellectual challenge, my parents, especially Pauline, had other plans. She was insistent that I attend a military college to learn "the little niceties" which, she contended, I lacked. Whatever made her think I would learn "little niceties" at a military school I do not know. Instead I learned to drink, swear, and chase girls. However, I also learned military discipline, which Clifford was heartily in favor of for me; it was probably for this reason that he gave in to Pauline's pleas. In any event, much that I learned at Kemper Military School in Boonville, Missouri, stood me in good stead when I enlisted in the Army and was called up in early 1943.

In the meantime the U.S. was edging closer to war. In early January 1941, at the urging of the President the Lend-Lease Bill (H.R. 1776) was introduced in the House and the Senate. It was designed to lend or lease war supplies to Britain and other allies. Hope, together with all members of the Kansas delegation except one, opposed the bill as introduced. In a speech he said he favored aid to Britain short of war — including gifts if necessary — handled by the British Purchasing Commission but he opposed giving FDR power to determine when to give, how much, and so forth, "making him a dictator with more powers than Churchill now has." The bill was amended in the Senate to allay these fears with the result that four of the seven Kansas House members, including Hope and Frank Carlson, ended up voting for it.

By the end of July Hope had modified his views further. He wrote to Mrs. B. H. Bainter of Hutchinson:

> Events which would have been considered breathtaking a few years ago are occurring almost daily now. I doubt if there is a full realization on the part of the American people as to the full extent of the danger which faces our country, and I am afraid there is something of an unwillingness to look this question in the face. I am very much opposed to our sending another AEF [American Expeditionary Force], yet if Hitler defeats Russia and takes Spain and Portugal, as well as the French forts on the west coast of Africa, we may be in the position where we will have to send troops to South America or to some of the island bases in order to protect this country. I think we have to look at all of these things realistically and meet situations as they arise. I think it is unfortunate that there is a tendency on the part of a lot of our people to want to avoid looking these facts fully in the face. We are a little soft — too much like France was a couple of years ago.

These concerns, however, had not convinced Hope that the one-year Conscription Act should be extended. In a letter to Mrs. Will Heiland of Ford, he wrote: "The President should keep his word to these boys that they will not be called on to serve more than a year." And in late September, in a letter to his old friend, C. C. Isely, he commented:

> Roosevelt's avowed policy is not defense; it is to carry the four freedoms to the ends of the earth, which simply means to carry the New Deal to the ends of the earth and while he is doing that to make sure it is pretty solidly planted in this country.

On Sunday, December 7, Clifford, Pauline, and Martha, then 12 years of age, were at home in Washington. In recalling that day years later, Martha wrote:

> Mom and Pop were in the basement at 3541 Brandywine Street, possibly considering how to create a "recreation room" there. The phone rang. I answered and found Cousin Georgia on the line. She said, "Tell your father the Japanese have bombed Pearl Harbor."
>
> "Bombed what?" I asked. I had no idea where Pearl Harbor was.
>
> Georgia repeated her message. I hung up, feeling perplexed and uneasy, and went downstairs to tell Mom and Pop. Pop's reply was something about Georgia being mixed up or excitable, and he and Mom continued their discussion. But after a few minutes, Pop reconsidered and came upstairs to turn on the radio. Georgia was right. And nothing was the same after that.

The surprise attack and tragedy at Pearl Harbor prompted Hope to write C. C. Isely:

> As you say, the whole war situation developed almost at once. While everybody regrets the debacle at Pearl Harbor, yet in a good many ways we are perhaps fortunate that the war started in that way. In the first place, it has brought about a feeling of national unity, which could never have been secured in any other way. In the second place, it is apparent that sooner or later we would have found out the Japanese army and navy is nothing to laugh off. It is a good deal better to find that out in the beginning than several months from now.

Hope's constant, voluminous correspondence during the period from 1942 through 1945 illustrates the many problems and concerns of the people of southwest Kansas and the actions and expressions of views in response to them. As historian Gilbert Fite has observed, World War II solved several farm problems at once: the need for food and fiber wiped out surpluses, the call for troops and war plant workers began to draw down on the excessive farm population, and wartime demands and good prices created a higher degree of prosperity than most farmers had ever known.[3] A case in point is Pauline's uncle and aunt, Perry and May Corkadel, who were able to install indoor plumbing and electricity at their farm with their increased income. Wartime legislation provided for price supports at 90 percent on basic (and other) commodities, including wheat, during and for two years after the official end of the war. At that, farm income per capita was still only 57 percent of non-farm income, and Hope's correspondence told of problems of farm gas rationing, farm machinery shortages, and the drafting of farm boys who were hard to replace on busier-than-ever farms.

Prosperity came to southwest Kansas in another form. Good flying weather most of the year and flat terrain resulted in the establishment of Army Air Corps bases in Pratt, Great Bend, Liberal, Dodge City, and Garden City and a Naval Air Station at Hutchinson. Hope spent much time working on these projects.

For the most part, people accepted wartime problems, restrictions, and shortages cheerfully. Mamie Axline Fay of Pratt, one of Hope's frequent correspondents, wrote in 1943: "These things are so small in comparison to the problems you are constantly facing that I hesitate to even mention them." Throughout the war Hope called on President Roosevelt to demand more sacrifices from the people. In a July 1943 Associated Press interview, he charged that the President had failed to impress upon the people the need for sacrifices with the result that "we have so many organized minorities all attempting to gain some advantages for themselves." He said he sensed people were eager and willing to make sacrifices but had not been given the opportunity to do so. He told the press:

> If the president would come out with an appeal to the people
> to make every possible sacrifice and to give up their demands
> he would do more to solidify the country and to halt inflation
> than anything that could possibly be done.

He recalled that when Winston Churchill had taken over as prime minister of Great Britain "all he could promise was 'blood, sweat and tears.'" He said that in this country "we [hadn't] heard anything along that line." Hope continued:

It has been the policy of the government here to give the news an optimistic tinge. Instead of impressing upon the people the need for sacrifices, the government has promised them higher wages, increased incomes, lower prices and subsidies. In other words, the policy of the administration has been to lead people to think that they can get a lot out of the war rather than make any sacrifices. That is what is behind the fundamental difficulty the country finds itself in today.

He also placed the blame for bickering among government administrators and the greed of organized minorities on the fact that "the seriousness of the situation hasn't been brought home to the people."

The GOP picked up 50 seats in the House and 8 in the Senate in the 1942 congressional elections. In Kansas, Republican victories were even more impressive. In the governor's race, Andrew (Andy) Schoeppel, a Ness City lawyer and an old friend of Hope, defeated Clyde Reed (former governor and senator), Paul Wunsch, and Carl Friend in the GOP gubernatorial primary and had a landslide victory over Democrat Bill Burke in the general election. Senator Capper was easily reelected, as were all six GOP representatives. Because of the 1940 Federal Census, Kansas lost a Congressman; Ed Rees and John Houston ran against each other, and Rees won handily. Sumner County, south of Wichita, was added to the old 7th District, which then became the new 5th. Hope defeated S. S. Alexander, a Kingman lawyer 54,653 to 27,381 in the new district. Hope's victory came in spite of Alexander's vigorous attacks on him for his pre-Pearl Harbor votes on defense and foreign policy matters. Alexander's campaign literature reprinted William Allen White's August 1941 chastisement of the Kansas Republican delegation for such votes. Apparently these attacks carried little weight. Hope's votes had been in accord with the views of the great majority of his constituents at the time, and 1942 was simply a strong Republican year in Kansas.

GOP victories were even greater in Kansas in 1944. Thomas E. Dewey won Kansas in a big way over Franklin D. Roosevelt, and Clyde Reed was reelected to the Senate by a wide margin over Thurman Hill. Albert M. Cole, a Holton lawyer, defeated Bill Lambertson in the 1st District primary election and was easily elected in the general. Ulysses S. Guyer died in office in 1943 and was succeeded by Errett P. Scrivner, Kansas City lawyer, in a special election. Hope defeated A. E. Hawes in the

Clifford Hope (fifth from right) with part of the Special House Committee on Postwar Economic Policy and Planning — The Colmer Committee — at Prime Minister Clement Attlee's offices, 10 Downing Street. Members of the Committee were part of an extensive study trip to Europe and the Middle East in 1945.

Finney County Historical Society, Garden City, KS

5th District, 72,370 to 32,577. In the Kansas legislature, Democrat membership was reduced to one in the Senate and to a slim five in the House.

There was an interesting 1944 post-election exchange of correspondence between Hope and W. L. White, son of William Allen White, who had become editor of *The Emporia Gazette*. The elder White had died, as fate would have it, on Kansas Day (January 29) in 1944. On November 10 W. L. sent Hope a copy of his editorial recommending Clifford for the U.S. Senate in a future election, stating that he had always voted to aid the allies in his pre-Pearl Harbor votes. Hope replied immediately to correct the record, stating he would be the "first to admit that he had made some mistakes" in his votes and that he did not "want to be sailing under false colors." W. L. responded that his editorial had been based on his recollection of what William Allen White had told him, and a telephone call to Harry and Mitta, Clifford's parents. (W. L. said he had been unable to reach Clifford via telephone.) Harry and Mitta, with parental pride, told W. L. that "Clifford always voted right on everything!"

Victory for the Allied forces was still a long way off in early 1944, but it was assured. Hope and other members of Congress began devoting considerable time to postwar planning. The Special House Committee on Postwar Economic Policy and Planning was established in February with 18 members under the chairmanship of William H. Colmer of Mississippi. Among the members was Hope's good friend Jerry Voorhis, Democrat from California, who had been born in Ottawa, Kansas, in 1901. (Voorhis was the congressman defeated by Richard Nixon at the beginning of Nixon's career in 1946.) Seven members of the committee, including Hope, made an extensive study trip to Europe and the Middle East in the late summer of 1945.

Several letters selected from many express Hope's views during 1944. In one, written in late March to C. J. Revere in New York, he explained:

> We are going to have some kind of a farm program after the war, no matter which political party is in power. Both party platforms this year will make definite promises in that regard, just as they have for the past several years and whichever party is in power will, undoubtedly, attempt to carry out some kind of a program to keep farm prices on something like the same level as other prices.

Hope noted that the support price program was operating more effectively in this regard than anything that had been tried and that farmers
much preferred this system to one of direct federal payments. After the
war, he predicted, there would be "strong political pressure" to support
prices on all commodities. But a lot depended on the level at which prices
were placed and on the government's foreign trade and domestic policy
choices. He wrote:

> If we are going to have a monopoly in labor as represented
> by the closed shop or in industry as represented by price under-
> standings, then it seems to me that it is inevitable that agricul-
> ture will demand a closed shop which would be approximated
> by higher support prices and control of marketing.

He thought farmers preferred "a program of abundance represented by
free and open competition on the part of both industry and labor," but he
did not foresee that kind of development for the postwar period. "In other
words," he concluded, "I don't think the farmer can last very long if he is
the only man who is operating on a supply and demand basis."

In May Hope disagreed strongly with Sheldon Coleman of the Coleman Lamp and Stove Company in Wichita, who espoused the view that
the U.S. should prevent "as far as we can, the development of manufac-
turing industries in the backward countries." To the contrary, Hope
believed,

> The greatest thing that could happen to this country and to
> the world would be to increase the standards of living every-
> where. That can be done only through the expansion of indus-
> trial production, not only in the advanced countries but in the
> backward countries. You have a market in Latin American
> countries for comparatively small amounts of your product at
> the present time. The reason the market is so small is because
> buying power is small. It can only be increased by the indus-
> trial development of those countries. I think that we would be
> serving our own interests as a nation and your interests as a
> manufacturer and exporter, if we could cooperate with the back-
> ward countries in their industrialization. I don't mean on a char-
> ity or "gimme" basis, but through the intelligent extension of

credit and the lending of technicians to assist in educating and training of native labor.

Hope informed his prominent Wichita correspondent that he was "not a free trader," but believed in a protective tariff system. He did not think this incompatible with the ideas he had expressed. Hope explained:

> I believe that where there is one person in a hundred perhaps in Latin America who can now buy our products, that if industrial development and buying power were increased this number would expand tremendously. Production, as I see it, is the only key which will open the door to national and world prosperity following the war.

In response to an inquiry from Governor Schoeppel in June about the Pick Plan for development of the Missouri River Basin, Hope said he was not enthusiastic about "this river development stuff." So far he thought the plan was a waste of money for river transportation. Concerning reclamation of land for irrigation, he felt it would merely place such land in competition with existing irrigated land and that much of the reclaimed land would never be irrigated anyway. On other occasions, Hope had observed that the Army Engineers like to "tour the countryside looking for bluffs to build a dam between."

Upon learning that Robert Isely had died while leading an air raid on Saipan in late June, Hope immediately wrote a letter of condolence to Robert's father, C. C. To the best of Hope's knowledge, Robert was the first of those appointed by him to Annapolis or West Point to be killed in World War II. Isely replied, telling of his concern for his other three sons. "Charles," he wrote, "is still in Italy, saw some hot fighting. Quentin is still in the South Pacific with his PT boat. Thornton is in the states riding a Hellcat." The indomitable C. C., at 69, was seeking a foreign news correspondent assignment for himself. Later that year, while I was serving in Europe, my father wrote that C. C. had been assigned to the Middle East.

The sudden death of President Roosevelt in April 1945 brought eulogies from friends and foes alike. After reciting the major agricultural legislation enacted during his administration and praising all who had participated — "farm leaders, practical farmers, members of Congress and

men and women in all walks of life who are interested in rural progress,"
Hope's tribute concluded:

> Nevertheless, too much praise cannot be given Franklin D.
> Roosevelt for furnishing the leadership which made these
> achievements possible. To him must go the credit of being the
> first President to fully recognize the economic problems of
> agriculture and to be willing to use the powers of the Federal
> Government toward a solution of these problems. His sympa-
> thetic nature enabled him to see the human side of agricultural
> life and to be prompt in affording relief from the results of such
> overwhelming disasters as droughts, dust storms and floods.
> Coming as I do from an area which suffered from drought and
> dust storms, I have a keen appreciation of the value of that relief
> in human terms. This humanitarian approach is also reflected in
> the efforts, not always successful, to afford relief to the under-
> privileged farmer through the Farm Security Administration
> and similar agencies.
>
> The greatest compliment which has been paid to the agricul-
> tural program and policies of Franklin D. Roosevelt is the fact
> that both political parties since 1936 have accepted the general
> principles of those programs and have pledged their continua-
> tion in one form or another.

Don L. Berry wrote in June 1945:

> I see you were the only Kansan to vote in favor of renewing
> the president's authority to negotiate trade agreements. Again I
> congratulate you. If the Republican party tries to go back to the
> old Smoot-Hawley basis it will be just too bad, the badder if we
> win on it than if we are defeated.

To this Hope replied:

> I agree thoroughly with what you say. In fact, I am getting
> farther away from the traditional Republican position on the
> tariff all the time, although I am, of course, a long way from
> being a free trader.

Years later Hope recalled his "conversion" from being a supporter of high, protective tariffs to an advocate of reciprocal trade agreements. He usually added that his conversion was not nearly as sudden as St. Paul's on the road to Damascus.

Perhaps the most fascinating and strange correspondence in Hope's congressional files is that between him and one Ray Jackson from 1939 to 1945. Jackson's letterheads show he was a broom corn grower and wheat farmer in southwest Kansas and later the owner and operator of the telephone company at Syracuse. Apparently he was a successful businessman and a great, uncritical admirer of the Soviet Union and the worldwide Communist Party. For six years or so, he and Hope appeared to relish insulting each other with sarcastic letters. (They did agree on some matters.) Regardless of content, Hope always ended his letters "with kind regards."

Russia invaded Finland in December 1939, and at that time American public opinion was overwhelmingly on the side of Finland. But not Ray Jackson. He protested that Herbert Hoover's collecting for Finnish relief was a violation of the Neutrality Act. Hope disagreed with him "100%." In March 1941 Jackson protested efforts to deport Harry Bridges, leader of the Longshoremen's Union, as an undesirable alien. Hope fired back:

> I am not going to spend a lot of time worrying about the problems which seem to concern you the most. You can rest assured that this administration, irrespective of what it does to the American people generally, will see that the rights of the aliens, the labor racketeers and all of those for whom you seem particularly concerned are fully protected.

Jackson came back with a three-page, somewhat nitpicking letter which ended:

> I believe I wrote you once before that I feel I have a perfect right at all times to convey my ideas to you as a congressional representative from this district, but I have no desire to receive from you any letters attempting to set forth your position if you cannot justify your position by facts and logical reasoning. If you can only use sarcasm and personal digs to justify your position, then your letters are of no interest to me. It is too much like

debating with a child. It would seem like a man holding the office you do should be able to justify his position by reason, logic, and statement of facts. Perhaps I am expecting too much of you.

This mutual blasting away continued throughout the war years. In December 1945, answering Jackson's criticism of pending legislation to control (in Hope's view) excesses of organized labor, Hope ended his letter:

> Really while I enjoy getting your letters and having your viewpoint it is hardly necessary for you to write and give it to me. I know what it will be on any question and if I don't all I need to do is to buy a copy of *The Daily Worker* and see what position they take. As far as I can find out you haven't varied in the slightest degree from their viewpoint on any public issue that you have ever mentioned in your letters.

My book *Growing Up in the Wartime Army: A GI in the 1940s* (1989) primarily covers my adventures and misadventures as an enlisted man in the Army from February 1943 to January 1946. It also tells something of what our family — Clifford, Pauline, and Martha — were thinking about and doing on the homefront during that period.

Pauline agonized more during the war than any other member of our family. By the time the war began in 1939, she was experiencing mental problems. By her description, she had occasional "fuzzy" or "mind wandering" spells. One of her physicians recommended that she not do anything that would cause her to worry; that was the worst possible advice. She stopped many of her usual activities and, with more unstructured time, she worried more. She was a religious person who prayed constantly for others, but prayer did not relieve her anxieties. Years later Martha wrote of that time:

> The years of World War II took a toll on Mom, as they did on many people. Her anxieties were heightened by the war and especially by having Cliff Jr. in the Army and in active service in Europe. Pop worked very long hours in those days and was away on committee hearing trips more often than she cared for.

I was in high school and busy with extra-curricular activities and meetings of the young people's groups at the Chevy Chase Presbyterian Church. Regrettably, I was often reluctant to be at home with her when she was upset by the latest war news or hadn't heard from Cliff Jr., or Pop was out of town. Her anxieties seemed burdensome to a teenager trying out her wings and unable to understand fully the problems and tragedy of those times. I often kept a distance between us, retiring to my room to do homework rather than stay with her to talk after the supper dishes were done. She busied herself with a group of Congressional wives who met regularly to fold bandages; that, I think, was a place where worries and sorrows could be shared. And she did not let a day go by, once Cliff Jr. was overseas, that she did not write to him or see that another member of the family wrote.

Unfortunately for Pauline, the war did not stop Aunt Coe's visits. Sometime before V-E Day, Coe joked, "Don't you know there's a war on?" That attempt at humor upset Pauline and Clifford. I was infuriated when they told me Coe had said she thought I would have "a safe desk job in the Army." (In fairness to Aunt Coe, she had many talents in addition to annoying people. She was a leader in many civic organizations; she gave speeches, and she took creative writing courses up to her death at age 91.) My last memory of her was in Topeka in the early 1950s. She was seated in a chair next to a pillar in the crowded lobby of the Jayhawk Hotel on Kansas Day, January 29. She could see Dolores and me nearby but could not get our attention because of the noise, so she reached out with her cane and swatted Dolores across the seat.

Early in 1944 Clifford started riding the bus from Brandywine Street to Capitol Hill and back every day without making a great production of it or even mentioning the subject to anyone except family members and his office force. Although as a member of Congress he could have obtained a C-Card (for practically an unlimited amount of gasoline), he felt it his duty to conserve gasoline and tires just as the average citizen had to do. His customary driving route took about half an hour — down Connecticut Avenue to Cathedral Avenue, left on Cathedral to the Rock Creek-Potomac Parkway, then on Virginia Avenue to Constitution Avenue and on east. The bus route was much slower: down Connecticut through downtown to 13th and

Pennsylvania, then transferring to a street car (I think) to the Hill. This route took an hour or more each way. Clifford learned to stand up on the bus and read his newspaper folded into quarter sections, right along with more-seasoned bus riders.

He also raised a victory vegetable garden as the government urged many citizens to do. I had written home about piles of manure in front of farm houses in France, Belgium, and Germany, and Clifford responded that he had two manure piles, but they were in the back yard instead of the front.

I was most appreciative of all his handwritten letters, most written late at night or on Sundays. In them he responded patiently and wisely to my constant complaints. My letters were more than just complaining; they were "bitching," a term common in the Army at that time. He gave a kind of tacit acknowledgement of my diatribes on all that was wrong with everything without disagreeing with me. Instead, he told me not to get too discouraged. He reminded me that when he was my age he was having a tough time making his way through school on "nothing a year," taking any kind of job he could get. "I didn't like it particularly," he wrote, "but it didn't hurt me a bit."

Sometimes he commented on interesting dinners or receptions he had attended. For instance, in the spring of 1944 he reported on Congressional Night at the National Press Club:

> The program was furnished by members of Congress from Dear Alben (Alben Barkley, a Senator from Kentucky and later vice president) on down to a freshman or two. Dear Alben got a big ovation. He didn't sing "Wagon Wheels" which is supposed to be his specialty, but played it on a mouth organ. Some of the audience yelled for him to sing Wagon Wheels but the master of ceremonies said he didn't have to because he wasn't in the rut any longer. They had a quartet of house members. Two or three others gave readings or sang. Senator Truman played the piano and Senator Walsh of New Jersey played the violin, something which he does very well. When the meeting started the master of ceremonies announced that they were going to pick out some of the best acts and send them out over the world to the camps of WACs and the WAVEs to entertain them like the girl movie stars were on tour entertaining the sol-

diers. However, I guess none of them were good enough because Jimmie Byrnes, who was the chairman of the judges committee, didn't announce that any had been selected when he made his report.

While campaigning for his reelection back in Kansas, Clifford took time to write a long letter on the last Sunday in October. He gently prodded me to write my mother as often as I could "even if you haven't anything to say except that you're all right." She and my sister were alone in Washington. From the war news, he assumed our front was getting ready for a big push soon and hoped we could "finish the job before winter." He said it looked as if the Jap fleet was nearly taken care of, "so that ought to hurry things along in that quarter." Many people asked him about me as he went around the district, and he said he was proud to tell them I was in Belgium. Many of his constituents told him where their boys were in the war. From some came the sad news that their boys had been killed. He said he appreciated learning from me about the goodwill toward Americans, and he agreed it had to be preserved.

The second day after the Battle of the Bulge began, Battery B of the 285th Field Artillery Observation Battalion was on its way to join our battalion when it was intercepted and slaughtered by Kampfgruppe Peiper, a unit of the dreaded 1st SS Panzer Division. At least 86 GIs were killed. This was the infamous Malmedy Massacre. It was a traumatic experience for my father. After V-E Day he wrote me:

> I didn't worry a lot at any time except during the Ardennes battle. . . . I figured you were able to take care of yourself pretty well and would pull through O.K. But it wasn't that way during the Ardennes battle. No one, not even Mother, has any idea of the agony I went through at that time.

He was in Chicago at hearings held by the Colmer Committee, he explained. Finishing up, he started back to his hotel. Newsboys on the street were crying out, "Nazis murder U.S. captives." He bought a paper and was first horrified, then stunned. He wrote:

> When I read it was an observation battalion, everything just about went black in front of me, because I felt sure you must be

somewhere in the neighborhood, and I knew there couldn't be a lot of observation battalions in that small area.

It was not until two days later, when he had returned to Washington, that he was able to verify that my outfit was not the observation battalion which had been massacred. Fortunately, Pauline, at home in Washington and terribly worried about the Battle of the Bulge, had not seen the massacre story and did not learn of it until he was able to give her the details.

During my spare time in Europe, I wrote and rewrote "peace plans" for a United Nations organization and sent them to Clifford, who read them carefully and responded. However, with his usual practical mind, he cautioned me not to do too much serious reading and thinking about peace plans until the fighting was over. "No use in going around with your head in the clouds thinking about peace plans and then stepping on a German mine," he wrote.

A letter from him in June 1945 told of his admiration for General Eisenhower. This was occasioned by the General's return to the United States and receptions for him in Washington, New York, Kansas City, and in his hometown, Abilene, Kansas. Clifford wrote about Ike's homecoming celebrations:

> I don't believe there has ever been anything quite like them. The people came out in the main to acclaim Eisenhower the general but they left acclaiming Eisenhower the man. He was so natural and modest about it all that he won everyone's heart. For all of his modesty, he wasn't the least bit embarrassed but took it all in his stride. His speeches in every case were statesmanlike and constructive. It is easy to see how he was able to wield the allied army into the great fighting force it was and to handle all the political and personal rivalries in such an effective way. He would be a great diplomat or rather is a great diplomat and statesman. Raymond Moley has suggested him for Secretary of State. He could have any office he wants. The Republicans would nominate him for President. But he doesn't want any office. Makes all of us Kansans proud to be from the same state.

Clifford's observation that Eisenhower "doesn't want my office," turned out not to be the case, but it appeared so at the time and probably was. In the following years Clifford became one of the earliest and most earnest backers of an Ike for President boom.

Of all the committees, commissions, and councils Hope served on during his 30 years in Congress, his membership and active participation in the work of the Special House Committee on Postwar Economic Policy and Planning (the Colmer Committee) had the most profound effect on his thinking and worldview. In 1982 Karen Hunt Exon, then a graduate student in history at the University of Kansas, completed her master's thesis (unpublished), "A House Committee Looks at U.S. Foreign Policy; The Colmer Committee's European Tour of 1945." This excellent, readable study covers the work of the committee from its creation in 1944 through its final report in December 1946. Additional source material includes Hope's diary, which covers only the first two weeks of the committee's trip to Europe, his detailed letters to Pauline and Martha, and his newspaper columns of 1958 and 1964-1965 in which he commented on the highlight of the trip, a 45-minute conference with Josef Stalin in the Kremlin.

Perhaps the best sources of the tour, for me, are my diary and memories. By sheer luck and coincidence, I was able to accompany the committee from London to Berlin and am, in this instance, in the enviable position of being able to say, "I was there."

The purpose of the Colmer trip was to study political and economic conditions in Europe and the Middle East at the end of World War II and to make recommendations for the future. Although the committee was in existence for three years, its major recommendations came from the tour. Government leaders and U.S. diplomats were visited in Great Britain, France, Luxembourg, Belgium, Norway, Sweden, Germany (Generals Eisenhower and Lucius Clay), the Soviet Union, Iran, Egypt, Greece, and Italy.

The tour began on VJ Day, August 14, and ended October 9. The 7 of the 18 committee members who made the trip were Chairman William Colmer of Mississippi, Orville Zimmerman of Missouri, Jessie Wolcott of Michigan, Charles Wolverton of New Jersey, Jay LeFevre of New York, Sid Simpson of Illinois, and Hope. Quite by accident, all were Republican except Colmer and Zimmerman. Other members of the touring party were Marion B. Folsom, director of the committee staff and treasurer of Eastman Kodak (Folsom later became Secretary of Health, Education and Welfare in Eisenhower's cabinet); W. Y. Elliott, Harvard professor and

The Colmer Committee, 1944-1945, at the Chrysler Tank Arsenal (Clifford Hope, center). Finney County Historical Society, Garden City, KS

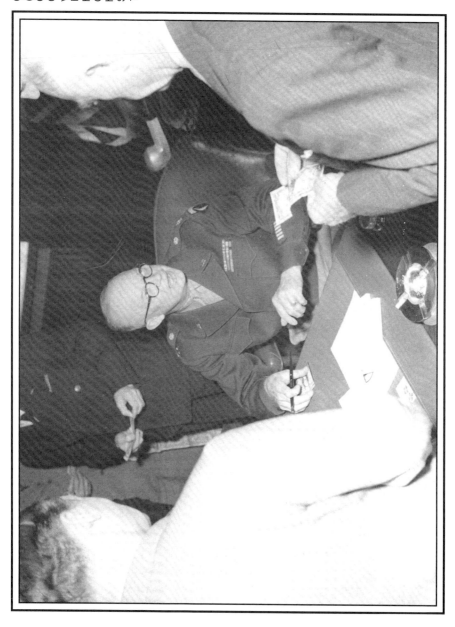

Clifford Hope (left) and the Colmer Committee visit General Eisenhower at his Frankfurt, Germany, headquarters, September 1945.

former vice-chairman of the War Production Board, consultant; James J. Farriss, the State Department representative; and Major Walter Mosmiller, military escort officer. (Committee members promptly dubbed the officer "Mossback.")

One day early in August my first sergeant, a guy I badmouthed regularly, overheard me saying I had a cousin in England and granted me a seven-day furlough to see him. My father was hoping to see me when the committee reached Germany but knew nothing of my furlough. My cousin, Wilmot Ragsdale — a correspondent for *Time* magazine, and I were able to meet the committee when it arrived at London's Waterloo Station. My father was flabbergasted.

Photographers of the *Chronicle* and *The Daily Sketch* had us do a repeat of our meeting. We checked into the Savoy Hotel and had a Scotch before a magnificent dinner. I wrote in my diary that it seemed almost criminal to be living this way after what I'd just left behind.

Three days after we got together, Clifford wrote to Pauline:

> Was I surprised when I stepped off the train here in London and found Clifford waiting for me. It was a mighty happy reunion and we've had a fine time since. He's right up here in the Hotel with me sleeping in my pajamas and on a soft bed once more. He seems to be able to accustom himself to it all right.

His next letter to Pauline was a classic, a perfect example of his blunt honesty. It contained a line that I have quoted many times. What he wrote could have been at once both comforting and worrisome to my mother. "I don't think you need to worry about the war changing him," he said of me. "I can't see that he's changed a bit for better or worse. I think he could come home right now and within two or three days you'd forget he'd ever been away." To that, he added, "We're having a fine time together and have had quite a little chance to talk things over about school and other things."

Next to the visit with Stalin, probably the most impressive conference was the one with General Eisenhower at his Frankfurt headquarters. Certainly it was for me, because I was not invited to most of the conferences. There Ike was, surrounded by a group of seasoned, professional politicians, and completely in command. By contrast, my diary told of my discomfiture in committing a great faux pas of military etiquette: I had remained seated while a lieutenant colonel and a major were standing at parade rest. I wrote:

> No one, least of all General Ike, gave any evidence of notic-
> ing me at all. A French lieutenant whom we called "Louie" was
> attached to the committee at the time. He was said to be the old-
> est lieutenant in the French army. He let it be known he had led
> a dashing, exciting life. Perhaps that's why he looked so old. At
> any rate, he, too, sat in Ike's presence but with total aplomb.

Concerning the visit, Congressman Hope wrote Pauline: "The Eisenhower conference was one of the high spots of the trip. I don't know of
anyone who has the ability to size up and outline a complex situation in a
direct and simple way as well as Eisenhower."

The committee met its first difficulty with the Russians when its plane
flew from Stockholm to Berlin. The Soviets refused to allow a direct flight
from Stockholm over Russian-occupied Germany. Instead, the plane was
forced to take a circuitous route back to Western Germany, then into
Berlin on the officially established air corridor.

My father had written a number of detailed, descriptive letters to
Pauline and Martha. His September 10 letter from Berlin was one of the
best. It read, in part:

> This place is certainly a contrast to Stockholm. I don't know
> that it is bombed any worse than some of the other places we
> have visited but of course the bombed area is much larger.
> There are miles and miles in the center of the city where prac-
> tically every building is destroyed although in many cases the
> walls or parts of them are still standing. There are supposed to
> be three million people here now but where they all live is a
> mystery. . . . The people look bad, much worse than in Frank-
> furt or anywhere in the American Zone. Of course part of that
> is because Berlin was in a state of siege for several months
> before it was finally captured and food was scarce before that
> time. The children especially look as if they were suffering
> from malnutrition. There's not much to look forward to this
> winter, because there will be no coal and far less than sufficient
> supplies of food. In a large part of the area it looks like a dead

The Colmer Committee left Berlin for Moscow, September 11, 1945, aboard General Dwight D. Eisenhower's plane, *Sunflower II.*

city especially in the Russian zone. . . . Water is now available in most parts of the city but lights are still off in most places. Street cars are running and the subway is open in some areas. The city still smells of dead bodies on a warm day and I suppose they will be digging bones out of the rubble for years to come. Misery and destruction are everywhere but if someone throws away a cigarette butt there are half a dozen people ready to pounce on it.

After a Sunday morning appointment with General Lucius Clay, the U.S. commander, the committee members visited the ruins of the Reichschancellery and I went along. That's when I learned congressmen were as good as, if not better than, GIs at souvenir collecting and looting. Each of them got a large splinter from Hitler's desk. (I did, too.) We had no positive proof that it was Hitler's very own desk, but we all convinced ourselves it was as we ripped it apart. I learned later that Hitler's desk was marble topped. Chairman Colmer also picked up a large metal hoop which apparently had been around a globe, and Sid Simpson latched onto part of a large light fixture.

The committee flew to Moscow on September 11, 1945. Hope described this visit in newspaper columns he wrote in 1964. His manuscript said:

> [The] week in Moscow was in many ways the high point of this trip. At the time we were there, the iron curtain was slowly coming down and we were the last official group of Americans to enter Russia for many years except diplomatic and military personnel and a few members of the press.

(Senator Claude Pepper visited Moscow on his own initiative at the same time.)

Recalling that the flight from Berlin to Moscow was aboard General Eisenhower's plane (the *Sunflower II*), Hope explained that they "were able to make the trip in such style because the plane was going to Moscow to take Ambassador Averell Harriman to London to attend a conference."

The climax of the committee's Moscow visit was a conference with Stalin and another meeting with Anastas Mikoyan, the minister of commerce and trade. There were also conferences with staff members of various government agencies dealing with economic and trade matters. Committee members soon discovered, however, that the duties of these operatives were mostly of a planning nature rather than decision making. Hope remembered:

> The representative of the Intourist Bureau assigned to our group was a Russian graduate of the Colorado School of Mines and had spent several years in the United States. He brought back with him a taste for American cigars; some of the cigar-smoking members of the committee kept him well supplied.

The committee's two Intourist guides were "charming and intelligent young women," Hope said. He continued:

> Both had been married — the husband of one was still in the army. The husband of the other had been in the army, but she had not heard from or of him for two or three years. Presumably, he had been killed or taken prisoner. When we expressed our surprise that she had not been informed of what had happened to him, she seemed even more surprised that we should raise such a question. She said families were never advised of the death or injury of a person in the service. They either came back or they didn't and that's all there was to it.
>
> Although the war has been over almost six months, there had evidently been little demobilization. About two-thirds of the employees in the industrial plants we visited were women. On the collective farm to which we were taken, there were only two men, both of whom appeared to be over seventy.

Hope remembered that the meeting with Stalin had begun at 9 p.m. and that George F. Kennan, Minister-Counsellor at the U.S. Embassy, had accompanied them to the Kremlin and served as interpreter. Hope wrote:

> When we arrived at the gates of the Kremlin, they were opened by heavily-armed guards and we were checked into the great walled enclosure. A guide took us to the building where Stalin had his office and escorted us through a number of labyrinthian corridors to the place of meeting. This was a fairly

large room in which the only furnishings were a table and chairs. In a few moments Stalin arrived, accompanied by an interpreter, and wearing the uniform of a marshal of the Soviet Army. I was surprised by his height, or rather the lack of it. His build was stocky, but he appeared to be no more than five feet four or five inches tall. His heavy shock of dark hair was turning gray. He was dark and swarthy — a reminder that he was not a Russian, but a Georgian.

We talked of many things and learned a great deal about the economic and physical condition of Russia at the war's end. It was not good, of course. In particular, its transportation system was pretty well shot, a very serious matter in a country as large as Russia. However, the total damage and devastation compared with its size and resources was nothing like as bad as that of Germany and Japan, or Poland and some of the Balkan countries.

The most important part of our discussion was on two points — one was the matter of a six billion dollar loan from this country to Russia, the other was what was happening in the countries of eastern Europe. The two questions were interrelated.

I don't know how seriously the Russian loan was ever considered by this country or Russia. However, there was a great deal of talk about it in the latter days of the war and for a while after it ended. This, of course, was while Russia was an ally and before we had fully learned how difficult it was to deal with her.

Our discussion with Stalin on the loan matter was mainly on what they would do with it and how it would be repaid. On the latter point, Stalin mentioned a number of articles which they were in a position to export including gold, manganese, chrome, lumber, wood pulp and furs. None of these articles were in short supply in this country.

The matter of Russian control over what later became the satellite countries was discussed at some length. It was already evident that Russia was moving to take over these countries in spite of the Yalta and Potsdam agreements. Stalin tacitly admitted that this was the case, but contended it was a partnership deal to build up the economy of these small countries, and on a temporary basis. But camouflage it as he would, it still looked like a case of the lion and lamb lying down together with the lamb inside the lion.

In its report, our committee recommended against the loan and called attention to what was happening in eastern Europe. However, I think the principal reason there was nothing further done about it was that Stalin realized that we would never make a loan nor would he get any other help from the West unless he gave up taking over eastern Europe. He was unwilling to do this. The alternative was to go behind the iron curtain and cut off relations with the West. This was the course he chose.

Although the committee met with President Truman on October 18, its recommendations were lost in the shuffle, in large part due to the advent of the Cold War. Ambassador Harriman, George Kennan, and others were giving the same advice at the time.

As for Hope, he was home scarcely a week in October before leaving to attend the first meeting of the new United Nations Food and Agricultural Organization (FAO) in Quebec. He had been appointed as a member of the U.S. delegation and thought it important that he attend to help get the FAO off to a good start. His letters to Pauline indicate he thoroughly enjoyed the many dinners and social events at the conference. While acknowledging the importance of his meetings and travels, she felt his long absences contributed to the state of her health. Near the end of one letter, he wrote to her:

> Hope you're feeling better again. You've got to stay with the doctor this time long enough for him to do you some good or find out that he can't and if he can't we're going to keep going to doctors till we get at the bottom of things.

Unfortunately, her worries and afflictions never improved for any sustained period. She and Clifford just learned to live with them for the rest of her life.

Chapter 9

Committee Chairman —
and the Cold War
(1946-1951)

C ONCERNS ABOUT THE developing Cold War, continuing wartime food production to feed the hungry of Europe
and Asia, labor disputes, and his aversion to self-seeking
publicity were concerns of Hope in the early postwar
years. All were alluded to often in his correspondence.

In response to a letter in January from Millard E. Hobson of
Kingman concerning the General Motors strike, he wrote:

Before going on to the strike, I want to refer briefly
to your statement that I should do something to make
headlines in the newspapers in connection with the
current labor dispute. Now, of course, that would be a
very easy thing to do. I could make some crazy statement and the crazier it was the bigger the headlines it
would get. However, I have never followed the policy of
trying to make headlines because after a great deal of
experience here in Washington, I know that that just

doesn't get anywhere. All the headlines that [Walter] Reuther and [Charles] Wilson have contributed to the strike situation in the last six weeks haven't done anything toward settling the strike. In fact, they have made it more difficult to settle. I just don't think we get anywhere that way.

(Reuther was head of the United Auto Workers and Wilson was president of General Motors.) As his experience in public office increased, so, too, did Hope's modesty and his disenchantment with headline hunting.

The most important agricultural legislation passed by Congress in 1946 was, in Hope's opinion, the Research and Marketing Act. He, with Democrats John Flannagan of Virginia and Stephen Pace of Georgia, were its most enthusiastic supporters. At the time, he believed marketing research held out the possibility of reducing or even eliminating government price supports. In a summary of legislation requested of him by the commentator George Rothwell Brown, Hope observed that in providing for research in agriculture marketing, the bill entered a new field. Acknowledging that research in production had accomplished wonders, he noted that practically no research had been attempted in the equally important realm of marketing and distribution. He asserted:

> In my opinion, much can be done. If this legislation succeeds
> . . . one of the most important pieces of legislation ever enacted
> on behalf of American agriculture will have been achieved.

The school lunch program, already in operation through congressional appropriations, was specifically authorized by legislation in 1946. It was one of Hope's pet projects, earning for him the title "Hot Lunch Cliff" from the same Kansas editor who had called Senator Capper "Old Zero."

The proposed loan to Great Britain, however, was the issue to which Hope directed more time and study "than any other question in the last twenty years," he said at the time. The proposal was for a loan of $3,750,000 to be repaid over a 50-year period at two percent interest. The loan would be advantageous for the people of the 5th District as well as the nation, he reasoned, because Britain was the United States' best customer for agricultural exports. In February he wrote to C. C. Isely expressing his belief that 95 percent of the people in Kansas were opposed to the loan, adding "but they don't know anything about the basic issue."

("95 percent" was probably an exaggeration, but undoubtedly a substantial number of Kansans were against it.)

He stated his views in no uncertain terms in letters to G. C. Robe of Ottawa on July 8 and P. S. McMullen of Norwich on July 18, warning that if the British Empire were allowed "to go down or become greatly weakened," the only other strong nation in the world would be Russia. He said he foresaw a struggle for supremacy between totalitarian and free governments in the next few years. It would not necessarily mean war, he said, but it did call for being prepared in every possible way to meet the issue. He pointed out that the British Empire and its constituent countries — Canada, Australia, and South Africa — were the nations nearest our own in political thinking and beliefs. Hope wrote Robe:

> We have managed to get into two wars in the last thirty years by foolishly sitting on the sidelines and not trying to do anything to prevent them from happening. I should think that would be lesson enough for us. From now on it should be our duty to prevent the catastrophe of a third world war, which may mean the destruction of civilization.

Hope said he was "shocked and surprised" at advertisements against the loan in *The Wichita Beacon*. "Every word of them is untrue," he charged. "I have never seen a more striking example of falsification in my life."

It would have been easier, he wrote the Kansans back home, to explain a vote against the loan "because such a vote yields itself to so many forms of demagoguery." Having written this, he was on a soapbox roll.

> It gives anyone who likes that sport an opportunity to twist the British lion's tail. It gives everyone who wants to pretend to be a great friend of the veteran a chance to say that we shouldn't loan the money to Britain but should give it to veterans. It gives everyone who wants to demagogue by claiming to be a great friend of the old people a chance to say we ought to give the money to old people. It gives everyone who wants to wave the flag and fight the Revolutionary War all over again a chance to do so.

Realizing all this, Hope admitted he was tempted to vote against the

loan. But considering the best interests of this country and the world —
interests he thought were the same — he could not do it. Nine-tenths of
the arguments in the House of Representatives against the loan were not
really against the loan but against the British, he wrote, adding, "I have no
particular love for the British, but that isn't the question involved in this
case."

Worthy of note in the long hearings held in the House and the Senate
was the lack of opposition to the loan. Support for it came from the United
States Chamber of Commerce, an organization composed of organizations
that are the heaviest taxpayers in the country, Hope said. "If the loan goes
bad or if it is not a good thing for this country, then they are the ones who
will have to pay the larger part of the bill." Among many other supporters
he named the American Farm Bureau Federation, the Farmers Union, the
CIO, and the American Federation of Labor on behalf of agricultural interests and laboring people. The Federal Council of Churches of Christ supported the loan. "They feel it is a step toward world peace which is the
objective and goal of all Christian churches," Hope wrote.

He ended his long letters to Robe and McMullen saying he was "sorry
indeed" that they were not in agreement with him on the loan, but he
respected their sincerity in opposing it and asked that they give him equal
credit for being sincere in his support of it.

The November 1946 elections brought control of Congress back to the
Republicans for the first time since 1930. Voters were upset over strikes,
price controls, and many other matters, so they took out their dissatisfaction on the Democrats. Frank Carlson was elected governor of Kansas, ful-
filling a longtime ambition, and a solid GOP delegation was sent to Congress by Kansas voters. Carlson was succeeded in the 6th District by Wint
Smith, a Mankato lawyer who was a staunch conservative and a veteran of
both World Wars. He became a strong supporter of Hope, following
Hope's lead in farm legislation. He reasoned that since we were continuing New Deal benefits for everyone else, the farmer should not be left
out. Herbert "Hub" Meyer, newspaper publisher from Independence, succeeded Tom Winter (who died in office in October) in the 3rd District.
Hope easily defeated A. L. Sparks, a young man running on a New Deal
platform, 54,478 to 32,538.

Upon the death of U. S. Guyer in 1943, Hope had become dean of the
Kansas House delegation. He now became chairman of the Committee on
Agriculture for the first time. George Reid moved into the post of clerk of

the committee and Clarence Everett, a Hutchinson businessman and a loyal supporter of Hope since the 1926 campaign, took Reid's place as Hope's administrative assistant. Congressman Stephen Pace wrote to Hope after the election:

> I am sure you know that I take no special delight in the defeat of the Democrats, but I want you to know that it does give me a great deal of satisfaction to know that in the change we have you as Chairman of the House Committee on Agriculture.

In replying to Pace, Hope told his Democratic colleague he had never known the committee to be partisan and certainly didn't want it to be that way in the next two years. He said there was no one on Pace's "side of the committee" that he could not work with wholeheartedly.

As committee chairman, Hope was entitled to more spacious office quarters adjacent to the Agriculture Committee's hearing room. He moved to 1309-10 in the Longworth Building and immediately planned a series of committee hearings around the country to receive input from farm organizations and farmers to assist in developing a postwar farm program. The wartime price supports were scheduled to expire at the end of 1948. Doris Fleeson, a national newspaper columnist and a native Kansan, described Hope's plans in a February column:

> Hope is using the present breathing space to lay plans for what must follow when the depression and war-bred support of farm prices shall expire. He will start hearings in April, after the first crush of legislation is over, at which he will develop the whole picture of U.S. agriculture in the post-war era. His ambition is to shape legislation that will prevent another of those farm depressions with its inevitable train of freak remedies and crackpots.
>
> As his technique shows, the quiet Kansan has come far from the lurid populism of his native state. But he puts this somewhat socialistic tenet at the basis of his efforts. The American people have accepted the principle that farm prices must not fall below the level of a living for the farmer in the same way that they have accepted social security for the worker.
>
> Hope asserts he will go into his hearings this spring uncom-

mitted to any program or panacea but intent only on discovering how the job can be done. He estimates that legislation can be shaped during the summer recess, considered for early next year, before the specter of the national conventions and presidential politics can haunt it. He says he expects help from members of both parties and has no doubt the legislative battle will cut across party lines.

The hearings were held in eight states during the congressional recess and were attended by more than 500 farmers from 40 states. Meanwhile, Kansas had produced a bumper wheat crop. Hope wrote his friend Don L. Berry in early June 1947 that farmers were busy figuring out how "to get the big wheat crop harvested and what to do with the money."

A continuing issue during the late 1940s was the question of whether universal military training (UMT) should be adopted to replace the selective service system or to substitute for a large professional army. (The Korean War began in June 1950, and the draft, with its many exemptions, continued through the Vietnam War.) In his correspondence, Hope indicated his belief that UMT should be adopted only as a last resort; he favored UMT over a large, permanent peacetime army.

In December 1947 Hope openly expressed his thoughts in a long letter to Reverend DeWitt L. Miller of McPherson. He began by saying he had not reached a clear-cut decision on the question of universal military training but was exploring the question from every angle. "There are a good many untenable arguments advanced on both sides of this controversy and a lot of the argument is more productive of heat than it is of light," he wrote. He gave both sides credit for being sincere and earnest, saying he hoped the discussion could be kept on a high plane.

One thing that irked Hope about UMT's opponents was that many ministers of the gospel seemed to be "setting themselves up as military experts and taking the position that they know just exactly how the next war is going to be fought." By implication at least, these ministers intimated "they know a lot more about the matter than men who have made military science their life work." This was as ridiculous as for military men to pretend to be spiritual advisors. Hope pushed his point, saying,

When I am sick, I go to a doctor. When I am in legal trouble,
I go to a lawyer. When the plumbing gets out of order, I go to a

plumber. In other words, I go to a man who has made a study
of the subject in question.

In his letter to Hope, Miller had written, "If we cannot make friends,
create understanding and learn to cooperate with all men, even those who
are different from us, we are done and the sooner we learn that the better."

That struck a nerve with the congressman. Citing that passage from the
preacher, Hope wrote:

> If you don't pay attention to anything else I have said, I do
> hope you will give me your answer to this question: What
> changes of national policy would you suggest in order to bring
> about understanding and cooperation between this country and
> Russia? You are offering that method as a substitute for military
> strength. What steps would you take to accomplish it and what
> assurances can you give that we can get along with Russia on
> that basis?

That was the whole question as he could see it, Hope wrote: "If we are
going to do anything along that line the time is now, not five or ten years
from now, because then it will be too late." Hope said he was giving the
matter a lot of thought but frankly had not yet come up with an answer that
he could put forward as being a safe policy for the country to follow.

A month later a letter came from a citizen in Anthony, Kansas, who
complained about everything under the sun and announced his intent to
vote against everyone in office. In answer, Hope fired back a letter that
began:

> Let me set you right in the first place by telling you that it is
> perfectly all right if you vote against me in the next election. I
> don't want anyone to vote for me except intelligent voters and
> certainly your idea of voting against everyone who is in office
> — no matter what they stand for or what their politics may
> be — is about the dumbest thing I ever heard of. So please don't
> change your mind and vote for me.

With that off his chest, Congressman Hope addressed some of the

Clifford Hope looks on as President Harry S. Truman signs legislation.

man's specific complaints and closed his letter with a cheery "Hoping that this finds you in a better humor, I am . . ."

This response was similar to those Hope always gave to constituents who threatened not to vote for him. It must have been disconcerting to those who made the threats.

A classic example of Hope's straight talk surfaces in his reply to a letter from Idella Henkle of Wichita. In April 1948 she wrote him:

> I beg of you in behalf of America's freedom, that you vote against President Truman's civil rights program. I am not against the colored man, but God Himself pronounced a curse upon Ham and his descendants, they were to be servants all the days of their life. I beg of you, in the name of Jesus Christ My Lord, that you vote against this bill. God will not hold you guiltless if you go against his will in this matter.

Hope answered:

> Until I received your letter I thought I had seen and heard about everything in the course of my twenty years in Congress. Your letter, however, takes the cake.
>
> There may be some good arguments against some phases of the present Civil Rights Program and I expect to consider any such legitimate suggestions.
>
> For one to urge as you do, however, that it should be opposed in the name of Jesus Christ is the most blasphemous thing I have read for a long time. I suggest that you hold a session of prayer with yourself or go to your Minister and try to find out something of the principles of the Christian religion.
>
> I am proud of the State of Kansas and I really didn't suppose there was anyone in the State who would go back so far to the dark ages as you do.

Not all issues faced by Congress in 1948 were as weighty as civil rights or the containment of communism. It is difficult today to explain to anyone under 60 the furor in Congress during the 1948-1950 period over repeal of the ten-cent-per-pound federal excise tax on colored oleomargarine. This was part of a larger battle between oleo manufacturers and dairy interests. Hope, as chairman of the Committee on Agriculture, was caught in the middle. He tried to be fair, but he was definitely prejudiced in favor of dairy farmers. As he wrote one Kansas soybean farmer, A. G. Thomson of Hiawatha, in April 1948:

> I am certainly not fanatical on the subject but there are certain things to be said for the dairy industry and for any type of animal agriculture that can't be said for any other type of farming. I am speaking particularly from the standpoint of conserving the soil and its fertility which I think is the biggest problem which faces agriculture today.

In March, after the committee voted to table all pending bills to repeal the tax, Hope appointed a subcommittee to study the matter. He pointed out that 23 states, containing two-thirds of the U.S. population, had laws prohibiting the manufacture and sale of colored oleo; hence federal repeal of the tax would have no effect on the laws of those states. Meanwhile, the oleo interests succeeded in getting the bill out of the committee by way of the discharge petition procedure. (House rules provided if 218 or more members signed such a petition, the bill was "discharged" from the committee and could be considered on the House floor.) In late April the vote to discharge was 235-121, and the bill passed the House by more than two to one, 260-106. It bogged down in the Senate, however, and repeal of the tax was delayed until 1950, prolonging the controversy.

Lester McCoy, still a political power in Hope's home district, advised Hope in a letter in May 1948 that his position on the oleo tax was not well understood throughout the district. He wrote:

> Most people who have mentioned the tax to me cannot understand why you support the idea of a tax on oleo; we are not a dairy district of any consequence. I do not find any organized support on either side of the picture, have not had anyone suggest to me they thought we should continue the tax, however, in view of the fact that oleo is made from American products.

Hope responded by informing McCoy that the Senate was likely to pass the bill, and as he saw it, the whole issue then would be quickly forgotten.

"By that time, the housewives will find out they aren't getting their oleo a bit cheaper than they were before, and will wonder why all the fuss about the matter."

Hope went on to defend his stand and to outline "sound reasons" for restricting the sale of "oleo colored in imitation of butter." Otherwise, he asked, why would the law have been on the books for more than 60 years, or why would practically every state have laws regulating the manufacture and sale of oleo, or why would 23 states prohibit its manufacture and sale? "In a state like New York," he argued, "the consumers outnumber the dairy men by at least fifty to one, so it's hardly possible to say the wicked dairy men are responsible for it."

Furthermore, Hope pointed out, Canada and New Zealand "up to this very day" prohibited oleomargarine, colored and uncolored, and France only recently refused to permit oleomargarine to be colored. "There is scarcely a country in the civilized world which does not regulate the man-ufacture and sale of oleomargarine in some way." He reminded McCoy that during the war Russia insisted butter be sent on lend-lease shipments.

"The present legislation is being pushed through Congress by perhaps the slickest propaganda campaign that has ever been conducted in this country," Hope wrote. He was not one who had been "overly excited" about this particular issue, but, he said, "the question has caused more dis-sension and hard feelings in Congress than any which has come up since I have been a member."

His whole effort, he told McCoy, was to prevent the question from "absolutely wrecking the Committee on Agriculture." He thought it was of paramount importance that representatives from agricultural regions of the country stand together. His opposition to repealing the oleo tax, he con-tended, helped hold the committee together, but the degree of harmony was not what it had been before the oleo question came up. "In short," Hope wrote McCoy, "I think the agricultural interests of our part of the country have been served by my taking the position I did."

Years later Albert M. Cole, representing the 1st (Northeast Kansas) Dis-trict, recalled the "colored oleo" times:

> He [Hope] understood the levers of powers in the House, and the importance of maintaining a working relationship with those who disagreed with him. He spoke to me about how important the margarine bill was to farm housewives, and there-

fore very important to him. They churned and sold butter to provide them with "a little money of their own." I responded that
the city housewives found it onerous to kneed each pound of
margarine to make it palatable for the family, and that I supported the bill. "Well," said Cliff, "you vote your conscience
and I'll vote mine. We will meet many times in the future in
concord."

Of far more importance than oleo legislation, especially in regard to the
1948 presidential election outcome, was the last-minute, patched together,
price support act passed on June 19, 1948, in the closing days of the 80th
Congress. The legislation, which became known as the Hope-Aiken Act,
was a combination of the temporary act passed by the House to extend 90
percent price supports on basic commodities for another year and the
"long-range" Senate bill devised by the Senate Agriculture committee
under the leadership of Senator George Aiken of Vermont. Despite the
extensive hearings Hope conducted, no consensus of a long-range program emerged in the House, and he thought it best to wait another year
when, he anticipated, there would be another Republican Congress and a
Republican President.

The Farm Bureau, led by its new president, Allan Kline of Iowa, strongly supported Aiken's "flexible" price support program, with supports
ranging from 60 to 90 percent of parity with an average of 75 percent. The
bill was also supported by outgoing Secretary of Agriculture Clinton
Anderson. The Senate bill revised the parity formula for wheat downward
from $2.20 per bushel for full parity to $1.79 per bushel. So the bill that
came out of the conference committee provided for 90 percent of parity
for an additional year (the 1949 crop) with the flexible provision to take
effect thereafter. Few members of Congress were happy about the final
bill, which was rushed through Congress just prior to the opening of the
Republican National Convention in Philadelphia.

Much has been written and many analyses made about the Republicans
snatching defeat from the jaws of victory in the 1948 presidential election.
Loss of Midwestern farm states by Dewey to Truman was a major factor
in the defeat. In Hope's mind, the overall cause was the overconfidence of
the GOP presidential candidate, Thomas E. Dewey. As Hope's friend, Don
L. Berry, observed the next year: "There is nothing so uncertain as a dead
sure thing."

Kansas historians James F. Forsythe and Virgil W. Dean have written excellent papers on the election. Forsythe's is titled "Postmortem on the Election of 1948: An Evaluation of Cong. Clifford R. Hope's Views."[1] Dean's title is "Farm Policy and Truman's 1948 Campaign."[2]

According to Hope's correspondence and my personal recollections, Hope's part in the campaign began when Dewey called Hope to his farm home near Pawling, New York, for a conference in mid-July. Hope was impressed with Dewey's knowledge of agriculture and its problems. When Hope visited Herbert Brownell, Dewey's campaign manager, in Washington on July 27, he urged establishment of a farm division of the Republican National Committee in Chicago as had been done in previous campaigns. He was careful to assure Brownell that he was not looking for a job and did not have time to be chairman of such a division in any event. Brownell appeared receptive, and Hope left thinking that a farm division would be organized and implemented.

Brownell immediately called Harry Darby, newly elected Republican National Committeeman from Kansas, and Darby wrote the same day to Lester McCoy at his summer home in Green Mountain Falls, Colorado. (McCoy was retired from his Ford dealership in Garden City but was still active in politics.) Darby told McCoy that Brownell had called him about Hope, saying that they had had a nice talk. Cliff had explained that he would help, but he didn't want a title. Darby explained that Brownell was trying to make sure that Cliff was "all right." Darby had assured him that Hope "was perfect with all of us and that to use him in any capacity would be very flattering to us and that we recommended him very highly."

When Hope learned of Brownell's call to Darby, he was upset. "Angered" might be a better word. Here Hope, a member of Congress since 1927, chairman of the House Agriculture Committee, and a Dewey adviser in the 1944 campaign, had to be checked out and approved by a brand new national committeeman. He expressed his feelings in a letter after the election to his friend, John M. Henry of *The Des Moines Register and Tribune*:

> One thing that rather irritated me as far as Brownell was concerned was that after I talked with him about the matter he called up Harry Darby, told him that I had been in to discuss the matter, and then asked Harry if he had any objections to my being used in an advisory capacity. Of course Harry told him

that would be fine but, in view of the fact that my only interest
in the matter was to get something started and that I wasn't
looking for any job or connection or anything of the sort — in
fact, expressly told Brownell so — I didn't feel any too good
about his handling it that way. Since he did, I had some reluctance about taking it up with him any further, particularly in
view of his statement when I was there that he thought it was
the thing to do.

For that reason, I didn't get in touch with him any more about
it. As a matter of fact, I haven't seen or talked with him from
that day to this.

No doubt Brownell was only following his standard procedure for "check-
ing out" campaign advisers, but he picked the wrong man to check out.

A farm division never was set up. Late in the campaign, a Farmers for
Dewey and Warren Committee was formed. Unfortunately, many of its
members were either farm leaders or farm managers for rich clients. It was
not a committee of "dirt farmers." In any event, the committee did little to
help Dewey's faltering campaign.

In early September Hope contacted Representative Hugh Scott, chairman of the GOP National Committee, to suggest that the committee dis-
tribute copies of Hope's *Congressional Record* statement titled, "What the
Eightieth Congress Did for Agriculture." Copies were distributed to all
GOP congressional candidates. Hope also got in touch with Representative Leonard Hall, chairman of the Republican Congressional Committee,
stating he anticipated the Democrats would "go back to the Hoover days"
in going after the farm vote. And that is exactly what happened. At Dex-
ter, Iowa, on September 17, Truman made his famous accusation that the
GOP had "stuck a pitchfork in the farmer's back." Charles Brannan, the
new Secretary of Agriculture, was equally vehement. Even though Truman had signed the Hope-Aiken Act, local Democrats in farm states
claimed the GOP wanted to roll back parity to only 60 percent. Republican responses to the charges were too little and too late.

I remember well the morning after election day, November 2. I had
come home from Washburn Law School in Topeka to vote. Clifford and I
were at his parents' home in Garden City sitting at the breakfast table with
Harry, Mitta, and their daughters, Mary and Mildred. All of us were feeling glum and — except for the sounds made by spoons and cereal — there

was dead silence. Suddenly, Mitta, who had turned 82 the previous day, slammed her spoon on the table and exclaimed loudly, "Truman's elected. The Democrats are back in control of Congress. What in the dickens is happening to this country?" This outburst from the quiet, always de-mure lady broke the spell. We all laughed and decided the world would go on.

Dewey had carried Kansas 423,039 to 351,902, but his majority was less than half his 1944 majority over FDR. Andy Schoeppel, former gov-ernor, defeated George McGill for the U.S. Senate seat vacated by Arthur Capper, and all six GOP congressmen were reelected. Hope defeated his friend, Henry D. Parkinson, Scott City farmer, by a little less than two to one. Frank Carlson easily won reelection over Randolph Carpenter, former congressman. Legal prohibition of the sale of liquor was repealed by a vote of 422,294 to 358,310. After enabling legislation was passed the next year, sale and possession of liquor in Kansas was lawful for the first time since the 1880s.

In an election postmortem report on November 24, 1948, to his friend, E. H. "Zack" Taylor of Curtis Publishing Company, Hope wrote:

> I have always liked Brannan personally very much and I agree with you that there isn't much substantial difference in our ideas. My only criticism of him is that he takes a pretty intensely political view of agriculture and I am afraid that he will be inclined to make a Democratic political machine out of the farm program setup. I think we'll have to watch that angle pretty closely.

As Hope and others anticipated, the activist Charles Brannan proposed a new farm price support program in the spring of 1949. The proposals, known as the Brannan Plan, were debated and defeated in Congress in 1949 and again in 1950. In essence, the plan would have continued high price supports for storable or "basic" commodities, but for perishable commodities which had not previously been regularly supported, direct subsidy payments from the U.S. Treasury would be made to farmers. The idea was to allow these commodities to find their own, presumably lower, level in the market place and to maintain high farm income with limited restrictions on production. The plan was to make both labor (consumers) and farmers happy. The concept of direct payments to maintain farm income had been floating around for some years and was actually allowed under the Aiken portion of the 1948 law; but under the Brannan Plan, for the first time, they were made mandatory for many commodities.[3]

Hope was convinced the Brannan Plan was, indeed, a political football. He found himself in agreement with the Farm Bureau, Senator Aiken, and conservative Republicans and Democrats. However, he was equally opposed to the Aiken flexible parity part of the Hope-Aiken Act. In one letter he referred to the Brannan Plan as the "Big Labor Plan" and to the Aiken Plan as the "U.S. Chamber of Commerce Plan."

In speeches and letters to constituents, he outlined his opposition, including the following reasons:

(1) The plan was introduced without consultation with farmers, farm groups or congressional committees.

(2) Its chief supporter was organized labor, whose support was solicited by the administration's promise to repeal the Taft-Hartley Act.

(3) Among farm organizations, it was supported only by the Farmers Union.

(4) Annual costs were not known but could range between two and ten billion dollars.

(5) Rigid production controls would be needed to prevent over-production and the resulting large outlays from the U.S. Treasury.

In addition, Hope pointed out that the 86-page bill contained 15 pages of penalties, including fines and jail sentences for failure to keep records. He emphasized this in speeches in a somewhat emotional way, uncharacteristic of his usual low-key, factual presentation. Because of this, Secretary Brannan wrote him a five-page letter of complaint in August 1950, stating that the fines and jail sentence provisions were actually a revision of existing statutes, providing for a reduction in some penalties. Hope responded with an accusatory press statement in which he said he was in "hearty accord" with the secretary's plea for cooperation and fair play since he had always sought to keep legislation out of partisan politics.

I have served under both Republican and Democratic Secretaries of Agriculture, from W. M. Jardine to Clinton P. Anderson. Every one of these men viewed farm questions from the standpoint of the national interest. . . . They worked with Republicans and Democrats, with farm organizations and farmers to reach a solution of the vexing problems of agriculture. That, I am sorry to say, cannot be said for the present Secretary.

Hope went on to say he was eager to cooperate with the Secretary of Agriculture and knew that leaders of farm organizations and members of Congress from both parties felt the same way. He continued:

There cannot be this cooperation unless Secretary Brannan is willing to treat agriculture and agricultural legislation as his predecessors have done — as an economic and not a political problem. Whenever Secretary Brannan is in the frame of mind to consider it from that standpoint, he can count on my hearty cooperation.

The dispute ended in a standoff between Brannan and Hope, but the issue was moot. The plan was already dead.

In place of the Brannan Plan and the Aiken flexible price support act, the existing 90 percent of parity price supports were continued for the remainder of the Truman administration, first under an extension written into the 1949 act and then in response to the Korean War. Hope's reasoning for advocating 90 percent of parity for wheat as opposed to 60-to-90 percent was simple. Both plans involved the same production and marketing controls; but under the 90 percent plan the farmer should receive more for a bushel of wheat, whereas under 60-to-90 percent, he could receive less, and the middleman (millers, bakers, etc.) would absorb the difference, while the price of a loaf of bread to the consumer would remain the same.

During this period Hope grew weary, I am sure, over the continuing battles involving different price support plans. He found much more pleasure and challenge in helping organize the National Association of Wheat Growers, strongly advocating the formation of such a group during the postwar years. In December 1949 a wheat growers conference was held in Denver with Oliver Brown of Liberal, Kansas, as chairman. That group set

a meeting in Kansas City the following April. Marx Koehnke reported on
that gathering in his book *Kernels and Chaff — A History of Wheat Marketing Development*:

> On April 21-22, 1950, 83 men met in the Phillips Hotel,
> Kansas City, Missouri, to adopt a constitution. Thus was
> formed the National Association of Wheat Growers
> (NAWG). . . .
> Among the people who addressed the sessions, Congressman
> Hope made a notable presentation. He pointed out that other
> elements of the wheat industry were organized, and it behooved
> the farmers to follow in their footsteps. He noted that the
> National Grain Trade Council, Millers National Federation, and
> two bakers' groups were already in existence. In addition, the
> American National Livestock Growers Association and the California Fruit Growers had active programs. Other organized
> groups were the Florida Fruit Growers, a Milk Producers Federation, the National Wool Growers Association, the International Baby Chick Association and associations representing
> sugar, hops, raisins and many others. All of these were in addition to the general farm organizations. He urged the formation
> of the NAWG as a commodity group to represent wheat producers.
> Hope pointed out that when the International Wheat Agreement (IWA) was under consideration in 1949, representatives of
> farm organizations, the grain trade and millers, and members of
> Congress were called by the Secretary of Agriculture to testify.
> Other than representatives from Kansas and the Pacific Northwest, no one appeared to represent the two-billion dollar wheat
> industry. He noted that many questions that needed answering
> by wheat-oriented people came before the Congress relating to
> the wheat industry.[4]

Hope said in his speech:

> I do not believe this organization should be what is commonly known as a pressure group. It should be the voice of
> wheat growers of the country. It should be in a position to speak

for them in matters which affect their welfare and the general welfare of the country as it is affected by wheat production and marketing. It will be a voice which . . . can be very helpful in keeping legislative bodies and government agencies informed and advised as to the problems of wheat producers and the relationship between those problems and the economic and social problems of the nation.

Officers elected at the first meeting of the NAWG were Herbert Clutter, Holcomb, Kansas, president; Jens Terjeson, Helix, Oregon, vice president; Herbert Hughes, Imperial, Nebraska, treasurer; and Kenneth Kendrick, Stafford, Texas, secretary. (Clutter was the Herbert Clutter who, with his wife and two children, was murdered in their farm home near Holcomb on November 15, 1959, as related by Truman Capote in his book *In Cold Blood.*)

A recurring complaint by small businessmen during Hope's years in Congress concerned farm cooperatives. Hope summed up his views on the subject in a 1949 letter to E. A. Davidson of Cimarron, telling him he felt this was a time for farmers and small business people to stick together to prevent big business and big labor from "taking over the country." Hope was concerned about the bad feeling which seemed to exist between some small businessmen and cooperatives.

Hope wrote Davidson:

I believe there is a field for both of them and they got along very well until some of the cooperatives grew enough to afford some competition against big business. That is when all the agitation about cooperatives began. The business interests of the district which I represent are those of small businessmen and farmers. Their interests are mutual. . . . All the benefits which come from cooperative organizations are kept at home and are spent in the local community.

Having served as secretary of the Republican Conference of the House since 1933, Hope was elected chairman in 1949. The conference consisted of all GOP House members. The chairmanship was not a position of power comparable to the position of Minority Leader and Assistant Minority Leader, posts then held by Joe Martin of Massachusetts and

Charles Halleck of Indiana. However, it was a position of honor and trust, and his election to it was indicative of the esteem held for him by his colleagues. He maintained the position for the remainder of his service in Congress.

R. L. Miller of Cimarron wrote Hope in late December complaining, "To talk plainly, you are a mighty nice fellow, but too timid a Republican and too afraid of offending Truman or some other Democrat. Every Republican should oppose everything Truman wants. . . ."

Hope's reply was a long one, dishing out a strong lesson on representative government:

> I don't believe that you are any better Republican than I am or that you have any more right to say what Republican policies are than I do. The fact is neither you nor I individually can determine what Republican policies are. The only organization which has the right to do that is the National Convention held every four years. I am enclosing a copy of the latest platform of the Republican Party adopted at Philadelphia in 1948 and I am asking you to kindly point out in what respects I have departed from that platform. You may not agree with it. I may not agree with it but it is Republican Party policy as officially stated by a group of men elected by the Republicans from every congressional district in the country. It is the platform upon which I was elected to Congress. It is the platform upon which every Republican candidate in the country ran and until the 1952 Convention, it will still be the Republican Party Platform. Now of course no party platform can bind your conscience or mine, but I don't think it is in very good taste for me to say that you are not a Republican or for you to say that I am not a Republican unless we can each show that the other is not in accord with the official Republican pronouncements on political questions. We probably have got forty or fifty different kinds of Republicans in this country. That is one reason why the party is in the bad shape it is, and unless these forty or fifty different kinds of Republicans can get together and everybody give and take a little bit, we will continue to be the minority party for the next one hundred years.

> You have a perfect right to believe what you believe but you

don't have the right to say that every Republican has to believe just as you do in order to be a Republican, and it is certainly presumptuous for you to try to read anybody out of the party who does not believe just as you do.

Now with respect to my votes in Congress, I repeat the challenge which I have already made that you show me where the votes I have made are out of harmony with the Republican Party platform. The fact is that many legislative matters which come up in Congress are not political. Many which are political have been endorsed by both political parties in their national conventions. Your idea of a Republican is some fellow who votes "No" on every proposal that comes up in Congress, because the fact is that all of them that come up are going to be Democratic proposals because the Democrats control the committees. I don't know of any Republican in Congress who has voted "No" on every measure that came up and if there was he would certainly do a poor job of earning his money because a robot could do just as well. There is no use sending a man down here and paying him $12,500 a year to do that.

Let me also point out that the Labor Unions and the Democrats do not give credit for voting Democratic no matter what you do. Labor's League for Political Education which is the political arm of the American Federation of Labor has just gotten out a booklet in which they list the votes of the Members of Congress on what they call "Key Bills." On this list there are ten bills. They say that I voted wrong on eight of the ten and voted right on two of them. One of the bills they say I voted right on was the bill to make loans for rural telephones along the same lines as REA loans, and the other is the bill to strengthen anti-trust laws. I am willing to stand pat on both of those votes, even if the A. F. of L. does favor these measures. The votes they say I voted wrong on are two votes on the repeal of the Taft-Hartley bill, one vote to reform the rules of the House, one vote on rent control, one vote on public housing, one on regulation of the distribution of natural gas, one on the minimum wage bill and one on the social security bill. It is true that I voted against the Administration and the American Federation of Labor's position on all eight of these bills and if that makes my vote wrong, it will have to be wrong. You no doubt would say it is right and I think it is right.

Hope's discourse did not close gently. He wrote:

> I hope this letter will also disabuse your mind of the fact that "I am a mighty nice fellow." You have got me all wrong there. I am just a guy in a tough spot trying to do the best job I can. If I do that I don't have much time to be nice.

The Cold War became hot in June 1950 when North Korea invaded South Korea. Reversing its previous policy of placing South Korea beyond the announced U.S. defense line in Asia, the Truman administration (and the United Nations) came to South Korea's defense. Hope supported this action although he had previously considered South Korea indefensible. In a letter to Harold Piehler of Lyons in late August, he expressed his views of events leading up to the war, the war itself, and Senator Joseph McCarthy's "communists in government" charge.

Hope did not see how anyone could have been particularly surprised by what happened in Korea, except perhaps by the timing of those developments. "It was practically certain when we withdrew our troops from Korea that eventually South Korea would be attacked by the Communists," he wrote. Hope sent Piehler a copy of the minority report on the Korean aid bill, which had been signed by five members of Congress the previous year. Piehler had referred to the bill in a letter to Hope, saying Republicans "voted against aid for Korea."

In response Hope explained that this had been a purely non-military aid bill.

> Not a dollar's worth of military aid was involved. What was contemplated was the furnishing to Korea of one hundred fifty million dollars' worth of economic assistance including the construction of roads, highways, hydroelectric plants, the building of factories and other types of assistance. These Republican members of the Committee on Foreign Affairs clearly point out in this [minority] report that it would be futile for us to furnish this economic assistance to Korea without making any provision to defend the country.

To do so, Hope wrote, would amount "to pouring money down a rat-hole."

Hope was insistent that the administration had had plenty of notice of the impending invasion of Korea: "The Intelligence Division of General MacArthur's headquarters sent a number of reports to Washington on the matter." He explained:

> On January 15, 1950, MacArthur notified Washington that the North Koreans were getting ready and the invasion might come in March or April. On March 10, 1950, a report was sent that the invasion might come in June. On May 10, 1950, it was reported to Washington from Tokyo that the North Koreans had increased their strength from six to thirteen divisions.

Continuing on the subject, he wrote:

> Our Central Intelligence Agency here in Washington repeatedly made reports of military activity on the part of the North Koreans but no attention was paid to them. Why? Simply because it was never contemplated until after the invasion had actually begun that this country would defend South Korea. Secretary Acheson said as much in a speech last January and on other occasions. In fact we just the same as told Russia and the Communists generally that we would not fight if Korea were invaded. That of course was nothing more nor less than an invitation for them to move in. When they did move in however the Administration suddenly reversed its policy and decided that we should go in and defend the country, announcing to the world at the same time that the Seventh Fleet would also defend Formosa.
>
> I do not mean by this that we did not furnish the Koreans a great deal of military aid. We turned over to them when our troops left the country millions and millions of dollars' worth of military supplies. However these supplies were not such as would enable them to defend the country against a foreign invasion but rather such as would enable them to protect themselves against riots and insurrections at home.

In his letter, Piehler remarked that he had not heard of Hope doing anything to support Senator McCarthy. Hope responded:

> I would support Senator McCarthy whenever he is right just as I would support President Truman whenever he is right. In my opinion McCarthy has done far more harm than good. What he has done was to make a lot of wild and reckless charges without having any information or facts to prove them. When I was out in Garden City in April I gave an interview to the paper there in which I said McCarthy's charges were all old stuff and that all the cases he was talking about had been reviewed by the Republican Eightieth Congress two years ago. And that is exactly the case as was later proven in the course of the investigation. It certainly doesn't do the country or the Republican Party or anyone else any good to have people go out making wild reckless statements such as were made by Senator McCarthy. I think it is a very bad thing for the country and no one can get very much comfort out of it except Russia.

Back on the Korean War, Hope wrote:

> I don't say everything is being done one hundred percent right but frankly I do think this Administration has done a pretty good job in the way the war has been conducted up to date considering that we started with practically nothing.

A week later Hope wrote at length to his friend, Marvin Brown, Congregational pastor at Garden City, who had expressed hope that the conflict between Communism and the western democracies might be resolved by a war of ideas rather than arms. Hope said the "disillusionment and shock to our ideas resulting from the developments of the last five years" had confused him at times. But out of all the conflict of ideas, opinions, theories and situations, Hope said a few recognizable, inescapable facts had emerged.

First among them was that the nation and its way of life were facing "the greatest danger we have ever known." Second, Communism was the one enemy to be feared. And third, the main objective of the country's foreign policy should be prevention of World War III. The matter of preventing a third world war hinged on the country's ability to convince Russia that she could not win by precipitating war. At the same time, Hope believed it was necessary to have united strength to resist if Russia resorted to war.

The question of convincing Russia that it could not win would depend, Hope wrote, upon the morale of the people of western Europe and upon our ability to convince them that there was a chance to win through resistance.

> I do not believe that they are going to settle this question among themselves on the basis of ideology. Their intellectuals are not of too much help to us now. A lot of them are clinging to the idea that resistance is hopeless and that in some way or another in a war between Russia and the United States they can escape if they don't resist. The whole history of communist policy since the war belies this, but nevertheless I am told there are many who believe and advocate this doctrine.

One reason for our "desperate plight," Hope thought, was clinging too closely to the notion that we could win the conflict with Communism as a war of ideas. He wrote Brown:

> The fact is the communists have licked the socks off of us in the war of ideas. They are so much more skilled than we are in propaganda techniques and so unscrupulous that we haven't had a chance with them.

The efforts of the U.S. to be scrupulous in dealing with other nations and to deal only with those we considered democratic "have gone to naught as far as getting that idea across to the world is concerned." This approach might pay some dividends in the future, but for the present, Hope was not optimistic. "We have our backs against a wall so to speak and unless we muster the kind of strength that the Russians can understand, I think we are going to sink."

Hope told Brown he had reached these conclusions reluctantly.

> I would much rather fight this out as a battle of ideas and ideals but I do not believe that we can defeat world communism

that way. At least not when it has reached the ascendancy which it has today.

Democrats retained control of both houses of Congress in the 1950 election, but the Kansas Republicans maintained a solid delegation.[5] The Democrat candidate for Congress in the 5th District was Robert Bock of Macksville, then the youngest member of the Kansas legislature. He was considered a comer in politics. Shortly after the primary election, Bock was called to active service (because of the Korean War) as a member of the Air Force Reserve, but he received a furlough to campaign in the last ten days before the general election. Some observers felt Bock's call to duty would help his campaign. This probably prompted Hope to include in his campaign ads that his son was an overseas veteran of World War II. On election day, Hope won by a good margin — 62,608 to 38,767.[6]

When Clarence Everett, Hope's administrative assistant, retired at the end of 1950, he was succeeded by Frances M. Griffin, a hardworking, efficient redhead from Culpeper, Virginia. Hope had to move from his "committee chairmanship" office in 1949, following the GOP debacle of 1948, to Room 1111 in the Longworth Building. He retained that office until his retirement from Congress, even though he became committee chairman again in 1953.

In the postwar period (1946-1951), my sister Martha and I finished college (and in my case, law school), married, and started families. Pauline, I am sure, was pleased and relieved to have her children happily married; but now, of course, she had two more children and then grandchildren to add to her list of constant concerns. Clifford also was pleased but for the most part kept his thoughts to himself.

When I returned from the Army in January 1946, I was interested in the U.S. Foreign Service as a career. Somewhat to my surprise, I passed the entrance examination and was admitted to Harvard College as a transfer student. Clifford had obtained much information on several colleges for me. By the time I graduated in the summer of 1947, I had switched my career objective back to politics and law. I attended Columbia Law School for a year and then transferred to Washburn Law School in Topeka, graduating in February 1950.

During the summer of 1946 I worked in Clifford's Washington office handling case work in the afternoons after attending a German language school in the mornings. Clifford paid me $150 a month out of his pocket.

Cousin Georgia Ragsdale, again working for Clifford and always a gossip, told George Reid I was going to take his job; she need not have worried. But I appreciated Clifford allowing me to work in the office because the experience renewed my interest in national politics.

Sometime when I was attending Harvard, Clifford gave me his only unsolicited bit of advice. I was floundering around fretting over a German girl who had just written me a "Dear John" letter and a Radcliffe girl who was giving me a bad time. His advice was simple, yet profound: "There's no sense in spending a lot of time liking someone who doesn't like you."

Martha was reminded of Clifford's strict policy concerning gifts. She said his carefulness about not being influenced by gifts from individuals or special interests, or even allowing the impression of such influence, was evident to her one Christmas when a box of various kinds of sugar arrived from the Revere Sugar Company. Martha recalled:

> Pop asked Mom to look through the box at the white sugar and brown, the confectioner's sugar and sugar cubes, etc., and estimate how much it would cost at the local grocery store. I don't remember how much it came to — five or ten dollars, I suppose — but it was a small enough amount that Pop said it was OK to keep it. I was relieved because I had my eyes on the sugar cubes, a special treat. But it was a time of first awareness of how special interests might try to influence legislators.

Clifford followed the same policy with respect to the annual gift of a Thanksgiving turkey from John Cowles of Cowles Publications. Pauline, Martha, and I were glad we got to keep the turkeys!

Martha graduated from Woodrow Wilson High School in 1947 and entered Swarthmore College in the fall, later transferring to Barnard College, but graduating from Swarthmore. During that time she met Frank West of Scranton, Pennsylvania; they were married in June 1950. Frank became a Presbyterian minister and later a psychotherapist in the New York City area.

Years later Martha recalled Clifford's advice to her:

> Pop rarely gave unsolicited advice. The only instance I can recall when he gave any to me was when I was considering var-

ious life courses and professional interests. He told me he thought taking some secretarial courses would be a good idea because women who could take dictation and type could always get work. I expect this was very true at the time, but I couldn't think of anything duller, so I didn't take his advice. The training would have been invaluable during all the years I've spent in higher education. I often recalled the advice, but didn't follow it even when its value to me as a student was obvious.

Clifford was irritated and embarrassed in January 1947 when the General Accounting Office closed down and froze all accounts in the Sergeant at Arms' office (the House bank) during an audit. Some of his outstanding checks were temporarily refused for payment. The bank passed the audit on that occasion and soon reopened.

After attending the GOP national convention in Philadelphia, our family spent the summer of 1948 in Garden City; Clifford, however, was gone much of the time working in the Dewey campaign. Lester and Hazel McCoy turned their spacious home on Seventh Street over to us rent free. As was their custom, they were spending the summer in Green Mountain Falls, Colorado. Martha, after her first year at Swarthmore, wanted to spend the summer with friends in the East, but Pauline insisted she come with us to Garden City. Pauline was suffering from cracked ribs incurred in a fall while packing for the trip to Kansas, so Martha got a real cooking and housecleaning workout. I had had much eye trouble in my year at Columbia Law School, and, therefore, took a job at a local lumberyard that summer to keep my nose out of the books for several months. Dolores was then city editor of *The Garden City Telegram*. We met on a blind date, immediately hit it off, and became engaged on Halloween.

Elinor Peterson of Larned, a loyal employee of Clifford, was in charge of his Garden City office that summer and fall. She was the daughter of Roscoe Peterson, longtime Larned lawyer. (A tall, thin redhead, she often stood up to type, placing the typewriter on top of a filing cabinet.) She and Dolores became special friends.

Dolores recalls an early December day after Pauline and Martha had returned to the East and I was at Washburn, when Clifford sat down at his parents' home and addressed envelopes for a thousand Christmas cards. He had no list, she said, he just wrote them out from memory. She understood then one of the reasons why Clifford Hope kept getting reelected.

Dolores and I settled on a December 30 wedding, to be held in McCook, Nebraska, which had been her parents' home since just before World War II began. This decision was based in part upon Pauline's reckoning. She, Clifford, and Martha would be in Kansas for Christmas anyway, she pointed out, so if we married then they wouldn't have to make an extra trip out for a spring wedding, which had been our first plan.

Pauline and Dolores's mother, Mary Sulzman, got along well from the very beginning, sometimes agreeing with each other for different reasons. This case in point: Pauline, a teetotaler and ardent prohibitionist, was deploring to Mary the repeal of Kansas' Prohibition Amendment. "Wasn't it an awful thing!" she lamented. It was indeed, Mary heartily agreed. It would all but eliminate liquor purchases by Kansans in McCook (just 15 miles from the Kansas line), causing a real blow to the town's economy, she said.

Dolores and her family were Catholic, creating great concern among some members of Clifford's immediate family. There never had been a Catholic in the Hope and Ragsdale families. One member expressed concern (to me) that Catholics were forbidden to read the Bible. I informed her this was not true, but I am sure she did not believe me. Another family member was more vehement. She reviewed for Pauline all the old wives' tales that had circulated about Catholicism since the Reformation. This was disturbing but not unexpected by Clifford and Pauline. Clifford calmly observed, "It will do the Hope family good to get some Catholic blood in it." In defense of the anti-Catholic members of the family, it should be said that after Dolores and I were married, they made the best of it and whatever their concerns might have been, they were never spoken of.

Clifford wrote Dolores and me a long letter in September, reporting on his recent trip to Europe to attend the Inter-Parliamentary Union meeting in Stockholm. He had taken some side trips with Hale Boggs of Louisiana (years later Boggs became Democrat Majority Leader, then died in a plane crash in Alaska) and Henry Talle of Iowa, visiting eight countries in all. Clifford was especially interested in observing the extent of European recovery during the first years of the Marshall Plan. Other representatives attending the Stockholm meetings were Albert Gore, Sr., Harold Cooley, and W. R. Poage, all from the Committee on Agriculture. A number of them brought their wives along, but Pauline did not accompany Clifford. By this time she dreaded traveling anywhere other than to visit family.

The trip to Europe was not all serious business, even for Clifford. He told about an evening in Paris:

> We had dinner at the Lido Club having been unable to get tickets to the Follies or the Bal Taberin. However, they had an excellent floor show at the Lido and after that we all went to a place called Monsignor's where they have about fifty violins playing all over the place, which is small. Really quite a remarkable joint. Will tell you more about it when I see you. Anyway we liked it so well that we didn't leave until five o'clock, so we really made a night of it. However, that was our last frivolity. From then on, we were pretty busy although there was quite a little social activity in connection with the Inter Parliamentary meetings.

Clifford and Pauline became grandparents in October when our daughter Christine was born. We were then living in veterans housing (half a Quonset hut) on the Washburn campus. The new grandparents used a photo of themselves holding Chris on the steps of the Quonset for their Christmas cards that year. By 1961 they had nine baby-boomer grandchildren — five from Dolores and me and four from Martha and Frank. They loved them all, but probably felt somewhat overwhelmed by the number — especially Pauline. They were in good company, because many of their friends and contemporaries were having the same experience. Sometime after Clifford's death in 1970 (Pauline died in 1969), cousin Margaret Hope, a single woman, told me she once asked Clifford how many children he thought Dolores and I would have. She said he replied, "Oh, probably about a dozen." Clifford and Pauline never gave advice to their children in that regard. What their reaction would have been to the birth of Dolores's and my sixth and last child, Megan, in 1973, is difficult to know. Undoubtedly it would have been a major worry for Pauline.

Dolores and I moved to Garden City after I finished law school in late February 1950. Clifford's old law firm took me in, somewhat to his surprise and mine. The firm consisted of Judge Hutchison and Judge C. E. Vance, both retired, and the work horses, A. M. (Art) Fleming and Bert J. Vance, son of Judge Vance. There was a wide-open race for county attorney that year, and I was encouraged by some to make the race for it. I sought Clifford's advice and, as usual, he wrote a long letter full of pros

Three generations of Harry and Armitta Hope's descendants. From left to right: Clifford, Jr., Armitta's grandson, with his daughter Christine, Armitta's son Clifford, Sr., and Armitta, *ca.* 1949-1950.

Curtis-Rintoul, Garden City, KS

and cons and sound thinking. He thought that his name on the ballot as a candidate for office for the 16th time would hurt my candidacy. He conjectured people would say that it was bad enough to have had Cliff Hope on the public payroll for 30 years and now "He wants the kid on too" or "Are we going to have the whole Hope family on the payroll?" It would not hurt him any, he went on, especially since he would be running in 32 other counties, but it could me. His parting observation was, "One other thing to keep in mind in running for this or any other office is to be sure you can afford to lose." I ended up deciding not to run for various other reasons, but I followed his last bit of advice when considering political adventures in later years.

Hope's public defense of President Truman's firing of General Douglas MacArthur in April 1951 was the most dramatic and publicized act of courage in all his 30 years in Congress. He was the only member of the Kansas delegation and one of the few Republicans in Congress to agree with the President's action. For this he was accused of treason and disloyalty to the Republican Party, urged to resign from Congress, and called — among other things — "dog manure."

When North Korea invaded South Korea on June 25, 1950, the Truman administration, revising its previously stated position, decided to defend South Korea. (Although Hope had thought South Korea to be indefensible, he supported this decision as the lesser of evils.) Nearly all of South Korea had been overrun by September; only the area around the port of Pusan was held by the South Korean-U.S.-United Nations forces. Then General MacArthur, in a brilliant maneuver, executed an amphibious landing at Inchon, just below Seoul, resulting in the liberation of South Korea and the invasion of the North. By November almost all of North Korea had been conquered. MacArthur ignored warnings that Communist China might enter the war, but that was exactly what happened. Chinese swept in, liberating all of North Korea and recapturing Seoul. The U.S.-U.N. forces set up a defensive line south of that city after evacuating many troops from North Korean ports.

At the end of December, MacArthur proposed blockading the Chinese coast, bombing Chinese industry, using the Chinese Nationalist forces in Korea and creating a diversion by landing on the Chinese mainland. The General admitted all these might lead to Soviet intervention, but he was not deterred by that possibility or probability. Early in 1951 the U.S. Field Commander General Matthew Ridgway commenced a counter-offensive, which resulted in the recapture of Seoul by mid-March. Truman and the UN made plans to propose a truce based more or less on the prewar 38th parallel boundary. Meanwhile, near the end of March, MacArthur publicly indicated that China could be defeated if his recommendations were followed. He offered to personally confer with the enemy, usurping the authority of the President. That act on his part torpedoed the chances for a negotiated settlement then. Joe Martin, Republican leader in the House and a great admirer, solicited MacArthur's views. The General wrote that Chinese Nationalist forces should invade the Chinese mainland. Martin used this letter in a speech on the floor of the House on April 5, 1951.

Four days later, Truman and his advisers agreed that MacArthur had to be fired. It was planned that Secretary of the Army Frank Pace would deliver the order to the General privately, but then a report leaked out that MacArthur was going to jump the gun and resign with a blast at Truman. Hence, on April 11 a public announcement was made that the General was fired, to be replaced by General Ridgway. MacArthur learned of it by radio. That's when all hell broke loose.

Previously Hope, in his usual studious manner, had been carefully reviewing all information available to members of Congress on the Truman-MacArthur clash of wills. On December 6, 1950, Hope responded to a letter from Charles M. Hardin, a professor of political science. The professor had enclosed a copy of a letter he had written to Truman, asking for Hope's comments on it. In his letter Hardin suggested that MacArthur be replaced by someone who would "have a willingness to support negotiation and compromise if negotiation and compromise became possible without sacrificing the national interest of the United States."

Although Hope respected the General's courage and qualities of leadership and unquestioned military ability, he stated flatly: "General MacArthur is not one of my heroes." But, in spite of his "luke warmness" toward MacArthur, he said he could not agree with the professor's criticism of him and did not believe "that criticism would justify his removal."

While Hope did not agree with all of MacArthur's views, he explained, "I find nothing in the record anywhere which would indicate that he has ever let those views influence his military activities." Hope acknowledged criticism here and abroad about MacArthur going further than authorized by the United Nations. There again, he said, he did not find anything to indicate MacArthur had failed in any way to strictly follow both the spirit and the letter of the authority given him even when it might have handicapped him from a military standpoint.

"I think it would be a great mistake from the standpoint of national unity to remove General MacArthur at this time," he wrote Hardin. He continued:

> I do not know whether you realize the great bitterness which exists in this country now over our Asiatic policy. I wish you could see some of my mail. However, the people who are the bitterest about this matter as well as many others who have not expressed any bitter feelings have a great deal of confidence in General MacArthur and should he be removed at this time when he is under attack in some of the countries of western Europe, it would in my opinion do more to split this country wide open at a moment when it should be standing together than anything else which could be done.

In response to Hardin's suggestion that MacArthur be replaced by someone willing to support negotiation and compromise, Hope countered, "That question is entirely outside General MacArthur's field or the field of anyone who might succeed him." Of course, he said, he (or a successor) should be consulted as to the military aspects involved in any political settlements of Far Eastern questions. In a final defense of MacArthur, he wrote:

> In spite of the great mistake which has been made in under-estimating the numbers and intentions of the Chinese communists, I question whether we have any other military leader who can offer anything like the sound military advice that General MacArthur can give.

All of this was written before MacArthur publicly defied the administration policies for a limited war and negotiated peace.

It is probably difficult today for anyone who was not an adult in 1951 to understand the furor against Truman and all who supported his decision. More than 40 years later, I perceive that Truman is regarded as a sort of folk hero who always did what he thought was right with the general approval of an admiring public. That was not so in 1951. The firing — and the way in which it occurred — was widely opposed by those who supported MacArthur's views and those who thought we never should have tried to defend South Korea in the first place. In addition, people were upset about charges of corruption in high places, hatred of Great Britain, the Alger Hiss conviction, charges of communism in government by Senator Joseph McCarthy, and many lesser irritations. The General's firing broke the dam of citizens' pent-up anger about many things.

"I have a high regard for General MacArthur and his achievements. His firing creates an unfortunate situation," Hope said on April 11, cautiously leading into his opinion of the firing. "I believe however that questions at issue are more important than personalities involved." He lined out the questions: "First, is MacArthur or the President determining the military and foreign policies of the United States? Second, should the war in Korea be localized or expanded to the mainland of China as advocated by MacArthur?"

Then Hope answered the first question. "Under the circumstances, the President had no alternative than to resign or fire MacArthur." Answering the second question, he said:

> An extension of war to mainland China would involve us in all-out war with China and possibly with Russia at a time when we are utterly unprepared. No nation has ever really won a war with China but millions of men have been sacrificed in trying. I feel it will be a mistake to follow MacArthur's policy.

Kansas's two senators and the other five representatives condemned Truman, and in Kansas they were the heroes of the moment for doing so. Hope was the villain. I remember getting telephone calls of protest about my father's position. Although I don't recall the details of the calls, I know for sure they were not complimentary. What I do remember vividly is General MacArthur's address to Congress on April 19. My law office was across the hall from that of Simon Zirkle, longtime Garden City realtor and insurance agent. On that day a dozen or more old codgers gathered around the radio in Simon's office (no television in southwest Kansas back then). One would have thought the General was God himself broadcasting.

The General gave a magnificent address. Hope commented upon it in his second press release in eight days:

A week ago it looked as if this country might be torn apart by the fratricidal controversy over General MacArthur's dismissal. His speech today is worthy to be compared with anything in the English language and must compel respect from every American regardless of his views or politics. Its high plane and the utter absence of partisanship sets a standard which can well be followed by everyone who discusses the great problems of war and peace which confront our nation today.

Criticism and comments on Hope's statement of April 11 concerning the General's dismissal were instantaneous. Letters and telegrams received may be divided roughly into three categories: outright threats and condemnations, criticism from friends questioning Hope's judgment and regretting his serious mistake, and compliments on his stand from friends and strangers. The latter definitely were in the minority.

R. F. and Lewise Todd, owners of an appliance business in Meade, wrote: "May you be advised that your pro-Truman expression in the Truman-MacArthur episode stunned your constituents as much as the episode itself stunned and embittered us in the first place." The Todds told Hope that "dozens and dozens of his faithful followers" came into their store waving the papers containing his statement and declaring, "I have always worked for and voted for Clifford Hope, but he has gotten my last vote." They said that one of his oldest friends, Robert Brannan, had asked them to include in their letter that he had voted and worked for Hope since the first time he ran but that he never would again. The way voter confidence was shattered by the stand he had taken "is pathetic," the Todds wrote Hope. They advised him not to defend his stand as other attorneys had with the argument that Truman had a legal right to dismiss the General. They were smart enough not to dispute that point, they said. The question as they saw it was whether Truman had the "moral right" to do it.

In the view of Mr. and Mrs. Todd, it was "the petty, lowly, selfish motives that prompted the little man to exercise that right" that people saw clearly and bitterly opposed. They advised Hope to "analyze and study the signatures on the Protest that was sent from Meade." They informed him that with more time, there would have been hundreds and hundreds more names on it, adding, "One of your most faithful supporters gathered these names out on the street."

A letter from Newton (not in the 5th District) told Hope he could "rectify his mistake" by voting to impeach Truman. If he didn't, he (Hope) should resign. A woman from Anthony closed a scathing attack with, "I would not give you my support if you were a candidate for the office to shovel manure out of the dog. I am sure the dog would be contaminated. May God forgive me for supporting such as you." From a Dodge City woman came a poem that ended:

> You'd better come home and sit by the fire.
> Western Kansans are through with your two-timing hire.
> You don't represent me, my sister, nor brother,
> Our dog, nor our cat, nor my poor old mother.
> Your farm legislation no more we'll need.
> We'll plow you under and try new seed.

Hope's friend, E. L. Woleslagel of Hutchinson, wrote:

> When you pull a "boner" you do a good job. Of course, you are entitled to your opinion but thousands in your district will be shocked to learn that you endorse Truman's position with McArther [*sic*]. The feeling is almost unanimous that McArther has something, even among the democrats. That Korea war is so rotten that it stinks to high heaven, and most of your friends are sorry to see you line up with the communist symsthizers [*sic*], including Dean Atcheson [*sic*].

Hope's old American Legion buddy, Bob Van Winkle, from Garden City, gave him a colorful account of how his defense of Truman played in the hometown. He wrote:

> I was in town today and things looks bad for you. Some say you are tanted [*sic*] so bad with New Dealism that you are ready to surrender to the reds. Even the Democrats want to hang you for taking Truman's side. Everyone knows Truman had the athority [*sic*] to fire McArthur [*sic*], but it was a dirty trick. And he only did it to please the Communists. People think that Atchison [*sic*] and his gang got Truman drunk at that midnight party and made him fire Mac. People want full scale war with

the Atomic bomb or get out of Korea. For my part, I want to stay in Korea with all out war. Well I guess this is about all. I thought you might want to know what is taking place.

The most organized opposition appears to have occurred in Sumner County, south of Wichita. Hope sent out mimeographed copies (most unusual for him) of his reply to James H. Taggert, the Republican county chairman. Taggert wrote Hope a courteous letter, dated April 18, which recounted the wide disapproval of Truman's dismissal of MacArthur and of Hope's agreement with it. He said some of the more active Republicans in the county wanted to circulate a telegram, "signed by any one who cared to do so," condemning him for his statement. "A few of us have succeeded in preventing this but have suggested that they send you letters expressing their feelings," Taggart wrote. Taggart said that in talking with many of the party leaders in the county, he found views similar to his: All agreed the President had the right to do what he did. However, he said, most felt it was done wrong. MacArthur should have been recalled to Washington as an advisor "in such a way that it would seem more of a promotion than a dismissal." This would have removed any of the bad features and "certainly not have caused so much excitement."

Taggart said he realized pressure on Truman from Great Britain, the U.S. State Department and others "must have been tremendous." He regretted Hope's action in that it split the Republican congressmen, and he could not see that as doing "anything to help the Republican party." He went on to counsel Hope:

> Rather than agree with him [Truman], if your conscience makes it necessary to do so, it would seem better to make no public statements in that regard. The voter who is not voting along party lines has a hard time voting Republican when its leaders divide the party on practically every major issue that comes up.

Hope's long reply, dated May 1, began on a note of appreciation for the spirit in which Taggert had written him. The disfavor with which leading Republicans had received his statement, Hope said, made him re-examine his thinking on the matter as would any expression of disagreement from them.

I have done this with respect to the MacArthur matter, but further consideration has made me feel even more strongly than ever that I am right as far as the real questions at issue are concerned. This does not mean that I am necessarily in accord with the way in which the President handled the matter.

Hope repeated his point on the supremacy of civilian authority over military authority as set up "by the men who wrote our Constitution." To ensure this, the Constitution provides that "the President be the Commander-In-Chief of the Armed Forces," he pointed out. "Our forefathers didn't want to take any chances of the military taking over . . . as they have done in so many countries in the past and in more recent years in Germany and Japan." Regardless of one's opinion on the merits of the controversy between the President and MacArthur, there could be no question that General MacArthur was guilty of insubordination. Official records showed that the General himself admitted it in his speech to Congress. Hope pointed out that had anyone under General MacArthur displayed the same insubordination to him, the General would have had him court-martialed in a hurry. No one in the history of this country typifies the military influence to the extent that MacArthur does, he continued. MacArthur, son of a 47-year career Army father, was born into an Army home and never spent a day of his life in a civilian atmosphere. Hope said he pointed this out not to criticize the General but "to make it clear that even more than usual the question of military and civilian supremacy is involved."

MacArthur's advocacy of carrying the war to the mainland of China was contrary to Hope's stand to localize the war.

To the extent the war spreads to other countries, the danger that it will become a World War is increased. . . . These views, which I held long before there was any controversy about General MacArthur, happen to be in accord with the present views of the President and Joint Chiefs of Staff. I do not believe that my Republican friends in Sumner county feel I should become such a partisan that I must switch sides whenever I find the President and I are in agreement on matters of policy.

Hope told Taggart that what really disturbed him in the present situation was the spirit of disunity prevalent in the country. He stated a need for "full and wide and constructive discussion" of important questions. "Much of the discussion which has gone on in the press and over the radio and even in the Halls of Congress has been on a pretty low level . . . much has degenerated into mere personalities and name calling." Hope hoped further discussions could be kept at the high level set by MacArthur in his speech before Congress.

All matters of foreign policy should be settled without "too much partisanship," Hope wrote. He mentioned the late Senator Arthur Vandenberg as an example in bipartisanship. "I am more interested in the next generation than I am in the next election," Hope wrote Taggart. "I have reached a time in life when what happens to my grandchildren seems a lot more important than what happens to me." He said he disagreed with President Truman on many things and would continue to criticize him when he thought Truman was wrong. "But I think I can agree with him when I think he is right and still be a good Republican."

Hope did receive some support for his position in Kansas newspapers. Probably the foremost editorial was written by Jim Cornish, managing editor of *The Garden City Daily Telegram*:

> Congressman Cliff Hope is in hot water in some Republican dining rooms around town because he said in Washington that President Truman had no choice but to fire General MacArthur for refusing to take orders.
>
> To this observer the worst angle to the MacArthur-Truman ruckus is that almost all the Republicans jumped over on the general's side of the fence five minutes after the news broke and all the Democrats fell into close formation behind their White House chief.
>
> The political odor of the affair stinks. It makes anybody with an open mind wonder.
>
> That's why it is refreshing indeed to read on the AP teletype last week that Congressman Hope broke party ranks to say what he believed.
>
> Whether we agree or disagree with the congressman, it is invigorating to see that he does his own thinking without looking the situation over through politically-tinted glasses.
>
> We're afraid that Cliff Hope's own hometown after all these

years doesn't know Cliff too well. Maybe that's because he spends most of his time doing his country's business in Washington — and doing it well.

The congressman, we've found on his visits home, has a frank opinion on all U.S. issues and they don't exactly follow the party lines.[7]

Hope wrote Cornish:

Thank you for that swell editorial. It more than makes up for some of the letters I received during the last week comparing me in most unfavorable terms with a skunk and intimating that I was a good deal worse than Alger Hiss.

At the same time, Hope continued, he had received some "mighty fine" letters as well. There was, in fact, a "slight preponderance of those which were favorable" in reference to his statement on the MacArthur-Truman issue. However, the bulk of the avalanche of mail was, he said, "pro-MacArthur or, more specifically, Anti-Truman" and didn't refer to his statement on the matter at all. He said he also received something like 1,200 Fulton Lewis questionnaires which indicated how strongly and emotionally most people felt on the MacArthur issue. (Fulton Lewis, Jr., was a popular, ultra-conservative radio commentator of that time.)

That his stand would be unpopular was something he knew from the start, Hope told Cornish. "I certainly don't feel like backing up a bit on the statement and as a matter of fact, I feel better about it now than I did when I made it." Again, Hope praised MacArthur's speech at the joint session of Congress, calling it "a masterpiece worthy to be compared with anything in modern oratory" and "a masterly presentation of his viewpoints." It raised questions that will have to be answered, Hope said, and left unanswered some questions that must be answered "before we have the entire picture."

Among letters of support was a handwritten note from Judge Hutchison, then age 90, as usual addressing Hope as "Dear Sir." The judge was succinct: "The President is Commander-in-Chief. I am with him officially but not personal or political." On June 30, 1951, Hope responded to a complimentary letter from W. A. Doerschlag of Ransom:

> I feel it is a mistake on the part of members of either party to exaggerate emotional issues for their supposed political value. In the long run, I think it is poor politics as well as a pretty poor thing to do in the interest of the country.

Fortunately for the Truman administration, its position was vigorously supported in testimony before congressional committees by Secretary of Defense General George Marshall, General Omar Bradley, chairman of the Joint Chiefs of Staff, and the three service chiefs. Bradley described MacArthur's plan as "the wrong war at the wrong time with the wrong enemy." The testimony put an end to the nation's hysteria. Truce talks began in July and dragged on for two years, but World War III had been averted. By 1952 most of Hope's irate constituents had forgiven him and some admitted he had been right all along. General MacArthur continued to make speeches around the country, hoping to be drafted for President by the Republicans in 1952, but the draft never came. Meanwhile, Hope, together with other Republican leaders, began working to draft another general, Dwight D. "Ike" Eisenhower.

Chapter 10

Eisenhower — and Last Years in Congress (1951-1956)

OPE'S LAST FIVE YEARS IN Congress were excit-ing, probably more so than any prior time. He played a major role in the pre-convention effort to nominate Dwight D. Eisenhower and in the fall campaign to elect him, but, with his usual modesty, Hope played down his part in the campaign. Then he was frustrated and saddened by Secretary of Agriculture Ezra Taft Benson's aggressive effort to lower and eventually abolish government farm price supports, with its resulting adverse effects on farmers and on Republicans in Congress. Hope was, however, heartened by the passage of the Watershed Protection and Flood Prevention Act of 1954 to conserve soil and water and by the passage of other measures with President Eisenhower's active cooperation. Finally, Hope's decision to retire at the end of his term in 1956 and return to Kansas fulfilled a long-standing promise to his wife, Pauline.

*In late May 1951, A. L. "Dutch" Schultz of **The Topeka State Journal** interviewed Hope in Topeka. Twenty-five years earlier, Schultz had interviewed Hope in Garden City to help launch*

Hope's first campaign for Congress. Hope lauded Eisenhower and Taft and emphasized the need for a presidential candidate who would appeal to independent and young voters. Eisenhower was then stationed in Paris as the first commander of NATO; by Army regulations he was forbidden to express opinions on political subjects. Ike's political affiliation was not yet known, nor was it known for certain that he would accept a nomination for President. All this did not deter his early supporters, including Hope. By fall Hope was convinced Ike could be talked into running.

During this period Clifford and I worked closely together in the "Draft Eisenhower" cause. I was the chairman of Finney County Young Republicans and was slated to become 5th District Young Republican chairman at a convention scheduled for October 27 in Garden City. This meeting resulted in the first endorsement of Ike for President by any Republican organization. Hope arranged for Representative Hugh Scott of Pennsylvania, former chairman of the GOP National Committee, to be the banquet speaker. The endorsement resolution and Scott's speech drew news correspondents and the GOP faithful and leaders from throughout Kansas and eastern Colorado and made the headlines in the Sunday papers. This was pretty heady stuff for me and even for Hope. That fall we spent much time together working on Ike's cause. It was as if we felt we were personally responsible for his nomination.

All this caused some ripples in our domestic tranquility. During the fall of 1951 Clifford and Pauline lived with us, occupying the upstairs bedroom. He and I talked politics incessantly, and we parked a small radio on the dining table so we would not miss a single political item on the news as we ate three meals a day. Clifford had been listening to the news during his evening meals in Washington for years. Although Pauline disliked it intensely, she never dared to do anything about it. When family members ventured to mention non-political subjects while Clifford was listening to a newscast, he shushed them sharply. This effectively stopped any casual mealtime conversation. One night Dolores had had enough. Clifford had shushed his wife once too often. Dolores got up, unplugged the radio and tossed it to the other end of the dining room where it landed unscathed on a sofa. Everyone, she said, had already heard the same news in the morning and at noon and if they had need to hear it again, it'd be on at 10 p.m. Clifford was nonplussed, more so than I. Never before had anyone dared disturb or question his radio listening.

Clifford and I, of course, continued to live in a political trance when at home. On November 18 Dolores's and my second child, Nancy, was born. Less than two weeks later, when Dolores made reference to the baby, I asked, "Baby? What baby?" On my birthday, December 21, Pauline and Clifford were in attendance at what was supposed to be my family birthday dinner. Dolores had spent the afternoon peeling shrimp and making a cake for a festive dinner. Although Clifford and I no longer had the radio on the table, we talked politics without pause. Dishes were cleared and the cake brought in. The every-evening summit to elect Eisenhower continued without pause. After waiting for a polite length of time for an opening to make note of the occasion, Dolores sighed, lifted the cake she was holding and dumped it, frosting side down, on my head. "Happy birthday," she said quietly. "This meal is over." I believe this startled Clifford even more than the radio incident. For her part, I imagine Pauline was secretly pleased although she was wise enough to say nothing.

On January 7, 1952, General Eisenhower revealed that he was indeed a Republican and would accept the GOP nomination if it were offered. Hope was more than ever convinced that Ike not only would be more electable than Robert A. Taft but also that, overall, he would be a better President. Hope was especially concerned about Taft's isolationist views.

In February, after a meeting of House members with Senator Henry Cabot Lodge (leader of the forces to draft Eisenhower), Hope prepared and circulated a letter to the General, signed by 19 GOP representatives including Gerald Ford, Hugh Scott, Albert Cole of Kansas, Christian Herter, Thurston Morton, and Jacob Javits. The letter read:

> This is a difficult letter to write but it comes to you from the hearts of some of your sincerest friends who have been working for your Presidential candidacy for months. It is prompted by the messages we are receiving daily from our constituents, from all parts of the nation, indicating that they want you to seek the nomination for President of the United States. They want you to come home; they want you to declare yourself on the pressing issues of the day; they want the inspiration of your dynamic honesty and the forthrightness of your statesmanship. The demands of these patriotic Americans have a right to be heard, and we beg you to listen to them because we agree with them.
>
> There can be no doubt that an overwhelming majority of the

people of the United States want you as their leader. They realize that for some time you have been devoting your energies to organizing and implementing the defense of Europe, and have accomplished much, but they also realize that if our own country is torn asunder by corruption and greed, by disloyalties and opportunism, by the avarice of selfish men, by the lack of vision of pseudo-statesmen greedy to retain public office, all the good and constructive work you have done will be destroyed. We feel deeply that those basic convictions for which you have stood and which are shared by so many millions of people deserve your personal leadership in this crucial hour. Your return home will unite our people as never before, and this is the surest way to preserve your efforts in Europe and to promote peace in the world.

Before signing this letter we discussed the foreign and domestic situation and your place in it from many angles, and with intense sincerity believe in what is said in this letter. We are practical and not hysterical and venture the thought that perhaps you do not fully appreciate the serious state of our country's domestic affairs. We pledge ourselves to your leadership without thought of any kind of reward — what we want to do is to save America and promote peace.

The letter was sent to Senator Lodge for hand delivery to the General, who sent individual replies to the signers. Eisenhower was quite circumspect in his reply, which read in part:

Under most circumstances, I would concede immediately the complete validity of your argument. However, as I am now situated, assigned to a duty that I firmly believe is of the utmost consequence to the peace and prosperity of America and the world, I am confronted by one dominant personal conviction — during the next few months no other job or mission that I can discharge seems more important than the one in which I am now engaged. My own personal inclinations, the advice of loyal associates and warm friends, the possibilities that lie ahead — none of these can be permitted to outweigh an inescapable and present duty.

There is no question in my mind concerning the propriety of answering a clear-cut call to another and higher duty, a call that is traditionally and universally recognized as the voice of the American people speaking through a national convention. Such a call imposes an obligation of citizenship on the man so honored.

It seems to me, however, that it is an entirely different thing to leave a critical assignment for the purpose of increasing the possibility or probability of such a summons. My friends, I know, will not expect me to act against my conscience. But, in the absence of a compelling call or relief by higher authority, I cannot see in any personal or political circumstances a sufficient warrant for me to leave this assignment during the immediate future.

No matter how others might interpret that action, for me it would be based on personal grounds and personal reasons. On the other hand, I assure you that I shall regularly re-examine my position, bearing in mind your message. World peace and human freedom; American solvency, prosperity, and unity — these things dwarf every American citizen's personal preferences and his personal decisions on his duty as an individual.

My thanks for your inspiring words.

It had been intended that this exchange of correspondence would be confidential, but someone leaked it to the press. Hope, after consulting with other signers, placed the text of the letters in the *Congressional Record* under date of March 20, 1952. Although Ike did not return home until June 1, the campaign on his behalf proceeded. He later acknowledged that the letter from the congressmen greatly influenced his decision to run.

In the meantime, Hope, for the first time ever, took an active role in the selection of Kansas delegates to the GOP National Convention. This activity was spurred in part by the election of Taft delegates from the 6th District in northwest Kansas. Hope drafted his old American Legion and Republican friend, Lee Kemper, of Garden City, and others to mobilize the Ike forces. By the time all district meetings and the state convention had been held, it was a solid Eisenhower delegation from Kansas, except for two Taft delegates. Hope also commenced an active speaking schedule on

Ike's behalf, addressing meetings in Kansas, Colorado, Oklahoma, Texas, South Dakota, Iowa, Maryland, Virginia, the District of Columbia, and elsewhere.

Pauline and Clifford, as well as Dolores and I, attended the National Convention in Chicago in July. Although Ike won before voting was closed on the first ballot, it was nip and tuck all the way. Most convention attenders (as distinguished from delegates and alternates) had no tickets to the auditorium. This included Dolores and me. For a large group of Kansans, Lester McCoy, the consummate host, provided a large television set and refreshments in his palatial suite in the Palmer House Hotel. It was a great place to celebrate a great victory.

The general election campaign proved to be an anticlimax. The Democrat nominee, Adlai Stevenson, governor of Illinois, saddled with the then-unpopular Truman administration and running against a war hero, was no match against the popular Ike, who received 55 percent of the vote nationwide. The GOP amassed 442 electoral votes in 39 states to the Democrats' 82 in 9 states. Hope was pleasantly surprised at the margin of Ike's victory, but disappointed that the GOP just barely carried the House of Representatives.

With the election, speculation, as always, turned to the question of cabinet appointments. In Kansas and among farm organizations and farmers throughout the nation, there was most interest in who would be the next Secretary of Agriculture. Many interested persons thought Hope had the inside track. Typical of the letters and contacts with Hope immediately after the election was a letter from Don L. Berry dated November 11. After exulting in Ike's triumph, Berry wrote:

> Now with Eisenhower in the White House and you in the Department of Agriculture, if I take a notion to visit Washington, I'll feel like a stockholder and not like a cat in a strange garret inhabited by hobgoblins.
>
> It would seem that even the Taft men should realize now that your judgment was right when you backed Ike. I believe now that Taft could have been elected, perhaps even after the asinine antics of his henchmen in Chicago. But it could never have been the overwhelming verdict of the American people such as we had last week.
>
> The chairman of P.M.A. [Production and Marketing Admin-

istration] and of the soil conservation district, Gilbert Fridley, called me yesterday and asked if there was anything we could do here to make sure Clifford Hope became secretary of agriculture. I told him I thought it was pretty well set already. He said absolutely nobody else would do, that Hope is the man for the farmers and for soil conservation and to tell you if you needed any help Warren County would go to Washington en masse to do anything we can.

My own feeling is that the matter is so well set that to even write to anybody endorsing you might raise the question that somebody had suggested another possibility. If there is any help necessary that we hereabouts could render, you know you have nothing to do but let us know. John Henry says he thinks it is all over but your acceptance.

But Hope's appointment was not to be. In fact, his advice on the appointment was not sought, nor was he even notified in advance of the appointment of Ezra Taft Benson. Hope read about it in the newspapers. He was deeply disappointed — but not bitter — that his opinion had not been solicited. Later Lester McCoy told me that Hope had quietly confided to him that "it would have been nice to be asked for advice." (I don't recall that Hope ever mentioned the matter to me. Although we talked often of many things, he never confided his innermost thoughts, nor did I ever press him for answers to such questions. We respected each other's privacy.) On November 25, after Benson's appointment, Hope responded to Don Berry's letter:

I appreciate what you say about Gilbert Fridley and his interest in my becoming Secretary of Agriculture. Frankly, I have never felt that there was much likelihood that I would be offered the appointment, and for that reason I haven't given the question of whether I would accept or not, if offered, very much thought. I suppose, however, that I probably would have accepted it if it had been offered to me. I am sure, however, that I will be very much happier as Chairman of the Committee on Agriculture in the House. I do not know Ezra Benson too well, but I do know him and have a very good impression of him. I think the General made a good selection in appointing him.

Why was Ezra Taft Benson appointed and why was Hope's advice concerning the appointment not solicited? It is easier to answer the first question than the second. Benson had a farm background and from 1939 to 1943 served as executive secretary of the National Council of Farmer Cooperatives. Then he resigned and returned to Utah to become a member of the Council of Twelve, the governing body of the Mormon Church. In the 1952 election he was a strong supporter of Robert Taft for President. The two men were distant relatives. Those involved in the cabinet selection process including, of course, the General himself, sought to include a spectrum of ideas and views among cabinet members. However, when the process was completed, only Benson was selected from the Taft wing of the party. Some historians state the selection was made by Ike's brother, Milton Eisenhower, then president of Pennsylvania State College and a former Department of Agriculture official and Ike's close advisor. Milton, a longtime acquaintance of Hope, stated Taft had originally suggested Benson. Other reported backers of the Benson nomination included Allan Kline, president of the Farm Bureau, and Tom Dewey, who had sought Benson's advice in 1948. On November 25 Hope wrote Milton concerning a proposed conference on conservation and natural resources, then added this paragraph:

> I was very much pleased over the General's selection of Ezra Benson as Secretary of Agriculture. I have known him for a number of years, and I feel he is eminently qualified by ability and experience for this position. In fact, I think all of the Cabinet choices which have been announced are excellent. Out there in Kansas we are still rejoicing over the big victory on November 4, and are happy that Ike's margin was so decisive.

Milton replied three days later:

> I'm glad you are pleased about Ezra Benson's designation as Secretary of Agriculture. I had not met him until the day the decision was reached. Confidentially — though this may be well known — he was originally suggested by Senator Taft. I believe geographic distribution operated in his favor. In my luncheon visit with him, I discovered him to be a man of sterling character and great dedication to helping the new adminis-

tration. He certainly seems to understand the economic, physical, and human problems of agriculture. Also, I discovered that he treasures good personal relations, and I therefore believe he will work hard to keep in close touch with Congressional leaders, farm organization leaders, and others — and that will be like a breath of fresh air.

Reportedly, General Eisenhower and Benson hit it off famously on their first meeting; Benson would have Ike's full support during eight years in office. That, of course, was the crucial point, rather than who recommended the appointment.

Why was Hope's advice not solicited, and why was he not even notified in advance of the appointment, as a matter of courtesy? I can only surmise as to the reasons. Perhaps it was thought that Hope would recommend someone, including even himself, whose views on agriculture would be incompatible with those of Dwight Eisenhower. (In November 1952 Ike's specific opinions on price supports were not generally known nor were they known to Hope.) Perhaps it was thought also that Hope might react adversely, in some way, if he knew of the appointment in advance. Or perhaps someone was designated to tell Hope and failed to do so. Whatever fears Ike's advisors might have had, indicated they did not know Hope very well. He never was one to brood over disappointments, and he had had his fair share in politics and government. Nor was it his way to "keep score" or "get even." He had a continued good relationship with President Eisenhower and Milton during Ike's administration and thereafter, as we shall see.

In 1953 President Eisenhower's true views on government farm price supports became known. Kansas farmers around Abilene were getting along all right without federal government assistance when he was growing up in Kansas, he thought, and there was no reason why they should not now. He wanted to reduce supports immediately with the long-term objective of abolishing them altogether. This repudiation of what had been a more-or-less bipartisan farm program since 1936 was in contrast to his administration's support for all other government programs initiated under the New Deal such as TVA and social security, according to his biographer, Stephen Ambrose.[1] These views account for his rapport with Ezra Benson. Unlike the conciliatory Ike, however, Benson considered his appointment a divine call to duty (according to his biographers Edward L.

Clifford Hope (middle row, second from left) and other House leaders were invited to lunch with President Eisenhower (center) and Vice President Nixon (third from left, front row).

Clifford Hope (seated, right) with President Dwight D. Eisenhower (center).

Finney County Historical Society, Garden City, KS

The House Agricultural Committee on the steps of the Farm Credit Administration Building, Springfield, Massachusetts, August 4, 1953. Front row, left to right: Carl Albert, Thomas G. Abernethy, R. D. Harrison, Clifford R. Hope, Paul C. Jones, August H. Andresen. Back row, left to right: John L. McMillan, Karl C. King, Paul B. Dague, Clifford G. McIntire, W. R. Poage, and Ralph Harvey.

Schapsmeier and Frederick H. Schapsmeier).[2] He was, in the words of agricultural historian, John Mark Hansen, "a zealous economic libertarian" who sought to make a moral and political crusade out of basic economic agricultural problems.[3]

Meanwhile Hope, again chairman of the House Agricultural Committee, spent 1953 defending Secretary Benson while attempting to maintain a bipartisan committee stance. The committee held extensive hearings throughout the country during congressional recesses; these hearings gave farmers in the field (as distinguished from farm leaders) a chance to sound off. The committee learned that most favored a continuation of 90 percent price supports. During that year, some Democrats and GOP Senator Milton Young of North Dakota were calling for Benson's resignation. Senator Wallace Bennett of Utah caused further problems for Hope by accusing *him* of calling for Benson's resignation so that he (Hope) might be appointed Secretary of Agriculture. In a speech defending Secretary Benson to the Salt Lake City Rotary Club on October 27, Bennett stated:

> For my fourth political observation, let me turn to my own party. Senator Milton Young of North Dakota was the first to oppose Secretary Benson and is now vociferously demanding his resignation. While North Dakota is predominately Republican, at least in name, the Farmers' Union represents a power that cannot be ignored — even by a Republican Senator. Then there is Congressman Hope of Kansas, Chairman of the House Agriculture Committee. He and his Committee have been holding hearings through the Farmers' Union area in the north and the cotton belt in the south, providing a platform for the political opponents of the administration's farm program and building a background against which Congressman Hope could ask for Secretary Benson's resignation. Hope was one of those most frequently mentioned last fall as a candidate for the position of Secretary of Agriculture. He wasn't selected. Ezra T. Benson was. Now he demands Ezra Benson's resignation and his name is again being mentioned as Ezra Benson's successor. I think the implications there are obvious.

A month later, Hope's friend, Gabriel Hauge of the White House staff, wrote that he had just read a copy of the speech and observed, "I found his

comments about you most implausible and I reject them completely."
Based on Senator Bennett's speech, the national columnist George Sokolsky wrote a column repeating the charges against Senator Young and
Hope. Hope wrote lengthy letters to Bennett and Sokolsky, enclosing
excerpts from his speeches and press clippings in which he not only had
defended but also had extolled Benson.

Secretary Benson's autobiography of his cabinet years, *Crossfire*,
describes his view of a private conference with Hope on December 15 as
"long and frustrating. He seemed more interested in outdoing the Democrats than anything else." By the end of the year, it was evident that
Benson — unlike Milton Eisenhower's description of him — was not
interested in the views of anyone except those who agreed with him. In
January the administration presented its plan for farm legislation, including flexible price supports ranging from 75 to 90 percent of parity. Hope
confided his thoughts at that time to Don L. Berry:

> I appreciate what you say with respect to the President's farm
> program. I am trying to keep out of taking any extreme position
> on the matter because I feel I should keep myself in a position
> where I can work with everybody in trying to bring out the best
> possible bill. I don't think that farmers are sold on flexible price
> supports and I don't think it will be possible to sell them under
> existing conditions. Much as I hate to admit it the farmers of
> this country just don't have too much confidence in the Repub-
> lican Party. They know that in the main it has been dominated,
> as far as its farm thinking is concerned, by the Eastern wing of
> the Party. That was so evident in 1948 that it is no wonder they
> turned against Dewey. The President went at this matter in a
> much better way and did what you and I have been urging for a
> long time.
>
> That is, he took it out of politics. The situation now is further
> complicated by the fact that although Ezra Benson is a fine,
> high-minded man and I like him personally, the farmers of this
> country have gotten the idea that he is in favor of low farm
> prices (and I think they are right about it). Consequently, their
> lack of confidence in the Republican Party generally which
> goes back to Coolidge's veto of the McNary-Haugen Bill is
> intensified when they consider that flexible price supports

would be administered by the man whom they feel will make them just as low as it is possible to do so.

At least that is the way it looks to me and I do not think that we can regain the confidence of farmers unless we give them some assurance in the law of the level at which prices will be supported. Too many farmers think that if they are flexible Benson will always flex them down and they simply aren't going to go along with that kind of a program.

I am not saying that the President may not be able to put his program across in the Congress and with the consumers in the country, but I am sure that he won't be able to put it across with the farmers.

The situation developed much as Hope had forecast. The House committee recommended, by a vote of 26 to 2, a bill including some of Secretary Benson's recommendations but not the 75-to-90 percent provision. In an effort to mobilize consumers, Benson and Vice President Nixon appeared on ABC radio in late June. A few days later, Hope and Representative Harold Cooley appeared to explain the provisions of the committee bill, especially refuting the claim that 90 percent supports had been responsible for the existing surpluses. The administration still did not have enough votes to lower supports to 75 percent, so the Republican Whip in the House, the skilled compromiser Charles Halleck of Indiana, proposed a reduction for the first year of 82.5 percent to 90 percent. That amendment made enough difference to carry 228 to 170.

Hope summarized his position in a news story, saying he did not think either 90 percent price supports or flexible price supports were the answer to the wheat situation. But, he pointed out, every objection to 90 percent supports could be made to flexible supports. "Our situation would be exactly the same if we had had flexible price supports during the past five years as it is now after 90 percent supports." The only difference, he said, was that farm income, "which has taken some pretty hard jolts already," would be further reduced.

Hope said he had a good record as a team player and he had supported Eisenhower measures, but he was not willing to settle for flexible price supports as a solution to the farm problem. "The real solution, I think, is a commodity-by-commodity approach." The best plan suggested for wheat, according to Hope, was the Certificate Plan covered by bills he and Sena-

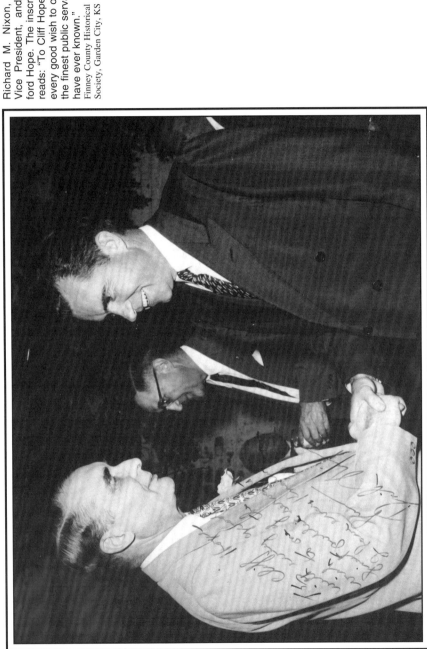

Richard M. Nixon, then Vice President, and Clifford Hope. The inscription reads: "To Cliff Hope with every good wish to one of the finest public servants I have ever known."
Finney County Historical Society, Garden City, KS

tor Carlson had introduced. Under this system farmers would be issued negotiable certificates equal to the difference between the computed 100 percent of parity price and the market price on the farmer's share of wheat used domestically. A tax paid by millers and passed on to consumers would finance the certificates, which could be cashed by farmers at any financial institution.

In 1954 and for his remaining years in Congress, Hope was under great pressure from the Republican leadership to modify his price support views. He did not complain, but his office staff and Pauline confirmed the pressure put on him. I complimented him in a letter I wrote in June 1954, telling him I thought he was showing great restraint and patience in not replying for the sake of headlines to "the unjust and unwarranted attacks which have been made upon actions of the House Committee on Agriculture." I assured him that eventually the truth about the whole matter would be known.

Hope always worked long hours and six-day weeks during his tenure in Congress, but probably worked harder during the Eisenhower first term than at any other period. In a handwritten letter to Dolores and me on the Fourth of July 1953, he reported he was working from 7:30 a.m. to 6:30 or 7 p.m. each day and that the Fourth was the first holiday he had taken in a long time.

By 1956 Hope had had sufficient time to size up Secretary Benson. In response to a letter from B. F. Hafer of Mayetta, in northeast Kansas, Hope observed:

> If you feel that Secretary Benson's policies, including flexible price supports with rigid controls of all basic commodities, constitute a good farm program then I respect your views and have no quarrel with you.
>
> Personally I am opposed to both flexible price supports and 90 percent supports, although I have said many times that I did not feel we should give up 90 percent price supports unless we had something better to take their place. I do not regard the present program with 76 percent price supports on wheat and 81 percent price supports on corn with exactly the same controls as we had with 90 percent supports as being a better program.
>
> My own thought is that we should approach the problems of the various commodities in the way that best meets the needs of

those commodities. We have some of these special programs which are working very well, for instance, on sugar beets, on wool and on tobacco. I am willing to go to any special program which the corn producers wish and which they may think is better than the present program. On wheat I have long been an advocate of the Domestic Parity Plan which provides for 100 percent of parity for that part of our wheat which is consumed domestically for human food and then letting the remainder sell for whatever it will bring on the market, thus getting away from marketing quotas and piling up wheat in government warehouses.

While I am not attempting to start an argument with you I do want to question the statement in the last paragraph of your letter in which you say, "Please do not forget that Mr. Benson is not a politician." So far he has won all his political battles. He was smart enough to realize when he first came to Washington that only 12 percent of the people live on farms and that a man could be a lot more successful politically by being with the 88 percent than with the 12 percent. What he did was to start out on a campaign to pit the consumer against the farmer in which he was most successful. It is my view that we all have to work together in this country, farmers, consumers and everyone else and that the last thing that we ought to do is to pit group against group and class against class. That was the Democratic policy for a good many years and I got pretty sick of it. I am just as sick of it when Mr. Benson and any other Republican uses it and I do not believe that such policies can be of any lasting value to the country or to the farmer.

We have a Secretary of Commerce in this country who fights the battles of the businessmen against all consumers. I have never heard him say that the automobile manufacturers were pricing themselves out of the market or intimating that steel prices are too high or that businessmen are making too much money. We have a Secretary of Labor who has taken up the cudgels for labor on every opportunity. Last year he sponsored a bill in Congress to increase minimum wages from 75 cents per hour to $1.00 per hour. He has stood up for labor at every opportunity. I don't know how you stood on the Right to Work bill in Kansas last year but when Governor Hall vetoed it, the Secretary of Labor wrote a letter congratulating him.

I like Secretary Benson personally but I would feel much more comfortable as far as the situation of the farmers of this country is concerned if he would stand up for them as the Secretary of Commerce stands up for business and the Secretary of Labor stands up for Labor.

The 1956 farm bill contained a different approach to the crop surplus problem. It provided for a soil bank program whereby farmers were paid for idling and conserving land, thereby cutting down on harvested acres. Hope reviewed the history of the soil bank legislation in an August letter to M. Frank Colter of Silver Lake, in northeast Kansas, who had advocated such a program for many years.

Hope told Colter he was entitled to a great deal of credit for having worked on the idea as early as 1940. The trouble, he wrote, was that before any program of the kind could be worked out, the country was at war and came up with shortages instead of surpluses for all agricultural products. "So your idea was not needed until we reached the surplus situation after the Korean War."

In 1953 Hope found Colter's ideas made a great deal of sense, but at that time, Hope reminded Colter, the Farm Bureau and the administration was convinced that the only thing needed to reduce farm surpluses was a system of flexible price supports. "It was impossible to secure any interest in your program . . . at that time," Hope wrote Colter. By the summer of 1955, it finally became apparent to the White House that the idea of reducing surpluses by flexible price supports was not working to deal adequately with surpluses. Hope said that in August of 1955 he had stayed in Washington after Congress adjourned to confer with Secretary Benson on a soil bank program but received no encouragement. He then took the matter up with White House aides and economic advisers who were working on farm problems and found them more receptive. Back in Washington in November, on his way to the Food and Agriculture Organization meeting in Rome, he talked with the White House aides again and found them "pretty well sold on a soil bank plan." He wrote:

It is a fact well recognized in Washington that the Secretary of Agriculture and his staff never accepted the soil bank of their own volition — it was forced on them by the White House and under those circumstances they went along.

Hope believed the enactment of this program at such a late date was unfortunate in that it could be put into effect for 1956 only in a meager way. However, a more extensive basis was being worked out for 1957. It would be a matter of trial and error for a while. Hope predicted that further changes in the administration of the soil bank program would have to be enacted after it was given a tryout in 1957. In closing his letter Hope told Colter:

> I think as I have always thought, however, that the idea is sound and I am sure that you must be gratified over the fact that it has been adopted by the Administration and is being given a thorough trial.

Secretary Benson's opposition to the soil bank was consistent with his overall opposition of federal payments to farmers. The respected agricultural historian Gilbert Fite wrote in 1964 concerning Secretary Benson:

> Benson held that if government restrictions were eased and finally eliminated farmers would adjust their output to meet the realistic demands of the marketplace. Consequently, the Secretary gradually lowered price supports after 1954.
>
> But the Benson argument proved fallacious, at least in the short run. Under fewer production controls and lower support prices, farmers actually increased their output. The government took larger quantities into storage and the cost of the farm program shot upward. By 1960 the Commodity Credit Corporation had more than $9 billion invested in farm commodities. There was enough wheat in government storage to meet the nation's needs for two years if not another bushel were grown.[4]

Years later Earl Butz, a plainspoken man who was an assistant secretary under Benson and later Secretary of Agriculture himself during the Nixon and Ford administrations, said,

> Ezra had the flexibility of the Rock of Gibraltar. But he and

Eisenhower had a love affair. . . . The press couldn't go after Eisenhower, so Ezra was a favorite target of the press. With Ezra, it wasn't hard. You didn't have to re-aim for your target with him, just reload.[5]

To my knowledge, Hope had few comments to make about Benson after the latter retired from public life in 1961. In a November 1969 newspaper column, Hope contrasted Clifford M. Hardin, President Nixon's first Secretary of Agriculture, with Benson. He was most complimentary of Secretary Hardin, quoting the secretary's testimony before the House Committee on Agriculture the previous September:

The charge given to me by President Nixon is to represent the farmers of this country in the councils of government. It is therefore my earnest desire to assist in the passage of good new legislation. This surely is a time when farmers and farm groups, acting through their enlightened self-interest, must find as much common ground as possible. I agree with the statement made by Chairman Poage last week in Texas to the effect that by themselves neither this Committee, nor the Administration, nor the Republicans, nor the Democrats, could pass a farm bill. We shall have to concentrate on the things which unite us if we are to rally the needed strength. It is in that spirit and in that framework that my colleagues and I desire to work with you.[6]

Hope himself could not have expressed better his feelings concerning the posture of a good Secretary of Agriculture. In comparison, he wrote this about Secretary Benson:

Mr. Benson was a strange man in many ways. He was very much an extremist and ran the office of Secretary under what seemed to be a curious mixture of religion and politics. His theology was mostly based on the old testament and he took great delight in smiting his political enemies hip and thigh.

He also had quite a martyr complex and following his retirement wrote a book called *Crossfire* in which he related his trials and tribulations — most of which he said he was able to overcome with the assistance of his wife, President Eisenhower and the Almighty. But as far as the nation's agriculture is concerned he made no significant contributions and left it worse than he found it.

Considering what Secretary Benson had said about Hope and other members of Congress, these comments seem rather restrained.

Fortunately for the nation's farmers (as well as all citizens), agricultural legislation much less controversial than price support programs was passed during the 1953-1956 period. Foremost — at least in Hope's view — was the Watershed Protection and Flood Prevention Act of 1954. I believe it would be accurate to say that of all the legislative matters before Congress during his 30-year tenure, soil and water conservation was closest to his heart. He wrote many letters and gave many speeches on this subject from the 1930s until the date of his disabling stroke in early 1970. He was fond of saying,

> Every drop of water which can be retained in the area in which it falls, either in the earth or in small retarding structures, is one drop subtracted from a potential flood and one drop added to our useful water supply.

The Soil Conservation Act of 1935 encouraged soil conservation by farmers on the land, and the Flood Control Act of 1936 provided for dams and reservoirs built by the Army Corps of Engineers and the Bureau of Reclamation on major streams. But until the 1954 Act, little had been done to encourage the building of dams or small watersheds "to catch the water where it falls."

Early in 1953 Senator Frank Carlson and Hope called on Ike in his White House office and were delighted to learn of his great interest in soil and water conservation. Small watershed legislation had been pending in Congress for the previous three years, but it took Eisenhower's message to Congress at the end of July to get the bill rolling. The Act passed in 1954 provided for local watershed districts, organized under state law, to construct dams and reservoirs with a capacity not in excess of 5,000 acre-feet [the equivalent of one foot of water covering 5,000 acres]. Cost sharing — with approximately 50 percent provided by the federal government — was based on benefits received. Watershed districts could not exceed 250,000 acres in area. Initiative for each project had to come from the people of the district, not the federal government. Support for the Act had a broad base; it was endorsed by the U.S. Chamber of Commerce, the CIO and AF of L, and major farm organizations. It was opposed by the Corps of Engineers, who still thought they should build and control all public dams. But with Eisenhower firmly in support of the Act, the Corps could not stop passage, even though it continued to oppose the program.

Another part of the soil and water conservation program illustrates how citizen initiative can sometimes succeed without great fanfare. In a speech at Chillicothe, Missouri, in September 1956, Hope told about two Chillicothe bankers, Mr. Simmer and Mr. Murray, who had visited him and other members of Congress two years earlier, proposing that the federal government insure loans for soil and water conservation purposes similar to federally-insured housing loans. "These gentlemen presented their ideas so clearly and forcefully that they made a deep impression on me, as I am sure they did with other members of Congress with whom they visited," Hope recalled. That same year (1954) late in the session, an amendment was passed to provide for such loans by the Farmers Home Administration.

In that same speech, as he would in many others, Hope spoke with almost religious fervor:

> If this were a sermon and I were to take a text, I would go back to the Book of Jeremiah in the Twelfth Chapter, verses 10 and 11, where the prophet spoke as follows: "Many shepherds have destroyed my vineyard, they have trampled down my portion; they have made my pleasant lot a desolate waste. They have made it a desolation, in its desolation it mourns to me, the whole land is made desolate, because no man layeth it to his heart."
>
> Therein lies the cause — "the whole land is made desolate because no man layeth it to his heart." Thus these citadels of ancient civilization fell victims to soil suicide.
>
> In these words of Jeremiah his meaning is at once a warning — a lesson to all of us today and to the generations to follow. I see in these words a sermon — teaching us that a nation's ultimate strength must lie not in its potential to destroy other peoples but in the simple, gentle and loving care of the soil, which is the source of all vigor in the growth of the physical,

the moral and the spiritual man. And in this ultimate strength —
the productive and protected land — is the key to peace among
peoples.

A hungry world is a dangerous world. Peace is not safe in it.
Hungry people are breeders of war. The Lord's land, the rich
earth, is hunger's only remedy. It is the place where all mankind
can find a mutual inspiration — it is the seedbed for permanent
peace.

The year 1954 marked the passage of other epochal legislation, an act
dealing with world hunger as well as with surplus commodities. The official title was the Agricultural Trade Development and Assistance Act of
1954, usually referred to as Public Law 480 (of the 83rd Congress). The
activities carried out under it became known as the Food for Peace program and, in amended form, it is the law today.

Hope wrote a number of newspaper articles about Public Law 480 in
the 1960s. In an October 18, 1964, column he explained that it was
designed to deal with surpluses and hunger.

> In some parts of the world science and technology were rev-
> olutionizing agricultural production. Not two, but several
> blades of grass were growing where one grew before. But these
> advances took place only in a few highly developed countries,
> our own in particular. Here, even with restrictions on produc-
> tion, we were producing more food than we could consume
> domestically or export in the normal channels of trade.
>
> At the same time, population was increasing faster than the
> food supply in many undeveloped and partially-developed
> countries. Thus while the world as a whole was producing
> enough to feed all of its people, there existed the paradox of
> surpluses large enough to be considered as a burden in this
> country while serious food shortages existed in others. It was a
> problem of distribution which could not be carried out through
> normal channels because the countries in the greatest need had
> no dollars with which to buy, and no way of getting them in any
> quantity.[7]

This situation was discussed widely during the early 1950s, and numerous bills designed to deal with the problem were introduced in both houses of the 83rd Congress (1953-1954). One such bill (S.2475), introduced by Kansas Senator Andy Schoeppel, passed the Senate in the closing days of the 1953 session, too late for consideration by the House before adjournment.

> During the Congressional recess and in the early days of the next session, the problem was given intensive study and consideration in many quarters. It was discussed in conferences attended by members of the House and Senate, members of the White House staff, officials in the Department of Agriculture, and other government departments and agencies, farm leaders, members of the food industry, merchandisers of farm products, and representatives of religious and philanthropic organizations. President Eisenhower indicated his strong interest in the matter.
>
> The result of all these deliberations was a bill considerably more comprehensive than the one passed by the Senate or any of the bills pending in the House. It was prepared in the Department of Agriculture and the White House and sent up to the House of Representatives for introduction by the chairman of the committee on agriculture [Hope]. After short hearings, the committee amended the Senate [Schoeppel] bill by striking out all after the enacting clause and substituting the House bill. The amended bill passed the House unanimously, was agreed to, with minor amendments by a Senate-House conference committee, and became Public Law 480 upon its signature by President Eisenhower on July 10, 1954.[8]

The original Act had three titles. Title I authorized the sale of surplus commodities to friendly nations for foreign currencies instead of dollars through private trade channels. Title II provided for outright donations for urgent or emergency food relief, and Title III authorized the Commodity Credit Corporation to make its surplus commodities available for school lunches and other domestic assistance programs and for barter for strategic materials. The Food for Peace program, as Hope wrote on the tenth anniversary in 1964, is a thrilling story. "It has helped us and helped others."

Hope's manuscript shows that in a 1969 column he gave credit to President Eisenhower for resolving by executive order the problem concerning the appointment of agricultural attaches to our embassies and the control of the attaches by the Ambassadors. "In situations where the interests of agriculture as an entire industry were involved," explained Hope, "the President was quick to take prompt action even if it involved conflict with other government agencies."

He noted that for many years attaches had served, for the most part, "as errand boys for the Ambassadors, although they were supposed to be working in the interest of U.S. agriculture." They were appointed by and responsible to the State Department. Agricultural organizations and members of Congress had long tried, without success, to correct the situation. Hope recalled how he and Senator Aiken, chairman of the Senate Committee on Agriculture and Forestry, had explained the matter to Eisenhower early in his administration. The President went into action, putting through a call to Under Secretary of State Walter Bedell Smith, the man who had been his chief of staff during World War II. He told Smith what was happening and said these attaches should be appointed by the Secretary of Agriculture and be responsible to him. Hope wrote:

> In five minutes, the matter was settled. The State Department bureaucracy had prevented any such action for years. Since that time these men have done the job they were supposed to do and have played an important part in expanding our agricultural exports.

During 1952 and until the truce arranged by President Eisenhower in July 1953, the Korean War was the foreign policy issue of most concern to Hope's constituents, as it was to all citizens. The volume of mail on the subject led him to prepare a two-page statement which discussed the matter at great length in addition to his answering each letter personally. In the statement he expressed his wish for peace in the immediate future, but he admitted it was something that no one could promise or do more than hope for under present world conditions. He wrote:

> I think I know what war means to every mother and to every

family. I served in the first World War as did one of my brothers and could not help but observe the concern and anxiety which this caused our mother. Our son served in World War II, and while he came back safely, no mother could have suffered more sleepless nights or more pain and anxiety than Mrs. Hope endured during his three years in the service. Experiences like that leave permanent effects.

He wrote that strength, firmness, and patience, combined with good judgment and experience might keep us out of World War III. While he hoped for a truce and final peace settlement in Korea soon, he felt there was no knowing what course the Russians and their communist allies might follow. He continued:

> They may precipitate war. Whether they do or not depends, in my opinion, on whether they think they can win. Any lack of firmness or show of weakness on our part will make the communists more arrogant and increase our danger. The military strength built up in the past two years might prevent further aggression. We are living in one of the most unsettled periods in history and powerful forces beyond our control may bring war irrespective of what we may do.

He likened the country's position to that of a ship at sea during a storm. "We can't do much about the storm. It will have to blow itself out. All we can do is to try and handle the ship so that it will ride through the storm successfully."

Meanwhile, during this period Hope was involved in his last two election campaigns. In 1952 he defeated Art McAnarney by more than two to one in the Eisenhower landslide. Hope's campaign contributions and expenses report showed contributions of $2,980, with $2,450 from Republican Committees, and itemized expenses of $1,441.04. All GOP representatives from Kansas were reelected with the exception of Albert Cole in the 1st District; he was defeated by Howard Miller, a farmer from Morrill, whose sole issue was Cole's support of the Tuttle Creek Dam project near Manhattan. The majority of voters in the district were against "Big Dam Foolishness."

Albert Cole had a distinguished career after leaving Congress. In 1953

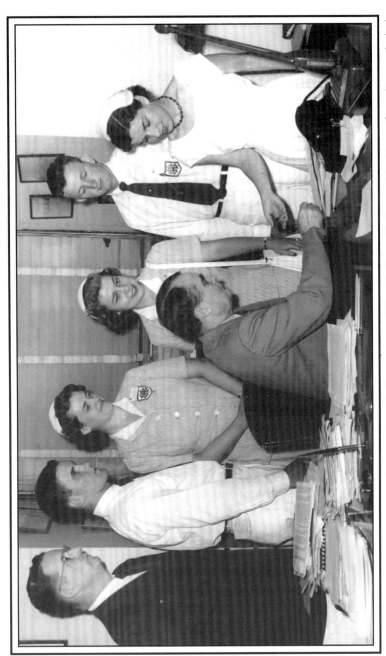

The Kansas delegation, *ca.* 1954, before lunching with Congressman Clifford R. Hope, Chairman of the House Committee on Agriculture, looks over the citation presented to their home state congressman for his great interest and support of the 4-H Club program during his 27 years as a member of the Committee on Agriculture. From left to right: J. Harold Johnson, state club leader, Manhattan; Jack Sexton, Talmadge; Luame Hicks, Goodland; Ruth Stinson, Ottawa; Tom Shinn, Conway Springs; and Virginia Armstrong, assistant state club leader, Manhattan.

USDA Extension Service, photo by George C. Pace

In March 1955, Congressman Clifford R. Hope of Kansas, 5th District, met the six 4-H Club delegates who came to Washington during National 4-H Club Week (March 5-13) to give "A Report to the Nation" on achievements of more than 2,000,000 Club members whom they represented throughout the country. From left to right: Congressman Hope, receiving 4-H memento; Leo Denise Corriveau, Millersburg, Michigan; Ralph E. Lamar, III, Southampton, New York; Sara Traughber, Springfield, Tennessee; Elden Holsapple, Mitchell, Indiana; Coleta Lou McAllister, Loyal, Oklahoma; and Cephas Williamson, Americus, Georgia.

Eisenhower appointed him administrator of the Housing and Home Finance Agency, the predecessor of the Department of Housing and Urban Development. He became a leading expert in housing and urban development. Years later Cole served as president of Reynolds Metals Development Corporation before retiring to practice law in Washington. Cole referred to Hope as a "role model congressman." Cole recalled:

> Cliff Hope became an internationally recognized authority in his field of agriculture through depth of knowledge, integrity, sincerity and dedication. Furthermore, these characteristics served him well in the House where his genial, assured manner placed him firmly among the leaders and honed his skills as an equal to the great, sometimes flamboyant, debaters of his time. A Congressman deals with an extraordinary range of concerns from the trivial to issues affecting the lives, well-being and security of the people. Cliff gave to each the same careful attention.

In 1954 Bob Bock, the 1950 candidate, again ran against Hope. This time one of Bock's charges was that "Clifford Hope Jr. is being groomed to succeed his father in Congress some day. I'm out to stop the Hope dynasty." Hope, however, did not believe in political dynasties. (A humorous anecdote from Bock's campaign concerns his sound-truck driver who announced, when pulling into a town, that Bock was running in the 1st *Congregational* District.) Hope used television for the first (and last) time that year on a very limited basis — his TV expense was $525.50! The final vote was 64,023 for Hope and 34,691 for Bock. In 1954 Andy Schoeppel was reelected Senator, running against the old Democratic warhorse, George McGill. All Kansas GOP congressmen were reelected, and William H. Avery, a Wakefield farmer who was later elected governor, unseated the first-term Howard Miller. Avery was also opposed to Tuttle Creek Dam, so "Big Dam Foolishness" was no longer an issue.[9]

Years later Bill Avery recalled Hope's counsel concerning the Tuttle Creek Dam fight:

> Not only did he counsel me on procedures during the floor debate, but after I lost the final vote, I shall always remember

his visiting with me about future planning and positions. In his own kindly way he suggested that I retain my position of opposing the project but anticipate that the dam would probably be built since it had the strong support of then Senator Andy Schoeppel in the Senate. Therefore, it might be beneficial to undertake to find ways of helping individuals and communities that would be adversely affected by the project. Although it took some time for me to become reconciled to this adjustment, the advice was appreciated and turned out to be useful and on target.

Avery concluded:

I never heard Cliff speak a harsh word against those with whom he disagreed either in debate or in personal conversation. He had the respect and admiration of all who knew him. He will always be remembered as an honest man with an infectious personality, kind to both friends and adversaries but unshakable in his convictions.

Hope was hospitalized in early June 1955 at Bethesda Naval Hospital with "coronary artery trouble," as he called it. Later that month he said he had "done less work in the last few weeks than anytime in the last fifty years and was feeling fine." His health problem may have hastened his decision to retire at the end of his term, in January 1957, but I am certain that was not the reason for it. He had considered retiring each election since 1950, but always had been persuaded against it by friends. Having made his decision and having no desire to pick his successor, he made his retirement announcement in November 1955 to give all prospective candidates plenty of time to reach their decisions. He wrote:

Knowing when to quit is a problem which confronts everyone in public life. Quite often the public decides the matter for us, and undoubtedly it will be decided for me if I tempt Fate long enough. But in the words of the preacher in the Third Chapter of Ecclesiastes, "There is a time for everything," and I believe this is the time for me to retire. If service in Congress is considered an honor then I have had far more than my share. On the other hand, if it is considered a difficult task, then it is not unreasonable that one who has held it for 30 years should be relieved of the burden.

He made it clear that he had not considered it a burden, saying he doubted if any member of Congress ever had a finer, more understanding constituency. The feeling that he had the confidence, respect, and good will of the majority of the people — although many may have disagreed with him on some matters — made his years in Congress "immeasurably easier." His retirement, wrote Hope, would mark the end of a relationship with the more than 300,000 people of his district, an association he treasured beyond expression.

But retiring from Congress, Hope said, would not mean retirement from activity. He looked forward to practicing law with his son, and he and his wife had long been eager to return to Garden City to settle down and renew associations with their friends. "When I return I want to do my share in the way of civic and community service and contribute what I can to the development of our state and especially to the great southwestern Kansas area which has vast potentialities."

Hope had been told there were "many willing hands ready to pick up the torch when I drop it," and he expressed confidence that when the time came, an able man, or perhaps a woman, would be selected. In the meantime, he reminded, "my present term does not expire for 13 months. . . . I hope the people of this District will continue to call on me for any service I can possibly render right up until the 3rd day of January 1957."

In the following weeks, Hope received many editorial eulogies and letters of appreciation from constituents. A letter from Nettie Bolmer of Conway Springs was especially moving:

> Did anyone ever write you a letter other than a letter of criticism? You know we human beings are so hasty to offer criticism but slow to praise folks when we are pleased. I was touched a couple days ago when I heard via radio that you would not seek another term of office. I just couldn't see how the government could function without you. I have written you many letters. I don't know how you ever did it, with untold thousands of letters coming in, but you always answered each letter promptly and satisfactorily. If you didn't know the

answers to my questions you took it up with the proper department and found out. I have always felt sorry for folks I talked
to, not in the 5th district, who would say they never received
any reply from their letters. My admiration for you was
increased several years ago when Capper's Weekly showed a
picture of you in your office. On a piece of furniture opposite
you, was not a picture from Esquire Magazine, but as I recall it
was a picture of your son and your daughter. Your ideals have
been high and your views most responsible. You will be missed
and it will be very difficult to replace you. You have served your
country well and we appreciate you very very much. We will
however welcome you back to Kansas and wish you all the success and happiness in the world.

In the months to follow, Hope was the honoree at various testimonial
dinners and receptions. The crowning event was a ceremony in the House
Committee on Agriculture meeting room on June 6, 1956, at which his
portrait was unveiled to hang with those of three Democrat former chairmen. Some months before, Hope's longtime friends R. N. Downie, Lester
McCoy, and George Reid had begun a low-key solicitation of funds to
have the portrait painted by a North Carolina artist, Mabel Pugh. About 70
persons responded, each with a personal letter. Contributions were limited
to $10 each. Downie, a courtly gentleman and Hope's banker for the fre-
quent loans Hope needed from one election to another, made the presentation. A number of members of Congress, including Frank Carlson,
Majority Leader John McCormack, and Joe Martin, former Speaker and
presently Minority Leader, responded. Carlson, a religious man, extolled
Hope as possessing the nine virtues of a perfect man as printed in Henry
Drummond's *The Greatest Thing in the World*. Carlson emphasized the
virtue of being without guile, and Joe Martin noted "in Congress there
isn't a single individual I know of that ever had an ill word to say about
Hope." McCormack gave this remarkable tribute:

As a Democrat from Massachusetts without a farm in my
district, somehow or other he and I always agree on farm legislation, because we view this great country of ours, 165 millions
of people, not a race, but a people, with our sectional problems,
and recognize that somewhere along the line there is an avenue

that we can all travel and should travel in the natural interests of our country.

And we both recognize that the agricultural community is a very powerful and important segment of our people, and of our national economy. And that buying in the protected market and selling in an unprotected market, there had to be some compensatory considerations given to them as a national policy — not as relief, not as charity, not as assistance, but as a national policy in the interests of our country.

After thanking his friends, Hope said,

I cannot help but think what a wonderful thing friendship is, because friends overlook all of our weaknesses and shortcomings and failures and for some reason seem to see things in our life and character that we did not know we possessed.

In acknowledging career personnel from the Department of Agriculture, he said many of them could have fared much better financially in private life, but they chose to make sacrifices and serve their country. Then he paid tribute to the American farmer:

All of us, some in the Congress, some in the Department, some in the farm organizations, have been working together on behalf of those engaged in the great basic industry of this country.

We realize how basic it is when we stop to think that a few inches of topsoil are all that really holds the world together. If we lose them, then famine and starvation would soon decimate the population of the earth. When we realize that the way we use that few inches of topsoil means the difference between starvation and plenty, then we realize the great part that farmers and the industry of agriculture play in the economy of this country and of the world.

Let me point out also that if there is any one reason why we have reached the high standard of living that we have in our country today, it is because of our fine, efficient agriculture.

Although Hope no longer had to give thought to his biennial race for Congress, he was as heavily involved in politics as ever during his last years in office. In early October 1955 before his retirement announcement, he received a handwritten letter from former governor Ed Arn urging him to wind up his career by running for governor. Hope politely declined, stating, "If I were 10 or 15 years younger I might have some ambitions along that line." Actually, I don't believe Hope ever had any great ambition to be governor. As a neutral party, he was agreed upon by both the Governor Fred Hall and anti-Hall forces to be chairman of the state convention to select delegates to the GOP national convention in the spring of 1956. Although everyone was for Ike, both sides had slates of delegates.[10]

The myriad of candidates which news commentators predicted for the race to replace Hope did not develop. George Reid probably wanted to run, but by 1956 he was too old. There were only two Republican candidates, State Senator John Crutcher of Hutchinson and State Representative Jay Berryman of Ashland. Crutcher edged out Berryman by 899 votes of 43,000 cast in the primary. J. Floyd Breeding swamped two opponents in the Democratic Party and edged out John Crutcher in the general election. Harry Dunn, Hutchinson lawyer, and other friends of Hope, dissatisfied with the GOP candidates, urged him to have me run as his replacement, and many people talked to me directly about the race. Hope would have none of it, and I agreed with him. I decided to run for the state senate instead.

My race for the state senate caused additional worries, if that were possible, for Pauline. As previously indicated, she basically thought anyone with a family to support should not be heavily involved in politics. Imagine her concern in September when she learned Dolores was pregnant with our fourth child. Clifford, who had known about it since spring, had put off telling her. Knowing how upset she would be, he waited until the night before they were to arrive in Garden City. Her first words were, "That boy has got to get out of the senate race and look after his family!" She loved having grandchildren but didn't want anything to happen that might give her any additional responsibilities and increased worries. Ironically, Holly Hope was born on election day!

Clifford and Pauline were fortunate in selling their Brandywine Street home in Chevy Chase for $28,500 — almost twice what they had paid for it in 1941. Clifford's beautiful rose garden enhanced the price. With the proceeds they were able to buy a home at 905 Lyle Avenue in a new addition in Garden City, two blocks from the Gillespie Place which Dolores and I had been renting from them since we returned to Garden City in 1950.

When the year ended, Clifford and Pauline had moved into their new home, and Clifford had begun preparation for what became a 300-bush rose garden. They were home at last.

Chapter 11

Interlude
(1957-1958)

*H*OPE WASTED NO TIME IN *resuming the practice of law in January 1957. Our second-floor law offices were located at 118 Grant Avenue in downtown Garden City. The firm of Hope, Haag, Saffels, and Hope had been established in March 1953. The other lawyers were two young attorneys, Lloyd H. Haag and Dale E. Saffels (who, years later, was appointed a federal district judge). They had formed a partnership in 1950. Hope did not become active in the firm until his retirement from Congress. During 1957-1958 he examined abstracts of title and handled a few decedents' estates and farmers' social security claims. In only one of the latter cases did he charge a fee. He wrote to the director of the Social Security Administration that he thought the manager of the Dodge City district office had "almost terrified these elderly people with his brutal cross examination and insinuations that they were wrongfully trying to get something from the government to which they were not entitled." He said he was familiar* enough with the cases to know they were bona fide and the people were acting in "utter good faith." They had good cases, he said, but that was not the point of his letter. He wrote:

>   American citizens are entitled to courteous treatment from government employees and this should especially apply to these elderly people who are not always in a good position to protect themselves.

Hope's files do not reveal the outcome of these cases, but they show he was fighting for his former constituents against government bureaucracy. In a 1966 letter to a friend, he explained: "The practice of law had changed so much during my thirty years in Congress that I found it rather boring." However, he kept practicing law for most of the two-year period without complaint or comment to his partners, and he did not draw any income from the firm. Fortunately, he found much else of interest to occupy his time.

He joined the staff of *The High Plains Journal,* at Dodge City, in July 1957 as a part-time advisor. Joe Berkely and Ray Pierce had plans to expand the *Journal* into a weekly farm newspaper covering all the Great Plains area, and Hope was eager to be of help. He began writing a weekly column, mostly — but not exclusively — on agricultural matters. This affiliation continued until early 1959.

President Eisenhower invited Hope to accompany him and Secretary Benson on the southwest Kansas portion of an aerial inspection of the Great Plains drought area in January 1957. The southern and central portions of the Plains had been inflicted with a severe drought from 1952 until 1957. Rainfall had been even less than in the early 1930s, but although there were dust storms, they were not as frequent and devastating as those of the Dust Bowl times. Governor George Docking and James McCain, president of Kansas State College, were also aboard the presidential airplane, *Columbine III,* when it landed at the Garden City Airport, on January 15, in a snowstorm! Ike greeted a crowd of 4,000 and spent an hour or so discussing the drought with local officials. Fortunately, spring rains brought an end to the dry cycle.

Hope was interested in establishing a Kansas wheat commission to promote increased and new markets, foreign and domestic, for wheat. Financing for the commission was to be provided by a small, refundable mill levy

Clifford Hope examines the wheat from the Kansas land that he loved.

DEDICATION

of the

CLIFFORD R. HOPE AUDITORIUM

The members of the Garden City Board of Education consider it a privilege to have the opportunity to name this beautiful new auditorium in honor of Clifford R. Hope, Sr., a local citizen who has gained national recognition and fame because of his outstanding work in the Congress of the United States for the past thirty years. This distinguished Congressman gave unselfishly of his time and knowledge to help make America a better place for all people, especially for those in the agricultural areas.

GARDEN CITY PUBLIC SCHOOL SYSTEM

January 16, 1957   Eight O'clock

Past and present board of education members and former superintendent who so generously gave of their time to aid in the planning and building of this auditorium.

Mrs. J. E. Dale   Paul O. Masoner
Mrs. L. R. Kester   Everett Miller
Charles F. Edwards   Charles L. Renick
Andrew B. Erhart   Claude W. Robinson
Harold Fansler, Sr.   Charles Schoonover
Kenneth M. Lyon   Helen Reed, *Clerk*

J. R. Jones (*Former Superintendent*)

on each bushel of wheat sold. As a new state senator, I was able to be of assistance by carrying the bill through the Senate. Although previous bills had passed the Kansas House several times, they had failed in the Senate, due in part to the strong opposition of my predecessor.

Hope continued to be a sought-after person in politics on the state and national levels. Some members of the legislature, the press, and others urged him to run for governor in an attempt to unseat Governor George Docking. Representative August Andresen of Minnesota, now ranking Republican on the House Agriculture Committee, asked him to come to Washington to write a general farm bill. Chairman Harold Cooley of the committee regretted that Hope was no longer the committee's peace-maker. National columnist Roscoe Fleming urged that Hope replace Sec-retary Benson. Hope politely declined the first three requests. Regarding his replacing Secretary Benson, there was nothing for Hope to say: Ben-son refused to resign and Ike refused to replace him.

Among the honors that continued to come to Hope, the most notable was having the auditorium of the new Garden City High School named after him in January 1957. This is the only public structure named in his honor. The ceremony was preceded by a dinner at Downing's Restaurant, during which Lester McCoy gave Hope what probably was the most flow-ery eulogy he ever received. Hope's two sisters and three brothers were present for the dinner and the dedication ceremony. R. N. Downie gave the dedication address and Hope responded. He paid tribute to his mother, Mitta, who had died five years before, saying,

> Our mother, especially, was determined that her children should have an education and sacrificed much to make it pos-sible. I don't think she cared a great deal about the material benefits which an education might give us. What she had in mind were the moral and spiritual benefits which should be a part of everyone's education. She wanted her children to be educated because she felt it would make them better citizens and better people in every sense of the word.

In the same year, Hope was awarded the Grand Prize of the Isaac Wal-ton League, a national conservation organization. For this, he received a congratulatory letter from Major General E. C. Itschner, chief of the Army Engineers, his old enemies in the small watershed battles.

On the home front Clifford resumed his membership in the Garden City Kiwanis Club — selling peanuts on the streets during a fund raiser — and participated in various charitable drives. As had been the case in Washington, the start and development of a rose garden was his most pleasurable activity. Pauline resumed her membership in Monday Club, a study group, and P.E.O., another women's club. They sold their home on Gillespie Place to Dolores and me for the appraised value under a GI loan, at four percent interest. Each purchased a new car — Pauline bought a Volvo, the only car she ever owned, which she kept until her death in 1969. At five feet in height, she could just barely see over the steering wheel of the small car. Clifford bought a 1958 Edsel, a choice he soon regretted.

Overall, 1957 and 1958 were good years for Clifford and Pauline, except for the experience of my running for Congress in 1958. The race was an emotional experience for them as well as for Dolores and me. I had dreamed of serving in Congress since I was a boy. In early 1955, months before his retirement announcement, I wrote Clifford inquiring as to his thoughts on my succeeding him in Congress. He replied in a handwritten letter, pointing out some of the difficulties. My best chance would be if he died in office, he said, "but I'll be darned if I'm going to die just so you can run." He foresaw objections, if I ran as his successor, to our family "trying to hog the office for two generations" and my "starting at the top." He quoted Ecclesiastes: "There is a time and place for everything under the sun." In other words, this was not going to be my last opportunity to run for Congress or other important offices. I took that advice; I was elected to the state senate in 1956 and decided to bide my time. Before the 1956 election, I expected John Crutcher to win the 5th District congressional seat and surmised he was ambitious and would be running for governor or the U.S. Senate in due course. When he was defeated by Democrat J. Floyd Breeding, that changed the picture entirely. My ambition was rekindled. It is accurate to state that in 1957-1958, there was no one in Kansas, not even Bob Dole or Keith Sebelius, who wanted to be a congressman more than I did.

Many Kansas Republicans thought Breeding's election had been nothing more than a fluke and it would be easy to return the district to the Republicans. Hope and I were under no such illusions. Breeding was personable and politically astute. He answered mail promptly and made many telephone calls to constituents, as my father had done.

As 1957 ended, my father and George Reid — in a gentle way —

warned me, "1958 is going to be a bad year for the Republicans." Clifford suggested I could run for Lieutenant Governor, an office where a familiar name and vigorous campaigning could be more effective. I appreciated the advice, but realizing the opportunity to run for Congress did not arise very often, I determined to plunge ahead. I figured if worse came to worse, I could afford to lose one race for Congress.

Once I was in the race, Clifford volunteered to help in many ways and to give advice, despite his misgivings about the year 1958. He was handicapped, however, by lack of experience in a campaign such as this. In 18 elections, he had never run against an incumbent, solicited funds on a mass basis, or employed an advertising agency.

After Harold Cooley, chairman of the House Committee on Agriculture, came to the district to boost Breeding's candidacy, Clifford volunteered to respond to Cooley at a GOP rally in Pratt. He also wrote newspaper columns in *The High Plains Journal* on timely subjects, including the Teamster's Union, the Right to Work Amendment, and recollections of campaigning during his time in Congress. He declined out-of-state speaking engagements during September and October and spent most of his time during those months on the campaign, including working with the advertising agency.

All was to no avail. Congressman Breeding won 53 percent of the vote. Statewide, 1958 was the worst GOP defeat of the 20th century. Thus in Kansas and in the nation as a whole, the returns were even worse than Hope and others had forecast. Democrats gained 47 seats in the House and 13 in the Senate.

My campaign expenses were about $20,000, a modest sum even for those times. There was a $4,000 deficit which Clifford quietly paid, at the same time giving a like sum to his daughter Martha; I learned after his death, years later, that he had cashed in insurance policies to accomplish this. Overall I do not believe the campaign hurt Clifford. He retained the respect most people held for him. He thought I had done my best under the circumstances, and that was good enough for him. As for Pauline, she did not want me to lose, but considering my family responsibilities, she did not want me to be a congressman either. She hoped her son had "gotten politics out of his system."

Congressman Breeding served two more terms, but in 1962 he lost to Bob Dole, the 6th District's congressman, when the 5th and 6th Districts were combined.

As the year neared its end, Clifford embarked on a new, full-time career, one which would occupy his time for the next 4½ years. He became president of the newly organized Great Plains Wheat Market Development Association, with headquarters in Garden City.

Chapter 12

Great Plains Wheat
and Afterward (1959-1970)

*URING THE LATE 1950s, farmers and farm leaders in
the Great Plains, including Hope, began efforts to create a regional self-help organization to develop new
markets for hard red wheat — both winter and spring
varieties, grown in the area to reduce burdensome and price-
depressing wheat surpluses and to feed hungry people throughout the world. The first meeting with definite accomplishments
was held in Dodge City May 19-20, 1958. In attendance were
representatives from Nebraska, Kansas, and Colorado along
with observers from Oklahoma, Texas, and North Dakota. Nebraska had taken the lead among Great Plains states in establishing a wheat commission in 1955, followed by Kansas in 1957
(as recited in the last chapter) and Colorado, with a wheat
administration committee, in 1958.*

*Subsequent meetings were held later in 1958 in Lincoln and
Denver. Hope was elected president and Herbert Hughes, executive vice president. There was great disagreement during a*

December meeting in Denver over whether to locate the organization's principal office in Wichita or Denver. In a compromise, Garden City was selected over Wichita by a 7-6 vote. Garden City won, I believe, only because the office location there would enable Hope to devote full time to his duties as president.[1]

Early in February 1959, Hope explained his new job to a friend in Washington:

> I have recently taken on a new activity as President of the Great Plains Wheat Market Development Association which is a non-profit corporation set up by the wheat growers organizations of Kansas, Nebraska and Colorado for the purpose expressed in the organization's title. We expect wheat organizations from other Great Plains States to come into the organization at a later date. I have been urging an organization of this kind for a good many years and believe so strongly in its possibilities that I am getting a lot of pleasure out of being associated with it. At the present time our most important sphere of activity is in the export field and to date we have established offices in Rotterdam, Lima, Peru, and in connection with the Pacific Northwest Wheat Growers have an office in New Delhi, India. These are not sales offices, you understand, as we are not merchandising wheat but offices for the purpose of developing markets working with the millers and grain trade and with the Foreign Agricultural Service of the Department of Agriculture. We are making preparations now for setting up an active campaign of domestic market expansion and have other projects in the mill including more equitable transportation rates and better facilities, and increased industrial uses for wheat.

In a letter to Frances Griffin, his former administrative assistant in Washington, Hope described the organization's plans and commented on a recent meeting of the Board of Directors which, he said, was "exceptionally harmonious considering the trouble we had at the meeting in Denver over the location of the principal office." The office in Garden City, he said, would be small until the Lincoln office, which had been handling all the foreign market development activities for the state wheat commissions of Kansas, Colorado, and Nebraska, moved to Garden City in July. By then there would be more activities underway. "I am sure that I am going to like this work very much," Hope wrote. "It gets me back in the agriculture field and I am working with a great many men I have known and worked with for many years." He mentioned that Lester Mort, the man in charge of the Washington office, was doing a fine job.

The Garden City office started from scratch. There were no funds available initially from the state wheat commissions, so Hope loaned the money for several months in 1959 to employ a secretary, Barbara Maddux, and to rent second floor office space in the old Walters Building on Main Street. Later, spacious, built-to-order offices were rented in the new Campbell Building on Eighth Street. Hope's salary for 1959 was set at $10,000. William H. Crotinger from Tribune, Kansas, was hired on a part-time basis to manage trade fairs, and Leslie Sheffield moved to Garden City as executive secretary in May with the move of the marketing office from Lincoln. In August Charles Burch came on the staff as director of information. Great Plains Wheat (GPW), a shortened title from Great Plains Wheat Market Development Association, was off the ground.

Hope's market promotion work involved a great deal of travel, including numerous trips to Washington, board meetings in the Great Plains area, speeches throughout the United States, and trips abroad. His most extensive trip was a 20-day trip in November and December 1959 to Rotterdam, Karachi, New Delhi, Hong Kong, and Tokyo. All this traveling was disturbing to Pauline. She seldom accompanied him.

During Hope's tenure as president, North Dakota and South Dakota became members and provided more funding for GPW activities. In addition to funds from the state wheat commissions, the Foreign Agricultural Service of the USDA provided foreign currencies for travel and for maintaining GPW foreign offices. Additional funding also provided for expansion of the staff in Garden City and other offices. Bill Crotinger became Hope's executive assistant in July 1960 and executive secretary a year later when Sheffield returned to the University of Nebraska to pursue a career in irrigation economics. Crotinger, whose background was farming, admired Hope greatly. Years later he recalled Hope's advice to him about the many detailed reports, surveys, and so on prepared by GPW. The basic admonition was "always make certain your figures are correct." In 1961 Howard Hardy, a wheat farmer from Beach, North Dakota, and Charles Potucek of Dodge City became administrative assistants in the Garden

City office. Secretaries and other assistants included Marie Dewey, Patricia Finney, Pat Collins, and Orvileta West.

Hope retired as president of Great Plains Wheat July 1, 1963, having reached his 70th birthday on June 9. In announcing retirement from his third career at the May meeting of the board of directors in Bismarck, he said:

> I have shared the gratification which I am sure has come to you in feeling that we in Great Plains Wheat are doing important and necessary work, and work which will make a better world. I have never been more interested in the success of the organization than I am right now, and wherever I am and whatever I am doing, that interest will continue.
>
> However, there are good reasons why I should leave at this time. In less than a month, I will observe my 70th birthday, which makes the span of life allotted to man in the Bible, and is somewhat past the usual retirement age in business and industry. Mrs. Hope, whose health has not been good, although improving, feels very strongly that we have reached an age where we should spend more time together and I must agree with her.
>
> Also, like all of us, there are many things I have hoped to do which I have not been able to work into a busy life. If I do them at all, they can't be put off much longer. Right now, I am about two years behind in my rose garden and even further behind in visiting my grandchildren, to say nothing of the stack of books gathering dust while I am trying to find time to read them.

After praising the GPW staff and incoming president, Howard Hardy, Hope issued a challenge to all concerned to cooperate in "telling the people for whom we are working what we are doing for them." He continued: "We have spent time and money on congressional dinners in Washington but have neglected Topeka, Pierre, Bismarck, Denver, and county seats all over the area. This has been and is a grassroots organization. In the future, we must make it even more so." Hope's "last report," according to those in attendance, was an eloquent testimony. Its closing lines were:

> I love the plains like a mariner loves the oceans. Their vast

expanse, their varied and unpredictable climate, their combination of rich soil and uncertain rainfall constitute a challenge which develops character and hardihood. Plains people have to learn how to take hardship and prosperity. The plains are no place for weaklings. To me, wheat is a symbol of the plains and its people. Like them, it is tough and resilient. It can take a beating and come back, if not this year then next year. The Great Plains is and will remain the world's greatest wheat growing area and in spite of so-called surpluses, the hungry world needs and will continue to need more wheat. And Great Plains people and Great Plains soil and climate are going to have a big part in supplying it.

During Hope's tenure, Great Plains Wheat grew from 4 offices and 12 full-time employees in 1959 to 8 offices with 47 employees, plus 20 more jointly associated with Western Wheat Associates, a similar organization supported by Oregon, Washington, and Idaho, organized in the spring of 1959. Hope continued as a consultant to GPW for three more years before resigning from that post, mainly at Pauline's insistence. She objected to his traveling and wanted him, as she put it, "close by my side."

At the urging of the majority of the board of directors, the Garden City office was moved to Kansas City, Kansas, at the end of 1966, and then to Washington in April 1969. Hope was opposed to both moves. He considered it important that GPW remain a "grassroots" organization. In his view, it was necessary to have a Washington office, but the principal office, he contended, should remain on the Great Plains. He thought, I believe, that the board of directors had succumbed to Potomac Fever. In January 1980, almost a decade after Hope's death, Great Plains Wheat and Western Wheat Associates combined to form U.S. Wheat Associates with U.S. offices in Washington and Portland. At the date of this writing (1995), the new organization has 15 overseas offices and is supported by wheat commissions from 17 states. I believe Hope would be pleased by this growth.

Hope maintained contacts with Harold Cooley, chairman of the House Committee on Agriculture and W. R. Poage of Waco, Texas, Cooley's successor in 1967 as chairman. He also became well acquainted with George McGovern and Orville Freeman. McGovern was head of the Food for Peace office in 1961-1963, and thereafter a senator from South Dakota.

Freeman, former governor of Minnesota, was Secretary of Agriculture in the Kennedy and Johnson administrations. Hope developed a warm friendship with both men. After his retirement as president of GPW, he had frequent contact with McGovern, a strong supporter of a domestic parity (voluntary wheat-marketing certificates) program for wheat which was finally enacted into law in the Cotton-Wheat Act of 1964. This program, re-enacted with little change in the Food and Agriculture Act of 1965, remained law during Hope's lifetime. He was pleased that the wheat price support program for which he had labored so many years had finally been enacted.

In the years after his retirement as president of GPW, Hope managed to catch up on some of the things he listed in his remarks at Bismarck, but by the summer of 1964 he was eager for more to do on a regular basis. He had started writing a column for *The High Plains Journal*, a regional farm weekly, during 1957-1959 even though he was busy with other matters at that time. Hence he thought about writing a weekly column for *The Hutchinson News*, *The Salina Journal*, and *The Garden City Telegram*, three daily newspapers that covered western Kansas. In an unobtrusive way, he considered it his duty to share the knowledge and opinions he had accumulated over the years with the people of the area.

In late July 1964 Hope wrote a long letter to his old friend, John P. (Jack) Harris, publisher of *The Hutchinson News* and chairman of the board of Publishing Enterprises, which then owned eight newspapers, including the *Journal* and the *Telegram*, and three radio stations in Kansas and Iowa. He began:

> Frankly, I am in no mood to retire from all activities. I feel I have some of the best years of my life ahead and I want to put them to some interesting and worthwhile use. The future of western Kansas is the subject of greatest interest to me. The area and its people have had a growing fascination for me ever since I came here as a boy. Much of the satisfaction which I got out of my years in public life and as president of Great Plains Wheat came from the feeling that I was in a position to deal with some of the problems peculiar to western Kansas.

He told Harris he was looking for some way to establish contact with people in the area and to develop definite area consciousness. He saw the three Harris papers west of U.S. Highway 81 as the best medium for that purpose and proposed writing a weekly column for them because of their excellent local and regional news coverage, wide circulation, and outstanding editorial pages, which already were doing much to enhance area consciousness. He wrote Harris:

> Western Kansas is as different from eastern Kansas as it is from Ohio or Maryland. Yet I am sure many otherwise well-informed area residents do not understand this, or if they do, don't think anything can be done about it.

He said he doubted if there were many — if any — area problems that he had not heard of when he was in Congress and that most of them continued to exist, some having grown more serious. His work with Great Plains Wheat's operations in 60 countries had given him an insight into world trade and world affairs generally that he could not have acquired in any other way. He continued:

> It has compelled me to keep in close touch with world economic and commercial affairs such as the European Common Market and the trade negotiations at Geneva. Because of the importance of food in the underdeveloped countries, I have been brought in close touch with their economic and political problems.

Hope wrote that these connections made it necessary for him to maintain contacts in Washington with members of Congress and governmental agencies and to be in touch with farmers and businessmen in all Great Plains states from Texas to Montana.

Harris was receptive to Hope's proposition to write a weekly column, provided *The Hutchinson News* editor, John McCormally, approved. He added only one caution:

> Of course you know enough about the ins and outs of Western Kansas to write books about it. The practical question is whether you have the knack of reducing your information to, say, no more than 500 words once a week that the mass of our subscribers would actually read.

(Hope handled this matter a number of times by writing several "to be continued" columns on subjects that warranted it.) And so it was agreed with the *News* and *The Salina Journal* to run Hope's column in Sunday editions. The column "Cliff's Comments" began in September 1964 and continued, with vacation periods from time to time, until Hope suffered a disabling stroke in February 1970. For his writing, Hope received what McCormally described as "the magnificent sum of $9 a week," barely enough to pay for the typing expenses. Even so, Hope was pleased to be writing again on a regular basis. As he said in a letter at the end of October 1964 to Frances Griffin, it gave him a good soap box. "I am making it strictly non-political but am discussing government policies, particularly as they affect Western Kansas." Hope confided that it was a lot more work than he was getting paid for, not as far as the writing was concerned but for the research that went into it. But then, he added, "I like that part of it . . . it keeps me up to date on a lot of things which I probably wouldn't trouble myself with otherwise."

Many of the quotations in this book come from Hope's columns, in which he wrote on a variety of topics. From time to time Hope wrote on strictly political issues. Perhaps the most interesting and popular columns were his political and personal reminiscences. Occasionally he despaired of continuing the column. For example, he wrote Whitley Austin, editor of *The Salina Journal* in September 1967:

> I believe my biggest problem in connection with the column is that I've been taking it overseriously and making too much of a chore out of writing it. I'm thinking now that I could start over and do it without so much mental sweat and probably do a better job.

In spite of periodic misgivings, however, Hope always talked himself into keeping at it.

During the decade of the 1960s, Hope maintained a keen interest in Kansas and national politics, mostly as an observer, but sometimes as a partisan of a particular candidate or cause. From 1960 to 1966 his work with Great Plains Wheat precluded his active participation in politics; he was hence somewhat embarrassed in the spring of 1960 at press reports that he was an advisor to Vice President Nixon, who by that time had the GOP nomination locked up. Nixon was most eager to distance himself from the person and policies of Ezra Taft Benson. A private meeting between Nixon and Hope was scheduled in Washington for March 29. Thinking it best to clarify his position, Hope issued a news release on the preceding day, denying reports that he was participating in the 1960 campaign as an agricultural advisor to Nixon. "These reports are not true," he said. While he had known Nixon for a number of years and held him in high regard, Hope "made it perfectly clear" that he had not seen or communicated with Nixon for almost a year and a half. Hope's only connection with Nixon or his office had been a brief contact with two members of the Nixon staff.

Hope went on to say he had no intention of returning to the political scene which he had left three years earlier and that he regarded his efforts in developing markets for agricultural products to be the most important activity in which he had ever been engaged. He would not enter into political activities, even in a small way, lest it impair his usefulness in this cause. However, he said, there was a difference between the purely political aspects of a campaign and the efforts of a candidate to be informed on public questions. The newspaper stories, Hope felt, gave the impression that he was dealing in the "political aspects," whereas he had been told that Nixon wanted to re-explore Republican policy on the farm question in light of present conditions. "I hope that he does so, and that in doing it, he secures the widest possible cross section of agricultural thought," Hope said in his statement to the press. "If his survey should be broad enough that he desires my views, I shall be very happy to give them to him."

I found no record of the Nixon-Hope meeting, but its subject matter can be surmised from Hope's letter to the Vice President on April 9. Hope had been concerned for some months about the constant criticism of farmers and farm programs appearing almost daily in the metropolitan press and in national weekly and monthly magazines. He wanted to make certain that Nixon understood the farmers' point of view and hence sent him a copy of an article by Dr. C. Peairs Wilson of Kansas State University, "Putting Agriculture in Proper Perspective." Hope also referred Nixon to an article in the April 9, 1960, issue of *The Saturday Evening Post* titled "The Farmer's Side of the Case." This article, written by the wife of a Kansas dairy farmer, gave a fair and factual account of problems confronting "educated, experienced and practical farmers who, until the present time at least, have had access to ample capital."[2] Hope pointed out that he did not know the author, Mary Conger, but had known her husband when he was a county agent in an adjoining county. On the same day, Hope wrote Mrs. Conger at her farm home near Iola, Kansas, to tell her he had previously called John Bird of *The Saturday Evening Post* urging him to publish Dr. Wilson's article. Bird informed Hope that the *Post* was already planning to publish Mrs. Conger's article. Hope wrote Mrs. Conger:

> I have read [your] article and have not been disappointed. . . . You have presented the facts and written your story in such a way that it can be understood by non-farm people. The tone certainly cannot be offensive to anyone who may have heretofore been critical of farmers based upon the misinformation which has been in circulation. . . . If non-farm people read it, it will do a lot of good.

(Mary Conger's long article set forth in clear, non-emotional language the cost-price squeeze on farmers who sold at wholesale and bought at retail.)

Mrs. Conger wrote Hope saying she felt highly complimented by his attention to her article. She said that the response everywhere had been gratifying and that one of the first letters to arrive was from the White House. "I worked hard on my reply to the President and tried to think carefully," she said. She had letters from a number of senators and representatives, many farm leaders, and people of all professions. Conger wrote to Hope:

> There are letters pouring in from men and women on every kind of farm in every state who tell me that this is indeed their story. Farmers look back with nostalgia to the more favorable era when we could depend on you for leadership. There is now an urgent need for a broad understanding and unity of purpose.

Hope's continued concern and leadership in the struggle to establish a fair deal for farmers was evident. Later in the same year, when another Kansas friend suggested Hope for Secretary of Agriculture in a Nixon administration, Hope didn't mince words:

My reaction to the possibility of being Secretary of Agriculture is something like that of General Sherman toward Texas when he made his well-known statement that if he owned both hell and Texas, he would live in hell and rent Texas out.

During the 1964 presidential election, when Senator Barry Goldwater was running against President Lyndon Johnson, Hope was still serving as a consultant to Great Plains Wheat; therefore, he felt he should not publicly express his opinion of the race. He was not reticent, however, in expressing his views privately both before and after the election. In brief, he was appalled by Senator Goldwater's campaign and by some of his fervent supporters. Hope was dismayed by Goldwater's convention statement that "extremism in the defense of liberty is no vice; moderation in the pursuit of justice is no virtue" and subsequent campaign "shooting from the lip" remarks. It was Hope's opinion that any presidential candidate should not be an ideologue, conservative or liberal. Goldwater proudly proclaimed himself a conservative and implied that anyone who did not agree with him was not welcome in the Republican Party.

In an October exchange of correspondence with Milton Eisenhower, Hope shared his concern about the future of the GOP. He said a crushing defeat of Goldwater and Miller would not disturb him, but he feared for the defeat of many able leaders who would be caught in the avalanche, and for the image of the Party being created by the Goldwater campaign. He wrote:

It may take quite a while to live that down. We probably could not win even with a strong candidate, but a man like Scranton or Nixon would have made a good race and left us with something to build on.

He and Eisenhower agreed that the party had a big job ahead.

On the day after the election, Hope included this note to John McCormally along with his column for the following Sunday: "What an election! I never expected to see the time when the party of Lincoln would get to the point where it was reduced to carrying five Deep South states on a racist issue."

The election results in Kansas and the U.S. were even more overwhelming than Hope had anticipated. Nationwide, Johnson carried 44 states and 62 percent of the popular vote to Goldwater's 6 states (Arizona plus the Deep South) and 38 percent. The GOP lost 38 seats in the House, giving the Democrats a 295 to 140 margin, and 3 in the Senate, giving a Democrat margin of 68 to 32. In Kansas Johnson received 55 percent of the popular vote and carried 39 out of the 58 counties in the conservative 1st District. In Hope's home county of Finney, the margin was 62 percent to 38 percent. Goldwater was the first GOP nominee to lose Kansas since Alf Landon in 1936.

In a long letter to his old friend Don Berry in January 1965, Hope noted that the Kansas GOP had survived the debacle even though it refused to go for Goldwater. He wrote:

> I am not sure, after reading your letter, just how strong you were for Goldwater, but I simply couldn't take him and there were certainly a lot of other Republicans in Kansas who felt the same way.

Hope said he could not remember ever having a weaker candidate or a worse campaign. "This state went for Goldwater at the convention, with the exception of two delegates, one of whom was the state chairman," he explained. "It was a very weak delegation." He pointed out that Governor John Anderson was not elected as a delegate to the convention because he would not go along with the "fanatical" Goldwater crowd. At this point, he said, he could not see that the election results had hurt the Party as far as Kansas was concerned. "In fact," he added, "I think perhaps it has been strengthened."

Backtracking a bit on Kansas politics, in 1960 Attorney General John Anderson defeated McDill (Huck) Boyd in the primary for governor and went on to beat Governor George Docking, who was running for a third term, 56 to 44 percent. Then in January 1962, when Senator Andy Schoeppel died in office, Anderson appointed his political ally, former state senator and GOP state chairman, James B. Pearson, to the vacancy. Pearson defeated former governor Ed Arn handily in the primary and Paul Aylward, Democrat stalwart, in the general election.

Hope liked Anderson and Pearson, regarding them as pragmatic, intelligent, and effective. He contributed $400 to Pearson's 1962 campaign, a sizeable contribution for Hope at that time. (The size may have been due in part to my serving as Pearson's campaign chairman that year.) In 1966

Pearson, running for the full six-year Senate term, was challenged by Republican Congressman Robert Ellsworth of Lawrence, who had been serving as the 3rd District's representative since 1961. Hope, no longer with Great Plains Wheat, endorsed Pearson in a July 3 newspaper column. Without mentioning Ellsworth by name, he cited Pearson's accomplishments and pointed out how much his five years of seniority in the Senate would mean to Kansas. The column was widely distributed by the Pearson forces and was quite effective, especially in western Kansas. Pearson won easily and went on to defeat Floyd Breeding in the general election.

Hope also attempted to help Governor William Avery win reelection against Democrat challenger Robert Docking, son of George Docking. After being elected as a congressman for five terms (1955-1965), Avery was elected governor in 1964 in a narrow (52 to 48 percent) victory over Harry Wiles. Avery sponsored a half-cent sales tax and income tax increases and withholding of income taxes (a first in Kansas) to provide more state aid for schools, with a reduction of local property taxes. Withholding income tax especially made Avery unpopular. Hope in his usual studious manner prepared a letter to the voters of Finney County citing Avery's long experience in government and explaining in great detail the reasons for the governor's actions. Avery lost Finney County by only 53 votes, but he lost the state to the astute Docking 56 to 44 percent.

Early in 1967 Senator George McGovern invited Hope to speak at a bipartisan recognition dinner in Mitchell, South Dakota, marking the Senator's tenth year of service in Washington. The plan, McGovern said, was to have a prominent member of each political party speak. He suggested that Hope be the Republican speaker. "Let me stress," he wrote Hope, "the entire evening is to be conducted in a nonpartisan fashion." Hope readily accepted. As previously indicated, Hope was grateful to McGovern for his services to agriculture, especially for his assistance when Hope was president of Great Plains Wheat and for his support of the Domestic Parity Plan for wheat enacted in 1964.

South Dakota Republicans, when they learned of Hope's acceptance, were greatly disturbed, to say the least. "Jesus Christ Almighty!" Congressman E. Y. Berry wrote: "How in the hell can you do a thing like this to us? You know, I hope, that this McGovern dinner is a fund-raising Democratic rally. No Republicans are involved." He asked, "What chance do Republicans have of electing Republicans when the most respected Republican in America comes into our state to support a left-wing liberal like George McGovern?" and then closed with, "I hope to hell, Cliff, you can get out of this trap."

Hope's reply was typical. He thanked Berry for his letter "even if you did give me hell about speaking at the McGovern dinner." He wrote that he was attending the event "because I admire George very much and think he is doing a good job, not only for his constituents but for my former constituents as well." Hope explained that he had come to know McGovern well when he was president of Great Plains Wheat and McGovern was director of Food for Peace. "He helped us a lot then as well as later, after he was elected to the Senate," Hope said.

It was a non-election year, and notwithstanding Berry's protest to the contrary, Hope reminded his friend that the meeting was bipartisan, adding,

> I understand that friends of Senator McGovern got the idea from a bipartisan dinner given in honor of my good friend, Karl Mundt, at which John McClelland (who is a whale of a lot more important as a Democrat than I am as a Republican) spoke.

Hope said he was sorry his attendance at the dinner offended Berry. "I have always held you in very high regard and will continue to do so irrespective of any differences of opinion which we may have regarding my participation in this meeting."

The GOP chairman of South Dakota wrote a courteous letter saying he would like for Hope to reconsider his decision. He, too, received a letter in which Hope gave his reasons for agreeing to speak. Hope probably received telephone calls about the matter, but he left no record of them. Hope and George Reid, still a legislative consultant in Washington, were bemused by the furor. George noted that the last time Hope gave a speech in Mitchell it was on behalf of Congressman Harold Lovre, who was defeated a few days later.

McGovern had not told Hope that the April 8 dinner would be a fund raiser ($25 per ticket); on the other hand, he had not said it would not be. I do not believe Hope, who had never had a fund-raising dinner for himself, thought much about that one way or the other. Senator Edward Kennedy, then serving his fourth year in the Senate, was the other speaker. Hope's speech, really a splendid one, dwelt on the history of South Dakota and the Great Plains during the previous 40 years of trials and tribulations and praised Senator McGovern for his work. Nineteen months later, McGovern was reelected to the Senate. It was doubtful Hope's speech affected the outcome either way; at least that was Hope's view.

As luck would have it, Hope, at the age of 75, became more involved in politics in 1968 than he had been since my 1958 congressional campaign. He supported Nelson Rockefeller for the Republican nomination for President and was an enthusiastic member of the Kansas for Rockefeller committee, of which Mike Getto of Lawrence was the executive campaign chairman. Phil Kassebaum asked Hope to serve on the committee. In his July 21 column, Hope gave a strong endorsement to "Rocky," citing his extensive experience in government and his broad appeal to a wide range of voters.

Unfortunately, Rockefeller's campaign got off to a late start, and Richard Nixon won on the first ballot at the convention. The Kansas delegation, as a courtesy, voted solid for Senator Frank Carlson. Mike Getto claimed Rocky would have received 15 of the 20 Kansas delegate votes if there had been a second ballot. Polls in Kansas had indicated strong support for Rockefeller over Nixon. Hope had little problem in supporting Nixon versus Vice President Hubert Humphrey in the November election. He was appointed to the Nixon National Agricultural Advisory Committee and to the Kansas Nixon-Agnew Campaign Committee. Nationwide Nixon won with only a 500,000-vote plurality over Humphrey (301 to 191 in the electoral college), but he carried Kansas by an almost 5-3 margin. As stated in a previous chapter, Hope was pleased by Nixon's appointment of Clifford Hardin as Secretary of Agriculture.

Near the end of 1967, Frank Carlson, Hope's best friend in Congress, announced his intention to retire at the end of his term in January 1969. Bob Dole, 1st District Congressman, announced for Carlson's seat the next day. As noted in the last chapter, Dole had defeated Floyd Breeding in 1962 to become the first congressman from the district constituting the west half of Kansas. Before that Dole had been elected to Congress from the old 6th District upon the retirement of Wint Smith in 1960. That year Dole had defeated Keith Sebelius by only 982 votes in a spirited primary. (In 1958 Sebelius had run against Wint Smith, losing by a scant 51 votes.)

Dole began his career as an ultra conservative; some observers dubbed him "Wint Smith, Jr." In 1963, his first year as Hope's representative, he sent Hope an editorial from *The St. John News* which referred to Hope as having been a conservative congressman. Hope wrote to thank Dole for the clipping but did not go along entirely with the conservative label. He told the young Dole:

> I am sure you know that we are not in entire agreement on some matters of public interest. However, I am sure that there is plenty of room in the Republican party for divergent views, and I have always been very reluctant to accept any designation of conservative or liberal as applied to my views on political and economic questions.

Both terms, he wrote, had been so abused that they did not really mean much. "As I think you know," he wrote Dole, "I, in general, took a middle-ground view during the time I was active in politics."

Hope was disappointed the next year when Dole and many other Republicans voted against the Cotton-Wheat Act, containing the Domestic Parity Plan for wheat.

In 1964 Dole was one of the original supporters of Barry Goldwater, campaigning hard for him. That fall Dole was opposed by Bill Bork, farm editor of *The Hutchinson News*, which Dole at that time referred to as the "Prairie Pravda." To the surprise of some, Dole won by a scant 5,000-vote majority, only 51 percent of the vote. Thereafter, Dole took a more pragmatic approach to issues, much to Hope's approval.

The next spring, in connection with consideration of the bill which became the Food and Agricultural Act of 1965, Hope wrote to Dole pointing out that the proposals in the bill offered the basis for a sound and practical wheat and feed grains program for the Great Plains area. There had been backing for the proposals from Republican and Democratic antecedence, he said, and Hope thought it would be "a great mistake" for Republicans from the commercial wheat-growing area to make a political issue of the matter. He pointed out:

> There has never been a time, since I first went to Congress, at least, when there was a real community of interest between the corn belt and the Great Plains as far as agriculture is concerned. Any attempt to go along with the corn belt program will leave Western Kansas holding the short end of the stick. I think our interests have always been more in line with those of other

farmers who produce export crops such as cotton, rice and tobacco.

Later that year Dole voted for the bill. He made a point of honoring Hope in many ways for his past service to western Kansas and agriculture. In the spring of 1968, Hope (I believe at the request of Bill Kats, a member of Dole's staff and a longtime friend) endorsed Dole for the Senate:

> Several years ago at ten o'clock on a Saturday night, I called Bob Dole at his Washington residence. His wife told me he was at the office. And sure enough he was. I don't think he spends every Saturday there but he is certainly not a Tuesday to Thursday Congressman. His attendance record at Committee and Congressional sessions is one of the best in the House. Frequently he spends his weekends in his District conferring with his constituents and speaking at public meetings. I know of no Congressman who works any harder at his job.
> While I have occasionally differed with Bob on public questions, I respect his viewpoint and independence as well as the study and consideration which I know he gives such matters.[3]

Dole defeated former governor Bill Avery in the primary and went on to a 5 to 3 victory over William Robinson in the general election. In one of Hope's last letters to Dole, in late November 1969, Hope, after thanking him for a courtesy, wrote:

> This brings me to another thing. While I have not always agreed with you on legislation and other public matters I think that you are doing a swell job. I don't see how you can accomplish all that you do and you always do it well. However, I can't help but add a word of caution, which is, the more you do the more you are going to be asked to do, and there is a limit to what any human being, even one as tough as yourself can do, especially in these days of year-long congressional sessions.

Little did he know then what lay ahead for Dole in his career, but overall I think Hope would not have been surprised. He always liked to see a poor, hard-working boy make good.[4]

For the most part the years from 1959 on were good ones for Clifford in his private and personal life, especially after he retired as president of Great Plains Wheat in 1963. He then had more time for his rose garden, which had grown to some 300 bushes. He delighted in studying rose catalogues in winter and experimenting with new hybrids and improving old favorites during the growing season. In Garden City he continued the practice of wearing a rose bud in his lapel on occasion. He regularly brought fresh roses to his secretaries and to his sisters, Mary and Mildred, and our home was seldom without a large bouquet during rose-blooming seasons.

By 1961 Clifford and Pauline had nine grandchildren (four in New York City and five in Garden City). They made a practice of visiting the New Yorkers at least once a year for several weeks, often during the Christmas season. For the Garden City grandchildren, Clifford was something of an oracle and confidant. Once a high school granddaughter complained endlessly to her parents about a recreation commission dance policy for young people. Failing to get the satisfaction and reaction she sought from them, she flounced out of the house saying, "Well, I'm going to talk to Grandpa." She soon returned, all smiles. "What did he say," her mother asked? She answered, "Well, he said the first thing I had to do was just 'cool it.'"

The years after Great Plains Wheat gave Hope more time to work on his longtime interest in sustaining and developing the Great Plains in general and western Kansas in particular. He sought to revive the Western Kansas Development Association, organized two decades earlier "to promote the general welfare of the people of western Kansas." (Western Kansas was defined as the west 46 counties.) Meetings were held but revival efforts were unsuccessful. The WKDA, however, had been instrumental in organizing the Western Kansas Manufacturers Association under the leadership of Dale Fry of Garden City and others. The WKMA became the sponsor of the 3-I Show (Irrigation, Industry, Implement), held annually to promote the Great Plains area. In 1967 the organization held Clifford Hope Day in Liberal, complete with an appearance of Senator Carlson, a telegram from Dwight D. Eisenhower, and recorded messages from Senator Everett Dirksen and other members of Congress. It was all organized by Jim Pearson and Bob Dole. It probably was the most spectacular event ever held in Hope's honor, and he was deeply touched.

L. C. Crouch, president of Garden City Community College, persuaded Hope to promote a bond issue for the college. Organized under the Community College Act of 1965, the college was a successor to Garden City

Junior College, founded in 1919. Hope and Crouch appeared at many meetings to discuss and answer questions. Two decades later, Crouch was still giving Hope major credit for the successful bond issue. During the 1960s Hope established a scholarship at the college, and debate and forensics scholarships at Garden City High School. Funding was provided by annual donations; Hope did not have sufficient assets to provide for perpetual funding. (His estate in 1970 totalled about $154,000, less — I am certain — than it would have been had he spent his life practicing law in Garden City or elsewhere.)

When Clifford was president of GPW, his and Pauline's total income exceeded $30,000 annually for the first and last time. His top salary at Great Plains Wheat was $15,000, and he received $11,340 from his government pension. Thereafter their income declined. It was sufficient to enable Clifford to continue buying and selling farmland. He had bought and sold dry farm land in Gray, Finney, and Wichita counties beginning (I believe) in the 1930s. Finally, in 1959, he purchased a half section (320 acres) in north Kearny County which he owned at the time of his death. By western Kansas standards his ownership was very small potatoes, but it was a manifestation of his love of the land. (He made a practice of keeping in close touch with his tenants. His grandson, Quentin, often accompanied him on inspection tours and received as "compensation" the proceeds from one acre of wheat each year — barring crop failures, of course.)

In the latter half of the 1960s, Clifford had more time to pursue his interests in history. In 1966 he was asked by Nyle Miller, longtime secretary of the Kansas State Historical Society, to become second vice president and move up through the chairs to the presidency of the society in 1968. Customarily the president gave an address at the completion of his term. Hope consulted with Miller, suggesting either a biographical sketch of Judge Hutchison or a report on Kansas in the 1930s. Miller's preference was for the latter. Hope spent a good deal of time researching and preparing the speech he presented at the annual meeting in October 1969. After his death the speech was published in *The Kansas Historical Quarterly*. (The substance of his remarks is noted in Chapter 7.) Hope also planned to write a history of the National Association of Wheat Growers but became involved in too many other projects to compose the detailed history he had proposed.

During Christmas week 1966, Clifford, his 12-year-old grandson

Clifford Hope speaking at the dedication of the Garden City Producers Packing Plant in October 1965.

Quentin, and I took a long-postponed trip to the Abraham Lincoln sites and shrines in Illinois, Indiana, and Kentucky. This trip had first been planned for the fall of 1955 but Clifford had become too busy. He felt so bad about the postponement that he gave me the recently published nine-volume *The Collected Works of Abraham Lincoln*, purchased at the princely sum of $75. (Soon afterward a book club was offering the set for $4 to new members!) On Christmas Day we headed toward Springfield. On our many trips back and forth to Washington over the years on U.S. Highway 36, our family had never taken time to see even Lincoln's home or tomb in Springfield. Those places we visited at leisure and many more (although not nearly all the sites we had marked on our maps). New Salem Village was closed for the winter, as I recall. We visited Ann Rutledge's grave in the Petersburg Cemetery and Lincoln Log Cabin State Park south of Charleston (the home of Tom and Sarah Bush Lincoln in Illinois). The ground at the park was snow covered, and a light rain was falling. When the caretaker came to unlock the cabin, he exclaimed, "My wife said nobody would be crazy enough to come out here today."

In Kentucky we began with Lincoln Homestead State Park, an ancestral home near Springfield, then Abe's birthplace in the log cabin near Hodgenville and Knob Creek Farm. Back in southern Indiana we saw the Lincoln Pioneer Village (then sadly in need of repair) and the Nancy Hanks Lincoln and Lincoln Boyhood National Memorial. I did all the driving, and by the time we reached Mt. Vernon, Illinois, on the return trip I was exhausted, but it was all worth it. It was a time for togetherness, which my father and I had not gotten around to since our early morning hikes near the Washington Zoo more than 30 years before. The morning we left Louisville headed for Bardstown, Kentucky, my father sat in the back seat, loudly singing some ditty from his boyhood. He seemed truly happy and content.

My father and I had another time for togetherness under different circumstances in early 1968. My decision then not to run for Congress — my last feasible chance to do so — caused me great anguish for some months. I did not mention this to anyone, believing it was my problem to resolve, but it was probably visible enough, certainly to my father. I busied myself with many activities to lessen the time I would have for brooding. Among other things, I enrolled in an estate-planning course held every Wednesday from 4 to 6 p.m. at the Hotel Lassen in Wichita over a period of 13 weeks, from late January through April.

I was accustomed to driving myself over the Kansas plains; in fact, I usually enjoyed it as a good time to think and dream. Then, however, I felt the need for companionship, so I asked my father, then almost 75, to go with me. He accepted without hesitation. We would leave Garden City in the late morning and have lunch at the highway restaurant in Mullinville. He would take his briefcase with him and sit in the Hotel Lassen lobby working on letters, speeches, or his newspaper columns while I was trying to get educated. At 6 p.m. we would load up for the long night journey home, a total of 420 miles round trip. I have neither record nor memory of what we talked about on those trips, but it was comforting to have him with me at that time.

Despite Clifford's many post-Congress activities, which gave him pleasure and satisfaction, Pauline's declining health cast a cloud on their lives. Although she was glad to be back in Garden City, the mental problems which she had had in Washington continued. She began seeing a psychiatrist in Garden City and in 1962 was referred to the Kansas University Medical Center in Kansas City. One of her problems concerned side effects from medications prescribed by various physicians over the years. Doctors at the medical center were appalled at their number and variety. After several weeks at the center, she was much improved and continued to improve for some months after, so much so that she made two lengthy trips to Washington with Clifford the following winter. After that, however, she entered into a slow decline.

Clifford took Pauline's condition philosophically: "She has her good days and her bad days," he would say in writing friends. In February 1969 he said, "While her illness is not critical, it is of a psychosomatic nature and my absence disturbs her greatly." Her problems, however, did not keep her from maintaining handwritten, voluminous correspondence with old friends far and near, including the woman who had purchased the Brandywine Street house in Washington 13 years earlier and Washburn classmates via a round-robin letter. (This was at a time when long-distance phone calls were costly and not used extensively.) She visited frequently with her old Garden City friends, Mae McAllister and Louise Dunn. She still worried about and sympathized with her cleaning ladies, her neighbors, friends, and relatives, and spent much time praying for the needs of others.

In early 1969 it was discovered that Pauline had colon cancer. Surgery was performed in March, and she appeared to be recovering until peritonitis set in. She never came home from the hospital. Clifford's card to her on her 70th birthday read, "Time will never change my love for you," to which he added: "No matter what I may say or do at times, this is the way it is." Quentin and I were scheduled to leave on a People to People trip to eastern and western Europe in late May, and she insisted that we go. She died on May 31, when we were in Stockholm on the way to Leningrad. It is one of the great regrets of my life that I did not return for her funeral; it would not have been easy, but it could have been done. Fortunately, Martha arrived two days before Pauline's death, and this was a great comfort to Clifford. For as long as I can remember, Pauline had had a worried look, but in death, I was told, she had a serene expression on her face. In early June Dolores wrote of Pauline in a *Garden City Telegram* column:

As her energies waned, we managed nicely on many projects — she providing the wherewithal and the worry and we the work. What we could not agree on, we joked about because, above all, she had a good sense of humor and an unequalled capacity for being razzed.

More than anything else, though, she was a sympathetic person, concerned with the troubles and grief and heartaches that come to people, not just to those whom she knew but everyone — those she read about in the news. She was impressed with goodness more than with greatness, and she was completely unpretentious.

Elinor Peterson of Larned, the tall, lanky redhead who had been one of Clifford's secretaries in the 1940s and 1950s, wrote to him:

Over the past twenty years there have been several occasions when I longed for the phrases to write a letter of condolence such as the immeasurably comforting ones you had dictated to me — right now I feel that longing more than ever before. Pauline was a darling — her merry brown eyes and twinkling charm completely captivated those who were fortunate enough to know her.

Perhaps the most touching letter arrived after Christmas from Nellie Thone of Fort Bragg, California. (She was the young woman who had befriended Pauline on the train from Portland to Topeka in 1912; she and Pauline had corresponded during the intervening years.) "She [Pauline] was a sweet child when we met on the train," Thone wrote. "I have always been thankful I could be her traveling companion for that short time."

Clifford spent most of July — together with granddaughter Nancy Hope — with Martha and Frank West and their family on primitive Spruce Island in Penobscot Bay off the coast of Maine. As he wrote at the time, he returned refreshed in body, mind, and spirit. He had taken a break from column writing in June and July but was eager to resume in August. He never mentioned Pauline's death in a column, but he told friends how much he missed her. I am certain he felt she had found relief from her constant anxieties. With his usual practical approach to life, he confided to Dolores and me his belief that marriage was for life but not longer.

In June 1964 Clifford had a mild heart attack, from which he had a full recovery. Thereafter he had annual checkups at the KU Medical Center and took meticulous care of his health. He was planning to live as long as or longer than his parents, both of whom lived to their mid-80s. He was looking forward to a continued active life, including traveling and what his generation called "feminine companionship." He was somewhat cautious concerning the latter, however. When a friend asked him to go for a drive in the country to test out her new car, he thought about it for several days and then declined.

In December Clifford was delighted to learn he had been selected by the Board of Directors of the National Association of Soil and Water Conservation Districts to receive its annual distinguished service award. No award could have pleased him more. He flew to San Francisco to receive the award on February 4, 1970, at the association's annual convention. Unfortunately he contracted a bad cold and lung congestion, which grew worse after he arrived home. He resumed eating dinner with our family, as he had done on most nights since Pauline's illness and death, but he was not his usual self. On Friday the 13th of February, he entered St. Catherine Hospital on Dr. Robert Fenton's orders and late that afternoon suffered a severe stroke.

Clifford lingered on for three months. Only on a few occasions was he able to speak a few words, and that with great difficulty. Friends far and near were saddened and shocked. Granddaughter Nancy Hope, then working in a nursing home in Denver, returned immediately to spend a few days. Later daughter Martha West, then an elementary school teacher, visited him during spring break and planned another visit in late spring or summer. Don Berry, Clifford's Iowa friend, was especially saddened. Four years earlier he had written:

> I passed my 86th birthday a week ago today. I think the show is about over for me. I am having a pretty good time passing through the foyer, eating peanuts and greeting old friends, but the show is over. The same period will overtake you one of these days. You may as well get set and take it in your stride.

Abe and Agnes Peters of Greensburg wrote on a get-well card, "You were always our friend in the farm industry." They signed it, "Just a farmer."

That spring there were tentative plans for Clifford to go to KU Medical

Center for therapy, possibly as early as July. However, he suffered two additional strokes the week of May 10, after which he went into a coma. He died in the late afternoon of Saturday, May 16, 1970.

Clifford's funeral was held the following Tuesday afternoon, May 19, at the First United Methodist Church. The pastor, Leonard Clark, kindly offered the use of the church sanctuary, which was much larger than that of the Presbyterian Church. The Presbyterians were then without a pastor, so I called the former minister, the Rev. J. Merion Kadyk, who came from his new pastorate in Gillette, Wyoming. There were about 500 in attendance. Among the pallbearers were Frank Carlson and Howard Hardy, who drove down from North Dakota with Paul Abrahamson of that state's wheat commission. Others in attendance were Congressman Keith Sebelius, former Representative Wint Smith, and John Rees, son of the late Representative Ed Rees. I chose "A Mighty Fortress Is Our God" and "Battle Hymn of the Republic" for the funeral music. I know Clifford would have approved the former, and I believe he would have appreciated the latter.

At the end of the procession to Valley View Cemetery on the ridge overlooking Garden City was Clifford's contemporary, Earnest Moody, a farmer from south of town, clad in bib overalls and driving his Model A Ford. Clifford was, Moody said, his special friend. The American Legion post, whose members had done so much to first elect Hope in 1926, provided the color guard and firing squad. My father was buried in the Hope family plot at the far north end of the cemetery, within several feet of an alfalfa field, with his parents, Pauline, and Baby Edward, who had been the first to be buried there in 1923.

In the days following, hundreds of letters and cards were received and editorials were written; tributes were given on the floor of the House and Senate. It is not my intention to burden the reader with lists of names or lengthy quotations from tributes, but a representative few seem worthy of mention. President Nixon, Clifford's former colleague in the House, sent a letter. (A *Hutchinson News* editorial recalled that Nixon had received a standing ovation less than four years before when he mentioned in a speech at Wichita that if he had been elected President in 1960, Hope would have been his choice for Secretary of Agriculture.) Secretary of Agriculture Clifford Hardin sent a telegram, and Orville Freeman, former secretary wrote: "During his years of service to agriculture, your father contended with many a hard row of stumps. He met the challenge superbly." Albert Cole, former Kansas congressman, observed in a hand-written letter: "His quiet and disarmingly unassuming manner made him truly unique in the Washington world of strident strivers." In another hand-written letter, John W. Berkebile, official of the Wichita Regional Office of the Post Office Department, wrote:

> My friendship and admiration for him goes back to 1926 when he first ran for Congress and I was in my first year of high school at St. John. He was my first "exposure to a politician." How fortunate I was to have known him and to have been influenced by one whose character and personality I wanted so much to emulate.

The Washington Post ran a lengthy obituary and quoted its editorial of December 2, 1955, after Hope had announced his retirement from Congress. Clyde Reed, Jr., editor of *The Parsons [Kansas] Sun*, observed, in part:

> Clifford R. Hope, it can be said without fear of contradiction, was the best congressman Kansas ever had.
>
> Always fair and moderate, Cliff Hope never catered to the expedient or the passing whims of the body politic to pick up a stray vote or two. If he ever took a cheap shot at anyone in his public career, which extended over 36 years including service in the Kansas legislature, it is neither a matter of record nor of political knowledge.
>
> An authority on agriculture, particularly wheat, the Kansas congressman gained national and even international stature on those subjects during his long years in Washington. "What does Cliff Hope think?" was a question which preceded action and even consideration of any farm measure, major or minor.
>
> Not only was he a good man in Washington, and a big one as well, but he had the excellent judgment to retire at the peak of his career at the age of 63 instead of clinging to the seniority ropes on Capitol Hill to claim a committee chairmanship or add to his congressional perquisites.
>
> His record as a congressman is a model for his time and for all yet to come.[5]

That editorial was from a man whose father had served as governor and senator and had died in office at the age of 78. Senators Jim Pearson and Bob Dole and Congressmen Keith Sebelius and Garner Shriver of Wichita read tributes in the Senate and House, respectively. Included were remarks from Hope's longtime friend from Oklahoma, Carl Albert, then the House Majority Leader and soon-to-become Speaker.

As for our family, Dolores expressed well the thoughts of all of us in her column in *The Garden City Telegram* in late May:

> Much has been written in the past two weeks about a man who came to be known as an outstanding citizen, statesman, agricultural leader, and lawmaker.
>
> On this Memorial Day weekend, I'd like to write a few thoughts about this same man who was my father-in-law and who was known in and around our household simply as Pop and Grandpa. Whatever others have written about his qualities of fairness, integrity and magnanimity in his public life can be said of his private life. There was never an occasion to doubt his sincerity or his intentions or his word. He was without pretense, without deceit, and that made a man very easy to get along with.
>
> As a reporter for this paper, I covered a number of his speeches and his trips home from Washington, so I knew him first as a public figure. One of my first memories of him, after I became the prospective daughter-in-law, was shortly before Christmas 1948. He was sitting at his parents' dining room table on Garden City Avenue addressing Christmas cards. While members of the family stamped and sealed, he addressed and signed hundreds of cards without consulting a list or a directory or anything. He simply took them county-by-county in his large congressional district. Those on his Christmas card list were his friends and constituents and he knew them that well.
>
> As a father-in-law, I knew I had a good one to begin with and each year, I knew it even more so. He didn't meddle, interfere or criticize. He ate what I cooked, planted gardens for me, gave advice when it was asked for and was delighted at the arrival of each grandchild. He turned out to be a whale of a grandfather. He knew silly songs and jokes and riddles and did skin-the-cat

with our children until they got too tall to flip. His rapport with children can be illustrated by the fourth grader across the street who, when her parents were deciding how many of their children would go to his funeral, said, "Well, if anyone from this family goes, it should be me. I knew him better than anyone else." After all, she reminded, he had attended the burial rites for her pet duck.

I was most impressed in recent years, particularly in the last year when he joined us every day for the evening meal, with his youthfulness. Backed with firm knowledge of the past, he was every bit a man of today and tomorrow. In all of our conversations, I cannot once remember his taking a dim view, viewing with alarm, or decrying the actions of the younger generation or wondering "what it was coming to." One felt he had faith that whatever foolishness might be on the surface, there was something solid beneath. When the first bearded, long-haired boy friend appeared at our table, he smiled just a little. His comments on the fads of the times were always mild and never critical or condemning. Ranting and raving were not his way.

Most of all, he was a thinking man. He thought more than he talked. And he always thought big. This limited him sometimes in small talk of small things, but you could always spend a very comfortable silence with him. I often did that.[6]

Epilogue

*T*HE UNITED STATES CONGRESS HAS, *perhaps, always been the most loved and hated of all American institutions. People often respect and appreciate their own representatives while deriding the institution in which they serve. During the 200-plus years of the existence of this great experiment in representative democracy, many men and women have served — a few with distinction, some less than honorably, but most, I am quite sure, with the desire to uphold a revered tradition. Clifford R. Hope certainly was one who embodied the best of that tradition.*

The Iowa-born, Kansas-bred congressman was a believer, as was most of his generation, in the two-party system, and early on he hitched his wagon to the party of Lincoln—a propitious choice for an early 20th-century Kansan with political ambitions. His guiding principles, which generally took precedence over party loyalty, helped make him a statesman and a Republican in the best sense of the word.

"In the Washington world of strident strivers," wrote his Kansas colleague Albert Cole, Hope's "quiet and disarmingly unassuming manner made him truly unique." Kansas editor Clyde Reed, Jr., said Hope's record was "a model for his time and for all yet to come." In the current atmosphere of cynicism toward anything "political," it is appropriate to examine what made Hope an exemplary politician for his own time and now.

First of all, Congressman Hope had a solid record of substantial legislative accomplishments. He probably spent more time from 1933 until 1957 on farm support legislation than on any other single issue, seeking to secure a safety net for farmers and, equally important, striving to ensure a stable supply of inexpensive food and fiber for consumers. During Hope's time in Congress, by trial and error, his efforts for the most part were successful. Like others in his time and since, however, he recognized that these legislative efforts were only a temporary substitute, and sometimes a poor one, for farmers' lack of bargaining power in the marketplace.

His more lasting legislative accomplishments were in the areas of soil and water conservation, agricultural research and marketing, and the Food for Peace program. While usually not an eloquent speaker, time after time in his later years, he delivered stirring speeches on the importance of preserving the soil and saving rainwater when it fell.

Although preoccupied with agricultural problems, Congressman Hope spent many hours studying and seeking the truth on all important issues and legislation, especially during the years leading up to Pearl Harbor, World War II, and the advent of the Cold War. When hindsight proved his judgment to have been wrong on particular issues, he readily admitted it. This was in keeping with his pragmatic approach to problems. He did not reach decisions based on "liberal" or "conservative" positions. His test of any piece of legislation was "Will it work?" or "Will it accomplish its intended purpose?"

Hope's legislative achievements and his pursuit of facts and truth regarding all proposals before Congress were not, in my opinion, the primary reasons he was considered a role model congressman by many of his contemporaries. He was a role model, rather, because of the virtues and values he held dear. In recent years in America, there has been a rediscovery of — or at least a renewed interest in — personal virtues.

William J. Bennett (*The Book of Virtues*) quotes stories and poems from the past which exemplify ten virtues: responsibility, self-discipline, compassion, friendship, work, courage, perseverance, honesty, loyalty, and faith.[1] Senator Frank Carlson, in the congressional ceremony honoring his friend Clifford Hope in 1956, cited Henry Drummond's list of nine virtues "that make up the stature of a perfect man": patience, kindness, generosity, humility, courtesy, unselfishness, sincerity, good temper, and guilelessness. Hope would be the first to disclaim that he was a "perfect man," as indeed he was not; but in large measure, he did possess the virtues cited by Bennett and Drummond. Five of these in particular were ones he imparted and taught to all with whom he came in contact, including his wife, Pauline, his two children, and his grandchildren. He taught by example, not by preaching.

WORK: My father worked hard all his life, from the time he hoed cotton and clerked in a grocery store as a boy until after he retired from the Great Plains Wheat organization. He loved hard work; it was second nature to him. On one occasion, when I wrote home complaining of hardships I perceived I was enduring in the army of occupation in Germany, he responded, "When I was your age I was working for nothing a year and it didn't hurt me one bit." As a congressman he worked six- and seven-day weeks, seeking answers to every problem presented by constituents, whether it was large or small, sending timely replies to all.

HONESTY: My father was a man of his word. He told colleagues and constituents exactly what he thought. If he did not have an answer, he said so. When new facts were presented on an issue, he did not hesitate to change his mind and admit previous errors.

GUILELESSNESS: This is not a common word. It has several definitions, one of which is "being without deceit or cunning." As applied to my father, the word means a man who did not believe in punishing enemies or those who had done him wrong. He never tried to "get even" with anyone, however tempting it might have been. He believed in the biblical admonition "Recompense no man evil for evil." Once when I complained to him about a man who was giving me a hard time, my father said, "Oh, that guy won't live forever." He handled those who sought to do him wrong by outmaneuvering them or killing them with kindness, or both. He treated those who disliked him with civility. Some members of Congress — and many other people — spend a lot of time trying to punish their enemies. One might observe that Congressman Hope used the time he could have used in this way for more productive ends, such as finding solutions to legislative problems.

RESPONSIBILITY: In my father's case, the word "responsibility" might best be defined as "sense of duty" to God, country, his constituents and other people, and to his family. His sense of duty to the people did not end when he retired from Congress. When former constituents or others wrote him for answers to their problems, he always responded. He accepted his duties as president of Great Plains Wheat eagerly and, afterward, made helpful observations on the past and the present in his newspaper columns.

COURAGE: The most spectacular examples of my father's courage are described in considerable detail in this book: his fight against the Ku Klux Klan in the 1925 Kansas legislature and his defense of President Truman's firing of General MacArthur amidst vitriolic personal attacks. But most examples of his courage were of the quiet nature he demonstrated in stating his views honestly and voting his conscience regardless of political consequences and in never giving wishy-washy, noncommittal answers to conceal his true feelings.

A quarter of a century after his death in 1970, Clifford R. Hope is remembered by the few survivors of his generation and many of their children in Garden City and the surrounding area of southwest Kansas, by some people throughout Kansas, by his few surviving congressional and Great Plains Wheat colleagues, and by historians of 20th-century American history, especially those who have reviewed his papers.

Clifford's name is known to most residents of Garden City because of the high school auditorium named for him in 1957. Although they know the name, probably most know little about the man. Some assume he was a teacher, because nearly all the town's school buildings and facilities are named for former, local educators. Unlike some members of Congress, he has no federal buildings, dams, reservoirs, or other public structures that bear his name. (It should be noted that there are no federal dams or reservoirs in the area he represented in Congress, only small watershed structures.) With his inherent modesty, I do not think he would be disappointed or even surprised. Those who do remember his legacy often cite him as "the best friend the farmer ever had" or "the best congressman Kansas ever had." Regarding his place in history, I think those simple, heartfelt words would please him most of all.

My father, Clifford R. Hope, was a good man who did some great things. He was a man of quiet courage who set a standard for moral conduct for his time and for all time to come.

Notes

Prologue
1. Jesus, son of Eleazer, son of Sirach, The Book of Sirach from The Apocrypha, *The New American Bible* (NY: P. J. Kenedy & Sons, 1970), 998.

Chapter 1
1. Joseph Frazier Wall, *Iowa: A Bicentennial History* (NY: W. W. Norton, 1978), 114-115.
2. *Ibid.*, 107-108.
3. Taken from Clifford Hope's typed copy.
4. From Clifford Hope's typed copies, marked "July 23" and "July 30." They were published in 1967 in two consecutive articles in the Sunday *Hutchinson News* and *The Salina Journal*.
5. Taken from Clifford Hope's typed copy.

Chapter 3
1. From a letter dated November 15, 1924.
2. Information and quotes on pages 72-80 are taken from Clifford Hope's typed copies, which were published in *The Hutchinson News* and *The Salina Journal*.
3. A column Hope sent to both *The Hutchinson News* and *The Salina Journal*, October 31, 1965.
4. O. H. Hatfield and Hope remained good friends until the tragic deaths of Hatfield and his grandson, when a B-29 bomber crashed into their farm home during World War II.

5. "1925 Lawmakers Return Home," *The Topeka Daily Capital*, March 14, 1925, 1.

Chapter 4

1. E. E. Kelley, "Clifford Hope for Congress," *The Garden City Herald*, Feb. 18, 1926, 1.
2. "Tincher Will Not Ask for Re-election," *The Hutchinson Herald*, Feb. 24, 1926, 1.
3. "Campaigning Now and Then," *The High Plains Journal*, Dodge City, Oct. 16, 1958, 2.
4. "Campaigning Now and Then" [Part Two], *The High Plains Journal*, Dodge City, Oct. 23, 1958, 2.

Chapter 5

1. From Hope's copy written for *The Hutchinson News* and *The Salina Journal* for Feb. 23, 1969.
2. Irvin M. May, Jr., *Marvin Jones: The Public Life of an Agrarian Advocate* (College Station, TX: Texas A & M Univ. Press, 1980), 80.
3. The Congressional Club's Register included these instructions:

Cards are left at the White House once a year by women in official life in Washington, as soon as possible after arriving in the city. A caller does not expect to be received but gives her cards to a footman at the door.

Upon the opening of the social season, cards should be left on the official receiving days, upon the wives of Supreme Court Justices, and as soon as possible, after the opening of Congress, cards should be left upon the wife of the Vice President and the wife of the Speaker of the House.

The exchange of first calls should be made in person and will cancel all obligations for as long as the two ladies are in the same position in official life. A repetition of a call made in person will be considered social, not official.

When making official calls, a woman leaves one of her own and two of her husband's cards; in other words, one of her own for the wife and one each of her husband's for the husband and wife. One each of her own and her husband's cards may be left for additional women of the household but not more than three of her own should ever be left at any one household.

There was this one saving clause:

Since it is practically impossible for a newcomer to make all official calls, it is suggested that the essential ones would include, in addition to the White House, the wife of the Vice President, wife of the Speaker, the ladies of her own State delegation and the wives of Chairmen and ranking members of her husband's committees. After that she may call where inclination and discretion lead.
4. Joyce Milton, *Loss of Eden: A Biography of Charles and Anne Morrow Lindbergh* (NY: Harper-Collins, 1993), 162.
5. Dec. 7, 1929, 1.

Chapter 6

1. "Capper, the Christ-like Statesman" is a chapter title in *Rascals in Democracy*, by W. G. Clugston (NY: Richard R. Smith, 1941).
2. *The Great Bend Tribune* editorial writer was, I believe, a brother-in-law of Will Townsley, Jr., the publisher. I do not know when he first coined "Old Zero" and "Hot Lunch Cliff." I just have a memory of these terms of endearment!
3. David Brinkley, *Washington Goes to War* (NY: Alfred A. Knopf, 1988), 30-31.
4. Homer E. Socolofsky, *Arthur Capper: Publisher, Politician, and Philanthropist* (Lawrence, KS: Univ. of Kansas Press, 1962), 229-230.
5. Clifford Hope, "By Any Other Name . . .," *The Hutchinson News*, Hutchinson, KS, Jan. 16, 1966.
6. Brinkley, *op. cit.*, 195-196.
7. Tip O'Neill, *Man of the House* (NY: St. Martin's Press, 1988), 163.
8. From a column Hope sent to both *The Hutchinson News* and *The Salina Journal*, Feb. 18, 1968.
9. In Kansas the veteran Homer Hoch lost to Randolph Carpenter, also an attorney from Marion, and Charles Isaac Sparks, a Goodland lawyer, was defeated by Kathryn O'Loughlin, a Hays lawyer, who had been the surprise winner of the nine-candidate Democratic primary. For the session that started in March 1933, the House line-up from Kansas was William Purnell Lambertson, a Fairview farmer who had succeeded Dan Anthony in 1929 (R, 1st District); U. S. Guyer (R, 2nd District); Harold Clement McGugin, a Coffeyville attorney who had been elected in 1930, succeeding William Henry Sproul, unsuccessful candidate for the Senate that year (R, 3rd District); Randolph Carpenter (D, 4th District); William Ayres, Wichita, (D, 5th District); Kathryn O'Loughlin (D, 6th District); and Hope of the 7th District. (Kansas had lost a Congressional district as a result of the 1930 census. Congressman Ayres, formerly of the 8th District, ran and won in the new 5th District.)

    In the U.S. Senate, Kansas was represented by two incumbents: Arthur Capper, who had been reelected in 1930, and Democrat George McGill, a Wichita Lawyer. McGill was first elected in 1930, defeating former governor Henry Allen who had been appointed to the Senate seat vacated by Charles Curtis in 1929. Senator McGill won a full term in the 1932 election. Thus, in 1933 Kansas had a senator from each party and a four-to-three Republican majority in the House.
10. Taken from an undocumented clipping.

Chapter 7

1. Michael W. Schuyler, *The Dread of Plenty* (Manhattan, KS: Sunflower University Press, 1989), 183.
2. R. Douglas Hurt, *The Dust Bowl: An Agricultural and Social History* (Chicago: Nelson-Hall, 1981), 2-3.
3. Ada Buell Norris, "Black Blizzard," *Kansas Magazine*, 1941, 103.
4. Hurt, *op. cit.*, 50.
5. *Ibid.*, 137.
6. James C. and Eleanor A. Duram, "Congressman Clifford Hope's Correspon-

dence with His Constituents: A Conservative View of the Court-Packing Plan of 1937," *Kansas State Historical Quarterly*, Spring 1971, 64-80.

7. Congressional salaries had increased to $22,500 (of which $20,140.81 was taxable) by the end of Hope's career in 1956. Clifford and Pauline's total taxable income that year was $25,281.15.

8. Years afterward I remembered a small boy, often crying, whom we picked up at the Tilden Gardens Apartments. His father, Mr. Smith told us, was the U.S. Civil Aeronautics administrator, Eugene Vidal. Smith didn't mention that the boy's maternal grandfather was Thomas Pryor Gore, the blind U.S. Senator from Oklahoma. That crying little boy grew up to become the famous author, Gore Vidal.

9. Clifford also enjoyed reading. Usually he read only non-fiction, serious books, but I believe he did read *Gone With the Wind*. Pauline usually read only mysteries and inspirational and religious books. She read most of the comic strips; Clifford read "The Gumps" (Andy Gump) and "Gasoline Alley" occasionally.

10. At that time there was no public school segregation in Kansas except in elementary schools in certain first-class cities, including Topeka (from which the landmark *Brown v. Board of Education* case arose in the 1950s). However, in Garden City, African-Americans and Mexican-Americans had to sit in the balconies in local theaters, could not eat in most restaurants, and were forbidden to use the city-owned, tax-supported, free municipal swimming pool. Years later I learned that Mexican-American students were not allowed to speak Spanish in Garden City schools. But it was not until I saw that rundown, ancient school building next to Alice Deal Junior High that I began to think seriously about the whole issue of segregation. It should be added that although I thought about it, I did not take any action until I returned to Garden City in the 1950s. And Clifford was not a leader in the cause, although he supported anti-lynching legislation in Congress and, after World War II, civil rights legislation in general.

Chapter 8

1. Manfred Jones, *Isolationism in America 1935-1941* (Chicago: Imprint Publications, 1990), 100.

2. *Ibid.*, 101.

3. Gilbert Fite, *American Farmers: The New Minority* (Bloomington, IN: Indiana Univ. Press, 1981), 80.

Chapter 9

1. James F. Forsythe, "Postmortem on the Election of 1948: An Evaluation of Cong. Clifford R. Hope's Views," *The Kansas Historical Quarterly*, Autumn 1972, 338-359.

2. Virgil Dean, "Farm Policy and Truman's 1948 Campaign," *The Historian*, Spring 1993, 501-516.

3. Virgil W. Dean wrote his doctoral dissertation on the plan: *America's Search for a Long-Range Policy for Agriculture: The Truman-Brannan Price Support Plan, Innovative New Approach or "Political Football"?* It is a comprehensive history of the plan.

4. Marx Koehnke, *Kernels and Chaff — A History of Wheat Marketing Develop-ment* (Lincoln, NE: published by author, 1986), 31-32.
5. Harry Darby was appointed to succeed Clyde Reed (who died November 8, 1949) as senator for the balance of Reed's term, with the understanding he would step aside for Frank Carlson in 1950. Carlson defeated Harry Colmery, Topeka lawyer and author of the GI Bill of Rights legislation in 1944, in the primary, and Paul Aiken, Democrat from Macksville, in the general election. Myron George of Altamont was elected to succeed Herbert Meyer, deceased, in the 3rd District.
6. In the state races Ed Arn, former attorney general and Kansas Supreme Court Justice, was elected governor and Fred Hall, Dodge City lawyer, became lieutenant governor, after winning a nine-man primary race. Thus began a power struggle between the Arn and Hall forces for control of the Republican Party in Kansas which did not end until the election of George Docking as governor in 1956. Hall was more liberal than Arn, but the main battle revolved around Hall's desire to build his own personal political machine.
7. Jim Cornish, *The Garden City Daily Telegram*, Apr. 16, 1951, 4.

Chapter 10

1. Stephen Ambrose, *Eisenhower the President*, Vol. 2 (NY: Simon & Schuster, 1984), 159-160.
2. Edward L. Schapsmeier and Frederick H. Schapsmeier, *Ezra Taft Benson and the Politics of Agriculture: The Eisenhower Years, 1953-1961* (Danville, IL: The Interstate Printers and Publishers, Inc., 1975), 127.
3. John Mark Hansen, *Gaining Access: Congress and the Farm Lobby, 1919-1981* (Chicago: The Univ. Press of Chicago, 1991), 127.
4. Gilbert Fite, *American Agriculture and Farm Policy Since 1900* (NY: Macmillan, 1964), 23.
5. Ray Hemman, "Butz: Ag programs failing," *The Hutchinson News*, July 29, 1990, 1.
6. Clifford Hope, "A Look at the Farm Heads," *The Hutchinson News*, Nov. 23, 1969, 7.
7. From a column Hope sent to both *The Hutchinson News* and *The Salina Journal*, Oct. 18, 1969.
8. *Ibid.*
9. Bill Avery has recalled some memories of Hope:

It's remarkable how an otherwise insignificant incident becomes fixed in a person's memory. The first time I had lunch with Cliff was in the House Restaurant soon after we were sworn into the Eighty-fourth Congress. At noon, the restaurant always placed a tray of hard crusted, oblong shaped rolls on the table. When they were passed I don't recall if Cliff took one or not. Not caring for such an item, I declined to take one when they were passed by me. With what appeared to be a somewhat embarrassed grin, he said, "Even if you don't want to eat it, you should take it, break it in two so it can't be served again. In that way you will be helping the Kansas wheat farmer." That is the only extravagant utterance I can recall he ever made.

There was another incident, firm in my memory, in the House Restaurant that reflects Cliff Hope's personality and temperament. On one of our early luncheons, he ordered watermelon for dessert. I immediately suggested that we split one of the generous portions that were being served. He casually mentioned that he liked watermelon and could eat the entire serving himself. I continued to insist (for what possible reason I cannot remember) and after a few more comments about his fondness for melon, he agreed. Not long afterward, I realized he really did want the entire portion and finally agreed to share only to be accommodating to an overly aggressive new member of the House. Had our seniority status been reversed, I probably would have ungraciously advised the new member that I wanted the whole serving for myself and that if he wanted some melon, "just order his own."

10. Governor Hall was available, it was rumored, as a nominee for Vice President if Richard Nixon were replaced. In the GOP gubernatorial primary, Warren Shaw, Topeka lawyer, defeated the unpopular Hall in a bitter contest; this resulted in the election of George Docking, the first Democrat to accomplish this feat in Kansas since 1936. At the same time, Ike and Senator Carlson won by huge majorities.

Chapter 12

1. Attendees from Kansas included R. L. Patterson and W. W. Graber (then chairman and administrator, respectively, of the Kansas Wheat Commission), Ora Martin, Herbert W. Clutter, and Hope. Nebraskans present included Leslie V. Sheffield (chief of the Nebraska Wheat Commission), Marx Koehnke, Herbert Hughes, Lester Mort, and Carl Bruns. Those from Colorado included Lloyd Kontny, Ted Fiedler, and Sam Freeman, then an assistant attorney general. Other leaders were Kenneth Kendrick of Texas and Otis Louett of North Dakota.

2. April 9, 1968, letter to Nixon.

3. Dated 4/23/68, the endorsement was attached to a letter to Bill Kats.

4. Bob Dole's race for the Senate led to a spirited GOP primary and general election races for 1st District congressman. Keith Sebelius, the only candidate from the north half of the district, was thought to have a decided edge. He had run for Congress twice before and had a good record as a hard-working state senator for the past six years. (Sebelius became a state senator when Bill Ryan of Norton resigned to become a district judge in 1962.) Moreover, since 1960 he had been a strong Dole supporter, endearing himself to most of Dole's key people.

In the south half of the district, Republican candidates began popping up all over, including four from Garden City. Bill Crotinger, then from Tribune, announced in late December. Gerald Shadwick of Great Bend, most recently an administrative assistant with Senator Carlson, made his intentions known early in the year. He was raring to go. Bob Wells, well-known Garden City businessman and director of Harris Publications' radio domain; Jack Barr, state senator from Garden City; and George Meeker, state representative, also from Garden City, and the 1968 president of the National Association of Wheat Growers, all expressed interest. Finally, there was me; I still had a great ambition to be a congressman. However, by February, after much consultation with my father and others, I concluded that my chances for winning were less than 50-50 and that with my family responsibilities, I could not afford to lose another race. My father agreed.

By the June 20 filing deadline, the situation was this: Sebelius, Crotinger, and Shadwick had filed as Republican candidates; Wells and Barr had dropped out, and Meeker, who had announced as a Republican in late February, switched parties in late May and filed as the only Democrat. Meeker had a strong dislike for Dole and accused him and Sebelius of being "two peas in a pod." In addition, Meeker argued, an agricultural district should be represented by a farmer, not a lawyer.

Sebelius won the primary, but Shadwick ran quite well. The count was Sebelius 48 percent, Shadwick 40 percent, and Crotinger 12 percent. Sebelius immediately sought Hope's advice on many issues. Hope served as co-chairman of Sebelius' farm advisory committee, spending much time on that project. The general election campaign was a lively one. Meeker surprised many by receiving 49 percent of the vote and losing by only 5,000 votes out of the almost 170,000 cast. As he had been with Dole, Hope was impressed with Sebelius's capacity for hard work and pleased with his appointment of Pat Roberts, a member of Carlson's staff, as his administrative assistant. (Roberts succeeded Sebelius in Congress when the latter retired in 1980. Sebelius and Roberts often received election majorities larger than Hope had ever received.)

5. Clyde Reed, Jr., "Clifford R. Hope," *The Parsons Sun*, May 18, 1970, 6.
6. Dolores Hope, "The Distaff Side," *The Garden City Telegram*, June 1, 1970, 4.

Epilogue
1. William J. Bennett, *The Book of Virtues* (NY: Simon & Schuster, 1993).

Index

by Lori L. Daniel